# IS-32.A: Mitigation eGrants Internal System

## By

## Fema

2/16/2018

# Course Overview

This course is a part of the comprehensive training program for the FEMA eGrants System. This course is the third in the series of Independent Study (IS) courses for eGrants and will address the functions in the eGrants Internal System used by FEMA Regional and Headquarters (HQ) staff to administer the Hazard Mitigation Assistance (HMA) grant programs. You can access the eGrants Internal System from the FEMA Intranet at: https://portal.fema.gov/famsVuWeb/home.

At the end of this course, you should be able to:

- Describe the eGrants System and workflows
- Describe the process for accessing the eGrants Internal System
- Describe the process for reviewing, approving, and denying pending external eGrants Applicant user registrations
- Describe all of the Program Office's review and approval processes for applications and subapplications
- Describe the process of monitoring federal awards through the review of quarterly reports

# Lesson Overview

This lesson provides an overview of the course and an introduction to various course features and functionality.

At the end of the lesson, you should be able to identify the:

- Course structure
- Course navigation
- Knowledge Check functionality
- Slideshow functionality
- Screen features and navigation tools

# Terms Used in this Course

The Office of Management and Budget streamlined the Federal Government's Administrative Requirements, Cost Principles, and Audit Requirements for Federal Awards into a consolidated set of regulations. These regulations are located in Title 2 of the Code of Federal Regulations, Part 200, and are referred to as the "Super Circular." The Super Circular also introduced new terminology, including "Recipient" instead of "Grantee" and "Subrecipient" instead of "Subgrantee."

Because terminology has changed, many of the terms used in the eGrants Internal and External Systems screens are not consistent with the current terms used in the Super Circular. This course will reference eGrants screen labels as they appear, but will use Super Circular terminology throughout the rest of the course. Below is a table to assist you in understanding the terminology you will encounter in this course.

| Super Circular | eGrants Screens | Definition |
| --- | --- | --- |
| Federal Award | Grant | The federal financial assistance received directly from FEMA |
| Subaward | Subgrant | The federal financial assistance received indirectly from a pass-through entity (Applicant to a Subapplicant) |
| Applicant | Applicant or Grant Applicant | A state agency, territorial government, or federally-recognized tribal government submitting an application to FEMA for assistance under FEMA's mitigation grant programs. |
| Subapplicant | Subgrant Applicant | A state agency, local government, territorial government, federally-recognized tribal government, or qualified private non-profit organization submitting a subapplication to an Applicant for assistance under FEMA's mitigation grant programs. |
| Application | Grant Application | Application for federal financial assistance directly from FEMA |
| Subapplication | Subgrant Application | Application for federal financial assistance indirectly through a pass-through entity (Subapplicant to Applicant, Applicant to FEMA) |
| Applicant acting as Subapplicant subapplication | Grant as Subgrant Application | A state agency or federally-recognized tribal government submitting technical assistance or management costs subapplications which will be included in an application for assistance under FEMA's mitigation grant programs. |

| Recipient | Grantee | An Applicant whose application has been approved and a federal award obligated. |
| Subrecipient | Subgrantee | A Subapplicant whose subapplication has been approved and a subaward obligated. |

**Note** The competitive Pre-Disaster Mitigation (PDM) grant program is referred to as PDM-C (i.e., PDM-Competitive) on eGrants Internal System screens. However, the acronym PDM will be used throughout this course.

# Course Structure

Take a moment to review the course lesson plan for this course. The lesson plan is labeled **Lesson List** and is located on the right side of your screen.

This course contains 12 lessons. The lessons may be accessed in sequence or independently. The time to complete each lesson varies. A page tracker is displayed at the bottom middle of the screen to help you gauge your movement through the lesson. The specific time required for each lesson will be stated on the lesson's first screen.

After completing the course materials, take the Final Exam to:

1. Gauge your knowledge of the topic
2. Receive credit for taking the course

# eGrants User Scenario

This course will cover the various responsibilities for an eGrants Internal System user.
As part of this course, you will participate in a scenario in which you are a first-time user of eGrants.
You will play the role of a new Flood Mitigation Assistance (FMA) Program Analyst at a FEMA Regional Office. Your supervisor, Alex Salazar, will show you how FEMA uses eGrants to process FMA and Pre-Disaster Mitigation (PDM) applications and subapplications and to manage federal awards.

Listen to Alex

Hello. I'm Alex Salazar, the FEMA Flood Mitigation Assistance Program Coordinator at FEMA Headquarters. Welcome to the Mitigation branch team. I will be working with you throughout this course as you learn to use all the functions in the eGrants system. To get started, I am going to explain the different interactions you are going to encounter in this course.

# Screen Features

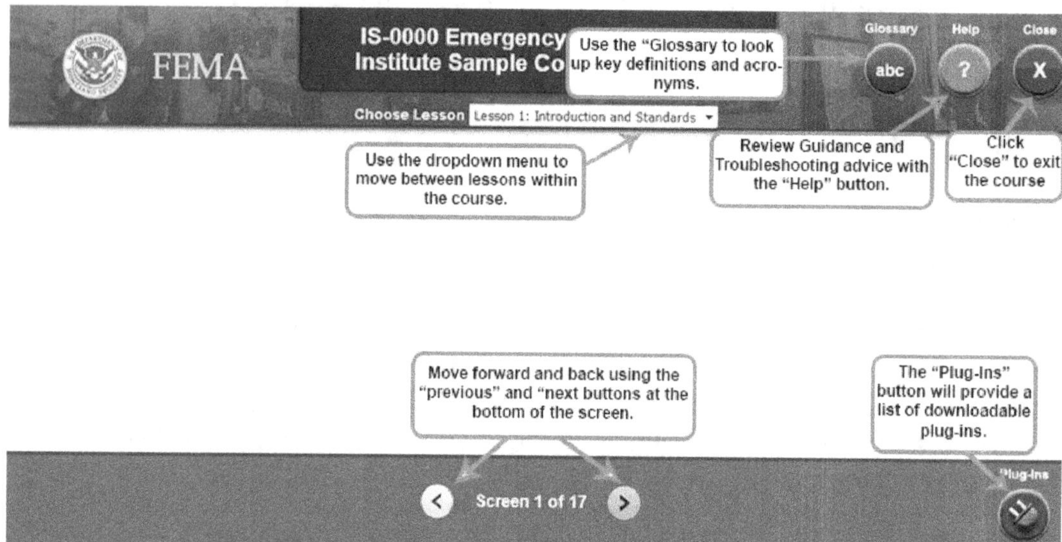


Click this link to access a narrative summary of the screen features.

# Navigating Using Your Keyboard

Below are instructions for navigating through the course using your keyboard.

- Use the "Tab" key to move forward through each screen's navigation buttons and hyperlinks, or "Shift" + "Tab" to move backwards. A box surrounds the button that is currently selected.
- Press "Enter" to select a navigation button or hyperlink.
- Use the arrow keys to select answers for multiple-choice review questions or self-assessment checklists. Then tab to 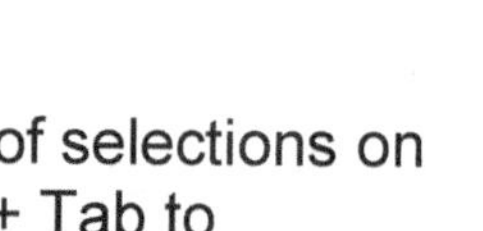 the Submit button and press Enter to complete a Knowledge Review or Self-Assessment.
- **Warning:** Repeatedly pressing Tab beyond the number of selections on the screen may cause the keyboard to lock up. Use Ctrl + Tab to deselect an element or reset to the beginning of a screen's navigation links (most often needed for screens with animations or media).

- Job Access With Speech (JAWS) assistive technology users can press the Ctrl key to quiet the screen reader while the course audio plays.

# Viewing Slideshow Simulations

Slideshows have been inserted into this course to display the eGrants screens a user would encounter when entering data.

You will see a "Scroll down to see slideshow captions" message. A shaded box with navigation buttons and a slide counter indicate the presence of a slideshow.
Select the slideshow's **Next** button to begin the presentation. Audio narration and captions will explain the data entry procedure. Select the link to hear the audio narration. A media player window will appear when audio narration is activated.

To navigate through the slideshow, select the **Back to the Beginning, Back, Next,** and **End of Presentation** buttons.
Select the **Next** button to move to the following slide.

The **Slide Counter** indicates the total number of slides in the presentation and which slide you are currently viewing. Keep in mind that the presentation is on a loop and will repeat.

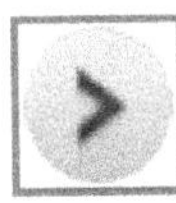

To exit the Slideshow, select the **Next** button at the bottom of the course screen.

## Receiving Credit

Students must complete the entire course and pass the final exam to receive credit for the course. Each lesson takes a variable amount of time to complete. If you are unable to complete the course in its entirety, you may close the window and reopen the course at any time. However, depending on the system used to take the course, it is possible you may have to repeat a portion of the last lesson you were studying.

## Lesson 1 Summary

You have completed the first lesson. In this lesson, you learned about:

- The goals and structure of the course
- How to navigate within the course using screen features and your keyboard
- How to access slideshows
- How to interact with Knowledge Checks

Remember, you must complete all lessons and pass the Final Exam to receive credit for the course.

Now that we have introduced the course goals and discussed the various navigation elements and features of the course, let's get started. To begin the course, select the **Next** button or choose a lesson from the **Topic** drop-down list.

# Lesson 2 Overview

This lesson provides an overview of the eGrants System, including the External System used by Applicants and Subapplicants and the Internal System used by FEMA users.

When we're done with this lesson, you'll be able to identify:

- The purpose of eGrants and the hazard mitigation grant programs it supports
- The categories of eGrants users
- The eGrants External System workflow
- The eGrants Internal System workflow

# eGrants User Scenario

Listen to Alex
Audio transcript

**Team Leader:** Alex Salazar, Flood Mitigation Assistance (FMA) Program Coordinator

**Your Role:** New FMA Program Analyst

**Office:** FEMA Regional Office

**Challenge:** State, territorial, and federally-recognized tribal governments use eGrants External System to create and manage subapplications and applications for HMA federal awards. FEMA uses the eGrants Internal System to review and process applications and manage federal awards.

**The Next Step:** Alex will describe how the eGrants Internal and External Systems function.

Hello. It's Alex here. It is important to know that there are actually two eGrants systems. At FEMA, we use the Internal system to review and process grant program applications from state, tribal, and U.S. territorial governments for flood mitigation plans and projects in their areas. The external eGrants system is used by Applicants and their Subapplicants to create and submit those applications. I'd like you to learn about both the internal and external eGrants systems and the mitigation grants programs they support.

# What is Mitigation eGrants?

FEMA's eGrants system was developed as a part of the eGovernment initiative to reduce the time and paperwork involved in managing the entire federal award lifecycle.

The eGrants system consists of two parts:

- An <u>External System</u> for Applicants and Subapplicants, which is available on the internet at https://portal.fema.gov/famsVuWeb/home
- An <u>Internal System</u> for FEMA users, which is available on the FEMA Intranet on: https://sso.fema.net/famsRuWeb/home

This course focuses on the eGrants Internal System. The FEMA Independent Study courses available on the Emergency Management Institute (EMI) website that cover the eGrants External System for Subapplicant users and Applicant users are Courses IS-0030.b and IS-0031.b, respectively. In order to provide a full picture of the overall system and to show how the External and Internal Systems interrelate, we will review the functionalities of the eGrants External System.

# The Purpose of eGrants

The FEMA eGrants system was developed to provide state and territorial governments, federally-recognized tribal governments, and local governments with the ability to apply for and manage the application processes for federal awards and subawards electronically.

Specifically, eGrants functions include:

- The creation and submission of pre-applications (when required) to state, territorial, and federally-recognized tribal government officials
- The creation and submission of FMA and Pre-Disaster Mitigation (PDM) subapplications to state, territorial, and federally-recognized tribal government officials
- The review and processing of FMA and PDM subapplications
- The creation and submission of FMA and PDM applications to FEMA
- The review and processing of HMA federal awards
- The creation and submission of quarterly reports on performance and financial status of FMA, PDM, and legacy Repetitive Flood Claims (RFC) and Severe Repetitive Loss (SRL) federal awards to FEMA

**Select an official** from each government to learn more about how they use the eGrants system.

Listen to the Local Official    Listen to the State Official    Listen to the FEMA Official

Select this link to access a summary of the screen content.

# eGrants Users Summary

### Local Government Official:
Local governments like ours, and some federally-recognized tribal governments, use eGrants to create and submit pre-applications to Applicants in state, territorial, and federally-recognized tribal governments, if they require them. Pre-applications only apply to project subapplications and, if required, must be approved prior to being granted permission to create and submit a subapplication. After our pre-application is approved, we can use eGrants to create and submit a subapplication to the Applicant.

### State Government Official:
As Applicants, we use eGrants to manage Subapplicant user access, and to review and process subapplications. If we approve a subapplication, we attach it to our application and submit it to FEMA. If we don't approve a subapplication, we may stockpile it for future consideration or we may ask the Subapplicant to revise and resubmit it. We can also create our own subapplications and include them in our application. FEMA may request revisions to our application or to a subapplication. For revisions to a subapplication, we can either make the changes ourselves or we can release the subapplication back to the Subapplicant and ask them to make the revisions. For revisions to an application, we'll just make them ourselves and resubmit the application back to FEMA for review. If FEMA obligates our

federal award, we can view the award package in eGrants. Afterwards, we use eGrants to submit our Quarterly Performance Reports to FEMA.

**FEMA Official:**
We use eGrants to manage Applicant user access and to review subapplications and applications for completeness, award eligibility, cost-effectiveness, the cost of the proposed project, and to document the status of Applicant mitigation plans. If we approve an application, we process it and the associated subapplications for federal award. We may make amendments to the award package later. If we don't approve a subapplication, we may ask the Applicant to make revisions and to resubmit the subapplication. After we obligate a federal award, we monitor its status by reviewing the quarterly performance and financial reports that the Applicant submits to us.

# eGrants External System Users

Applicant users must be approved by FEMA before they can access the eGrants External System. The process of managing Applicant registrations is covered in Lesson 4.
Subapplicant users must be approved by their respective state, tribal, or territorial Applicant organization order to access the External eGrants System.

# Types of Federal Awards

As a FEMA Reviewer you'll be able to use eGrants to review applications and subapplications and manage federal awards for the two current HMA grant programs supported by eGrants. You'll also be able to monitor the status of federal awards that were awarded under the two legacy HMA grant programs: SRL and RFC.

**Pre-Disaster Mitigation (PDM)** —Funding for the PDM grant program is provided to assist state, territorial, local, and federally-recognized tribal governments in implementing cost-effective hazard mitigation activities.

Learn more about the PDM grant program at https://www.fema.gov/pre-disaster-mitigation-grant-program

**Flood Mitigation Assistance (FMA)**—The FMA grant program was created to reduce or eliminate claims under the National Flood Insurance Program (NFIP). FMA federal awards provide funding to assist communities in implementing measures to reduce or eliminate long-term risks of flood damage.
Learn more about the FMA grant program at https://www.fema.gov/flood-mitigation-assistance-grant-program

# eGrants External System Workflow

The application process in eGrants follows a specific workflow:

- Initially, a Subapplicant creates a subapplication and submits it to the appropriate Applicant for review (either electronically or on paper). The Applicant may require a Subapplicant to submit a project pre-application for review before allowing a project subapplication to be submitted.
- Next, the Applicant reviews the subapplication.
- If revisions are requested by the Applicant, then the Subapplicant may revise and resubmit the subapplication.
- Once the subapplication is reviewed and approved, the Applicant may include it in an application that is submitted to FEMA. (FEMA reserves the right to disapprove any of the submitted subapplications.)
- Applicants may also create their own project or planning subapplications and may also create subapplications for management costs and technical assistance and include them in their applications to FEMA.
- If FEMA requests revisions to a section(s) of a subapplication, then the Applicant may revise the section(s) of the subapplication, or release the section(s) to the Subapplicant for revision and resubmission.
- Once FEMA reviews and approves applications, FEMA creates a federal award for the Applicant, who is then referred to as the Recipient.
- The Recipient issues subawards to the Subapplicant, who is then referred to as the Subrecipient.
- Throughout implementation of the federal award, the Recipient submits quarterly performance and financial reports to FEMA.

# eGrants Internal System Functions and Users

The functions supported by the eGrants Internal System include:

- Reviewing and approving Applicant registrations
- Reviewing applications for eligibility and completeness, which include:
    - Documenting the status of the mitigation plan

- Reviewing costs
    - Ensuring cost-effectiveness of mitigation projects
- Creating original and amendments of award packages
- Reviewing Quarterly Financial Status and Performance Reports

The people who use the eGrants Internal System include:

- FEMA Headquarters and Regional staff with HMA grant program responsibility
- Regional Assistance Officers

**Note**

Users must have approved eGrants roles in order to access the system. Access to eGrants is covered in Lesson 3.

# eGrants Internal System Workflow

The application review process follows a specific workflow in the eGrants Internal System:

- An Applicant submits an application to FEMA.
- FEMA reviews the application. If revisions are requested by FEMA, then the Applicant may revise and resubmit the application.
- After FEMA reviews the subapplications contained in the application, FEMA creates an award package for the Applicant—who then becomes the Recipient—that includes the approved subapplications.
- Over the period of performance of the federal award, the Recipient submits Quarterly Performance Reports on the federal award to FEMA. If FEMA requests revisions, then the Recipient may revise and resubmit the Quarterly Performance Report.

# eGrants Internal System Workflows (continued)

There are three workflows in the eGrants Internal System that detail the processes we discussed:

- **Pre-Award Eligibility Workflows:** Outlines the steps in FEMA's process for reviewing the submitted applications and subapplications for eligibility. The Pre-Award Eligibility Workflow for non-competitive FMA applications and subapplications differs from that of the competitive

PDM applications and subapplications because the PDM grant program requires the National Review Process to be followed.

- The **FMA Pre-Award Eligibility Workflow** will be discussed in detail in Lesson 5. You can view the <u>FMA Pre-Award Eligibility Workflow</u> diagram. <u>Select this link for a full description of the FMA Pre-Award Eligibility Workflow diagram.</u>

- The **PDM Pre-Award Eligibility Workflow** will be discussed in detail in Lesson 5 and Lesson 7. You can view the <u>PDM Pre-Award Eligibility Workflow</u> diagram. <u>Select this link for a full description of the PDM Pre-Award Eligibility Workflow diagram.</u>

- **Awards Workflow:** Outlines the process for creating federal awards. The Awards Workflow will be discussed in detail in Lesson 9.

- **Quarterly Reports Workflow:** Outlines the process for monitoring the implementation of federal awards through reviewing quarterly reports. This workflow is discussed in detail in Lesson 10. Select this link to view the <u>Quarterly Reports Workflow</u> diagram. <u>Select this link for a full description of the Quarterly Reports Workflow diagram.</u>

# Lesson 2 Summary

In this lesson, you learned about the general functions of the:

- Mitigation eGrants External System
- Mitigation eGrants Internal System

The key points from this lesson are:

- The eGrants system consists of two parts:
  - External System for Applicants and Subapplicants (on the internet)
  - Internal System for FEMA users (inside the FEMA firewall on the Intranet)
- Application submitted under the two existing grant programs FMA and PDM are managed in the eGrants Internal System.
- You can also monitor the status of federal awards under the two legacy programs SRL and RFC.
- Three separate workflows are used in the eGrants Internal System:
  - Pre-Award Eligibility Workflow for managing the review of submitted applications and subapplications
  - Awards Workflow for creating and amending award packages
  - Quarterly Reports Workflow for monitoring federal award implementation through review of quarterly reports
- The Pre-Award Eligibility Workflow; the Workflow used for PDM applications differs from the Workflow used for FMA applications because there is a National Review Process that is a part of the competitive PDM grant program.

# Lesson 3 Overview

This lesson describes the roles needed to access the eGrants Internal System to perform the various functions. At the end of this lesson, you should be able to identify:

- The eGrants Internal System positions and their associated queues
- The steps to access the eGrants Internal System

# eGrants User Scenario

**Team Leader:** Alex Salazar, Flood Mitigation Assistance (FMA) Program Coordinator

**Your Role:** New FMA Program Analyst

**Office:** FEMA Regional Office

**Challenge:** You need to access the eGrants Internal System for the first time.

**To Date:** You understand the functions within the Internal and External eGrants Systems.

Listen to Alex
Audio transcript

**The Next Step:** Alex will demonstrate how to assign roles and provide access to eGrants through FEIMS.

# Users, Positions, and Roles

The eGrants Internal System, like the External System, is developed on a role-based scheme. The eGrants roles are driven by positions on teams in the FEIMS System. This means that each eGrants Internal System user has roles assigned based on his/her FEIMS position(s) and teams. Each queue in the eGrants Workflow may be performed only by users who have the appropriate role(s).

# Workflows, Queues, and Positions

Each FEMA review team member is assigned eGrants roles based on his or her position on teams in the FEMA Enterprise Information Management System (FEIMS).

The eGrants Internal System review process comprises groups of actions called **workflows.** Each workflow is broken down into **queues.** The queues are available to users based on their assigned user roles.

The table below shows the workflows and queues applicable to the FMA and PDM grant programs and the roles that can perform each queue.

| Program | Program | Workflow | Queue | Position |
| --- | --- | --- | --- | --- |
| FMA | PDM | Pre-Award Eligibility | Receipt and Delegate | Assistance Officer |
| FMA | PDM | Pre-Award Eligibility | Initial Review | FMA Coordinator, PDM Coordinator |
| FMA | PDM | Pre-Award Eligibility | Cost Review | Cost Reviewer |
| FMA | PDM | Pre-Award Eligibility | Cost Effectiveness/Engineering Review | FMA Coordinator, PDM Coordinator |
| FMA | PDM | Pre-Award Eligibility | Planning Review | Plan Reviewer |
| FMA | PDM | Pre-Award Eligibility | Notification Coordination | FMA Coordinator, PDM Coordinator |
| | PDM | Pre-Award Eligibility | National Technical Review | Contract Technical Reviewer, HQ Technical Reviewer |
| | PDM | Pre-Award Eligibility | Subgrant Selection (for Award) | Approving Federal Official, Contract PDM Coordinator, HQ PDM Coordinator |

| FMA | PDM | Pre-Award Eligibility | Environmental/Historic Preservation | Environmental Reviewer, Historical Reviewer |
|---|---|---|---|---|
| FMA | PDM | Pre-Award Eligibility | Pre-Award Review | FMA Coordinator, PDM Coordinator |
| FMA | PDM | Awards | Create/Amend Award | Assistance Officer, Grants Management Specialist |
| FMA | PDM | Quarterly Reports | Quarterly Review (Programs) | Quarterly Reports Program Reviewer |
| FMA | PDM | Quarterly Reports | Quarterly Review (Grants) | Quarterly Reports Grants Reviewer |

# Requesting Access for a User

Certain FEMA personnel have a Submitter role in FEIMS that allows them to submit requests for new positions. These are usually Team Leaders, Branch Chiefs, or Managers. The Submitter role also may be assigned to a user with a position, such as Division Chief, due to hierarchy in FEIMS. You will need this FEIMS Submitter position if you will be requesting positions for yourself or others in FEIMS.

Alex is going to show you the process to request a new position for an eGrants user in FEIMS. As an example, he will show you how to submit a request for a Region 1 Hazard Mitigation Assistance (HMA) Coordinator position. The first step in the process is to search for the user in FEIMS.

Scroll down to see slideshow captions.

From the FEMA Intranet Homepage, enter the **eGrants Internal System URL:** https://fema.net/fams/RuWeb/home. It is a good idea to **bookmark** this page because you will be returning to it frequently.

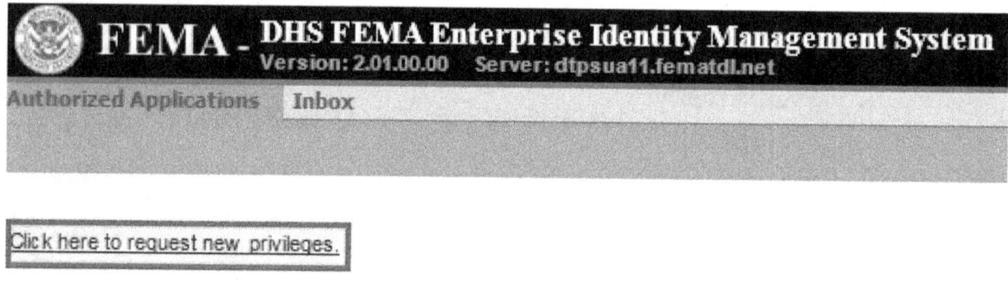

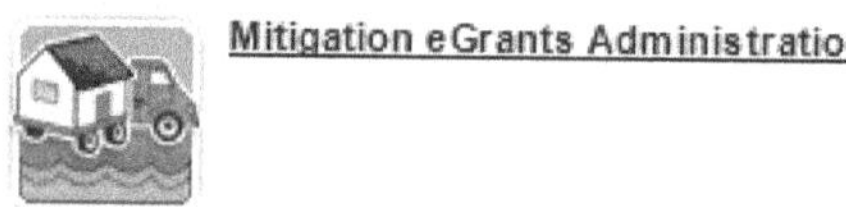

Mitigation eGrants Administration

The FEMA Enterprise Identity Management System (FEIMS) Authorized Applications screen displays. Select the **Request new privileges** link on the upper left side.

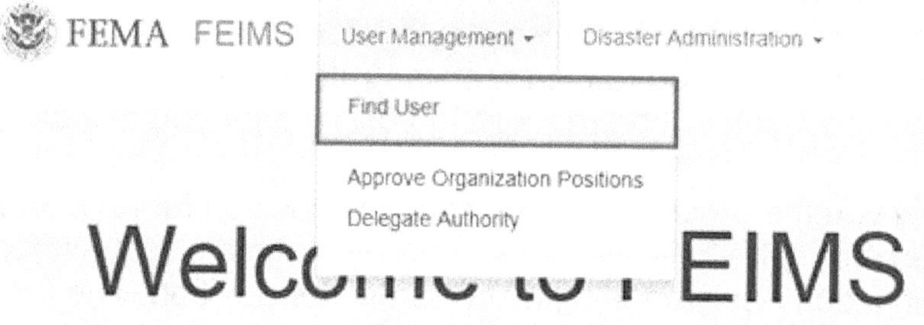


The FEIMS Portal Welcome screen displays. From the User Management drop-down menu, select the **Find User** option.

# Find User



The Find User screen displays. Type Smi* in the **Last Name =** field. Then select the **Search** button.

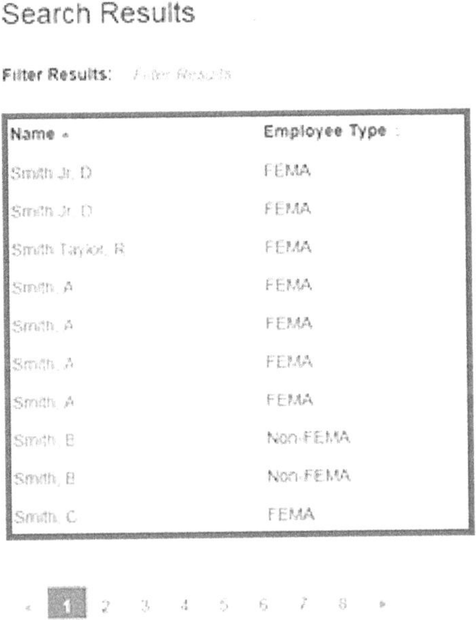



At the bottom of the screen, below the search criteria fields, the results of the search are displayed.

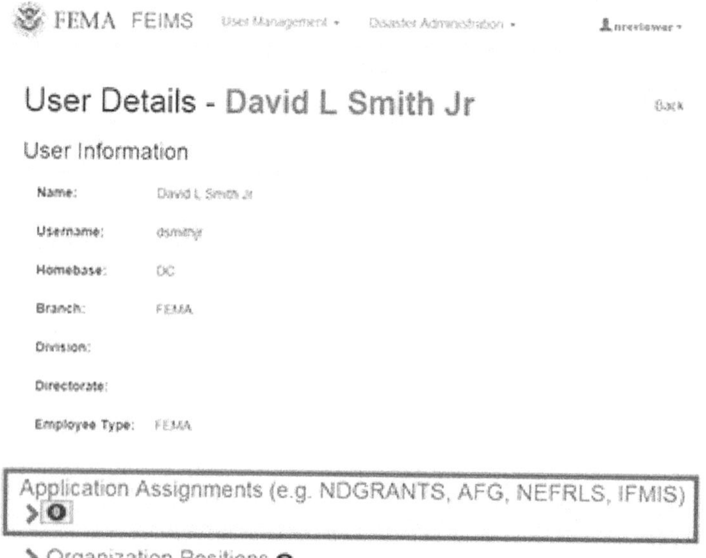


The User Details screen displays. There is a zero to the right of **Application Assignments** dropdown arrow because eGrants is not one of the application systems that you need to request specific access to. There are more steps to the process and we will continue them in the next slideshow.

# Assigning Positions and Teams

Organization Positions are based on the FEMA organizational structure. A user may have access to more than one application in FEIMS.

Alex will demonstrate how to select the correct organizational position to allow David Smith, Jr., to access eGrants so he may perform his job.

Scroll down to see slideshow captions.

We need to assign this user an Organization Position. You can see by the number 2 to the right of the **Organization Positions** drop-down menu that this user already has two team assignments. We want to assign him another position so he can process Hazard Mitigation Assistance federal award applications. Select the drop-down arrow to the left of Organization Positions.

Below Organization Positions three choices are displayed: Positions, Current Roles, and Authorities. Select the arrow to the left of the **Positions** option.

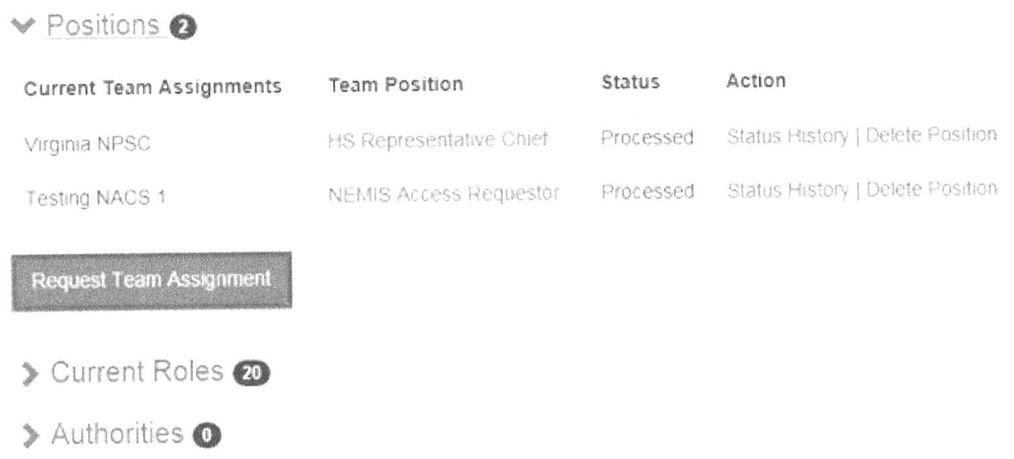


The list of the user's current team assignments and positions are displayed. From this screen, you can check the status history of an assignment or you can delete an assignment, if necessary. To add another, select the **Request Team Assignment** button.

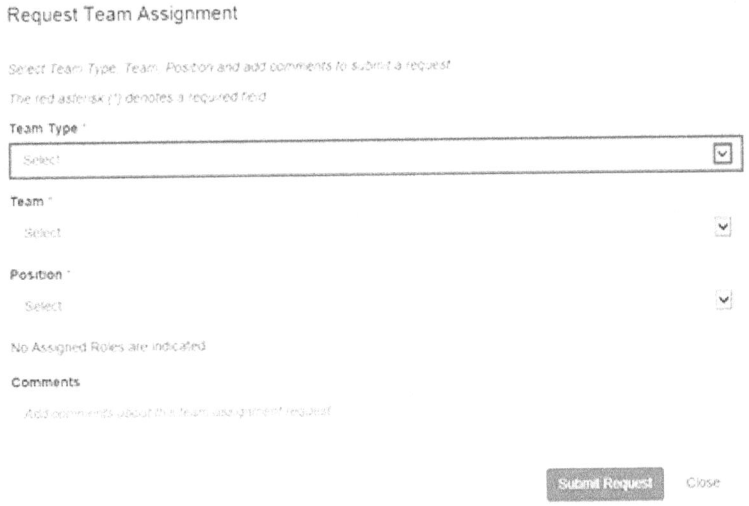


The Request Team Assignment dialogue box displays. You will note that several fields on this screen are marked with a red asterisk. The asterisk indicates a required field. Select the arrow for the dropdown menu under **Team Type.**

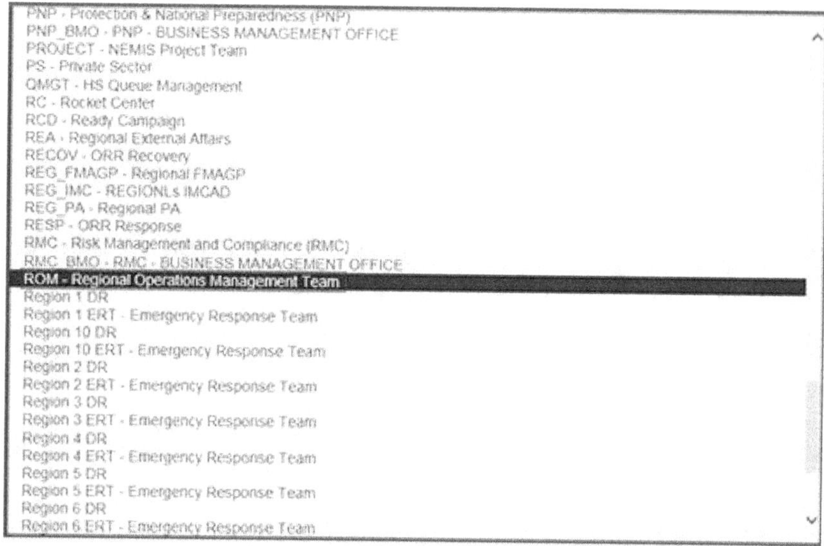

Select the **ROM — Regional Operations Management Team** option from the **Team Type** list.

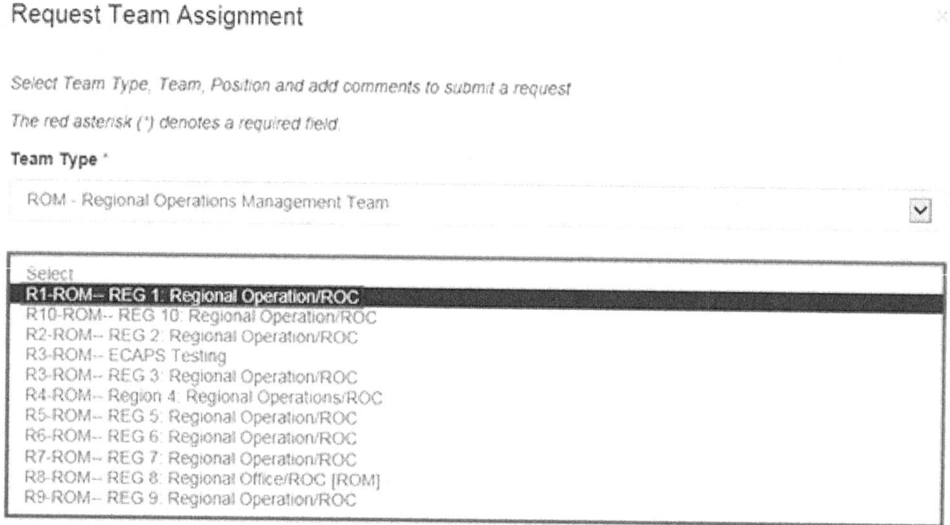

Then, from the **Team** drop-down list, select the **R1-ROM— REG 1: Regional Operation/ROC** option.

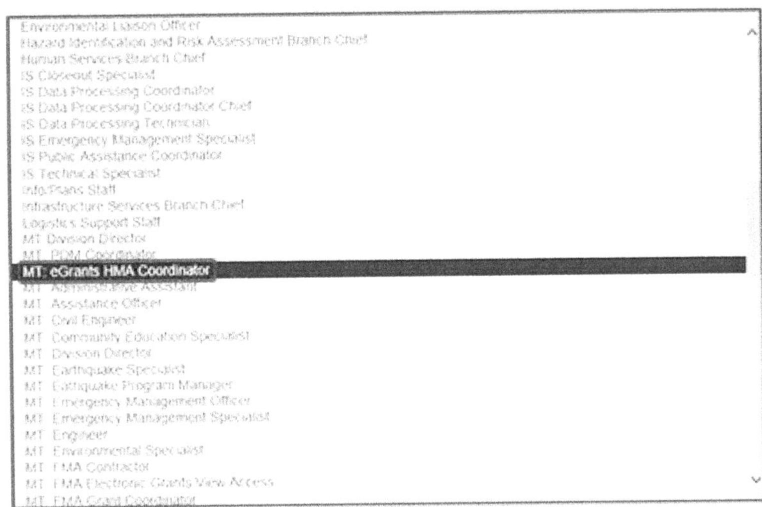


Then select the **Position** drop-down menu. Scroll through the list to find the positions that start with MT, which stands for Mitigation. These positions provide access to eGrants. We need to select the **MT: eGrants HMA Coordinator** option for this user.

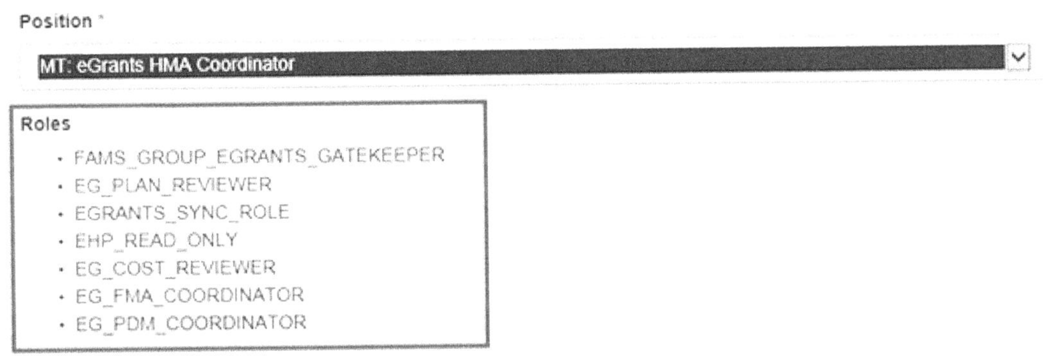


All the **Roles** associated with the selected position are displayed at the bottom of the Request Team Assignment box.

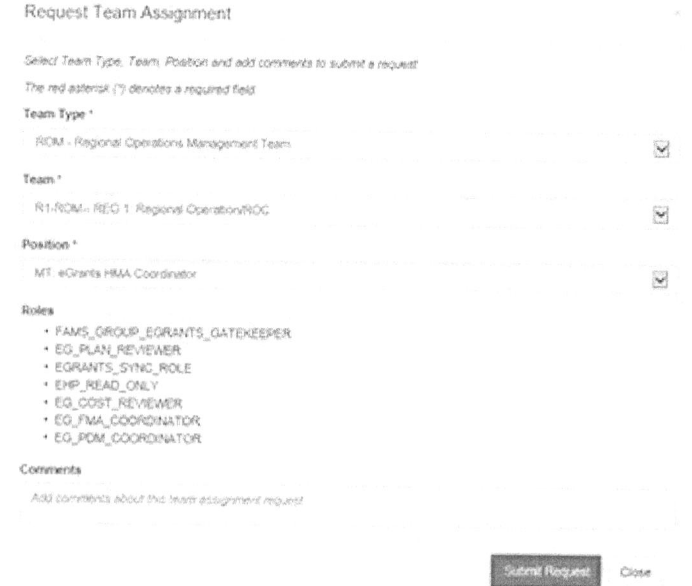

The Request Team Assignment box displays the selected Team Type, Team, Position, and associated roles. Select the **Submit Request** button.

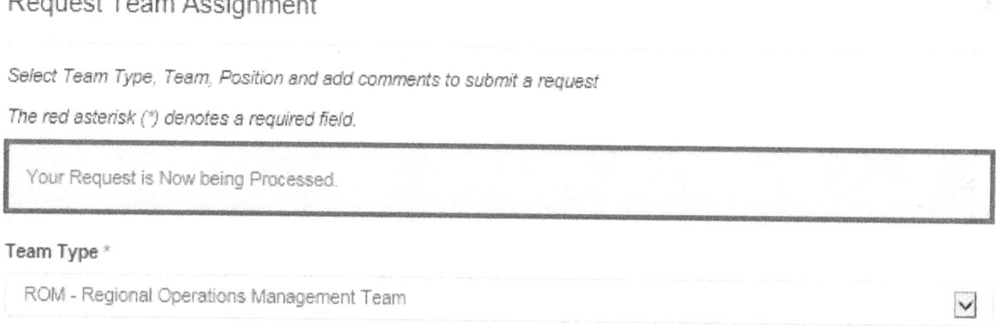

The notice, **Your Request is Now being Processed,** is displayed.

Select the **Close** button to return to the User Details screen.

# Contact the Approving Official

A person with the FEIMS Approver position will then need to approve the new role before it can be activated. This is usually a Team Leader, Branch Chief, or Manager at FEMA. The Approver role also may be assigned to a user with a position, such as Division Chief, due to hierarchy in the FEIMS, allowing him or her to approve every position below that level.

| **Note** | The Approving Official is **not** automatically notified. The submitter may want to notify the Approving Official to ensure that the request is processed in a timely fashion. |

# Logging In

The <u>eGrants Internal System</u> can be accessed only behind the FEMA firewall at URL: https://sso.fema.net/famsRuWeb/home.
Enter your **FEIMS Personal Identification Number (PIN)** and then select the **OK** button. If you mistyped your PIN, you can select the **Cancel** button to reset the information you entered.

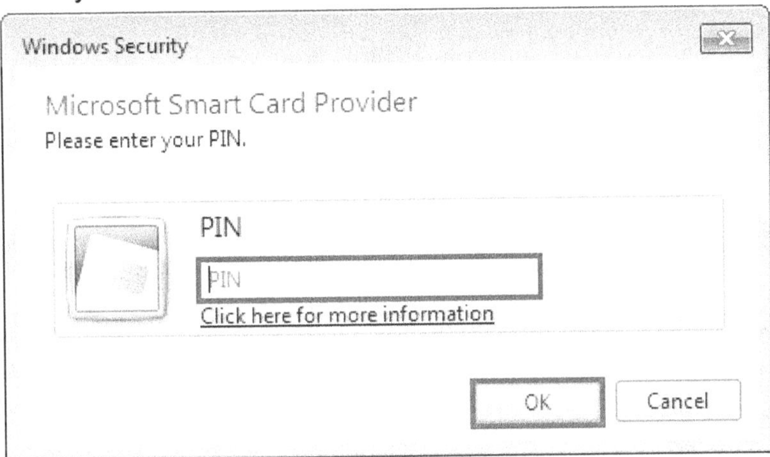



# Accessing the eGrants Internal System

Once you have logged in to the FEMA Portal, the Authorized Applications screen displays. You will see a list of all the systems available to you based on your FEIMS position. From this page, select either the **Mitigation eGrants Administration title** or **icon** to access the eGrants Internal System.

Select this link for the full text of the image.

# eGrants Internal System Homepage

Alex will describe the various features of the eGrants Homepage. Scroll down to see slideshow captions.

Once you have selected the Mitigation eGrants link, you are taken to the eGrants Homepage. The **program icons** and **links** take you to the Inbox for the selected program area.

This screen will also tell you **how many queues** for submitted applications are available in the Inbox for you to work on for each program, based on your roles.

eGrants Home

There are several links on the left sidebar as well. The **myRoles** link, which we will cover in this lesson, will allow you to view your specific eGrants roles.

Several **Registration links** are available to users with Grants Administrator, Pre-Disaster Mitigation (PDM) Coordinator, and Flood Mitigation Assistance (FMA) Coordinator roles to manage Applicant registrations for access to the External System. This functionality will be covered in Lesson 4.



The **Program Administration** link is available for FEMA Headquarters Program Administrators with Headquarters PDM Coordinator and/or Headquarters FMA Coordinator roles to manage the federal award programs in the system. The Program Administration function will be covered in Lesson 12.

# The myRoles Screen

The myRoles screen can be accessed from the eGrants Internal System Homepage, as well as from any other Internal System screen, by selecting the myRoles link in the sidebar menu on the left of the screen. This screen shows you the roles you have been assigned in the eGrants Internal System.

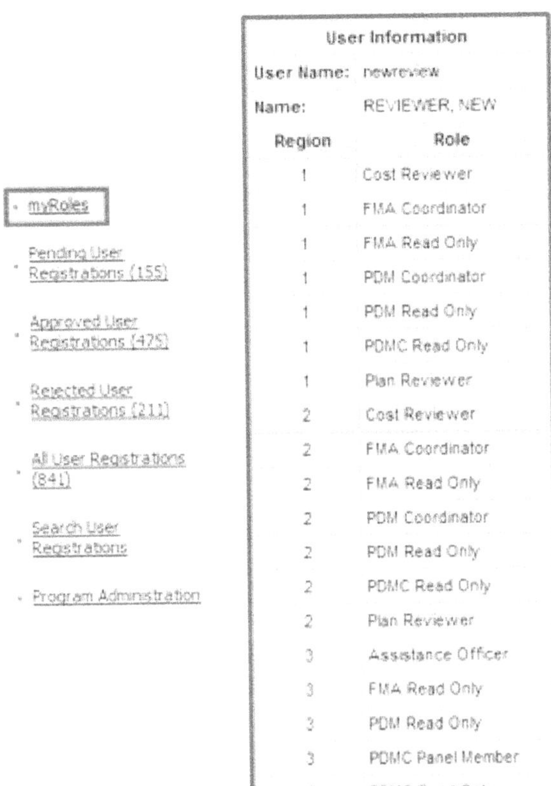


Select this link for the full text of the image.

# Logging Out

To log out of the eGrants Internal System, select the **Logout** link in the upper right-hand corner of the screen.

In compliance with FEMA Information Technology (IT) security policy, there is a time limit of 30 minutes of inactivity in the eGrants Internal System before your session will expire. An **expiration notice** at the top right-hand side of your screen informs you of how much time you have left before the session will be terminated. If you do not resume activity in eGrants, the system will automatically log you out and you will lose any unsaved data.

# Lesson 3 Summary

In this lesson, you learned about the:

- Mitigation eGrants Internal System roles
- Process for requesting access and roles in the eGrants Internal System
- Process for logging into the eGrants Internal System

The key points from this lesson are:

- You must be behind the FEMA firewall, i.e., use the FEMA Intranet, to access the eGrants Internal System
- eGrants roles are based on FEMA Organization Position and Application Assignments in FEIMS
- You will need your FEIMS User ID and Password to log into eGrants
- You can navigate to a grant program Inbox by selecting the grant program link or icon from the eGrants Internal System Homepage

# Lesson 4 Overview

This lesson describes the process used in the eGrants Internal System for administering the Applicant user registrations for the eGrants External System.

At the end of this lesson, you should be able to identify:

- The process for managing eGrants External System user registrations
- The process for searching the eGrants Internal System for Applicant user registrations
- The process for reassigning applications from one registered Applicant user to another approved user from the same Applicant organization

# eGrants User Scenario

**Team Leader:** Alex Salazar, Flood Mitigation Assistance (FMA) Program Coordinator

**Your Role:** New FMA Program Analyst

**Office:** FEMA Regional Office

**Challenge:** Processing eGrants user registrations

**To Date:** You have logged into the eGrants Internal System and understand how to request eGrants privileges for an eGrants Internal System user.

Listen to Alex
Audio transcript

**The Next Step:** Alex will show you how to assign or update access privileges for eGrants External System users.

Hello. I'm Alex Salazar, and I will be training you to review FMA grant program applications. People in communities, tribal regions, states, and territories have to register to be able to use eGrants to create and submit applications and subapplications. I will show you how to review and approve external eGrants user registrations and assign them the appropriate application access privileges.

# Granting Access Privileges to the eGrants External System

Applicants must register and request access to the eGrants External System. Those eGrants External System registration requests are pending in the eGrants Internal System for review by FEMA users. While eGrants Internal System users have roles and positions, eGrants External System users have privileges and access levels. The privileges given to Applicant users determine what they can do in the eGrants External System. There are privileges for applications, subapplications, award packages, and quarterly financial and performance reports. In addition, the levels of access that can be granted for each of these functional areas are View, Create/Edit, and Sign/Submit—or any combination of these. A user's privileges and access levels may not be the same under the FMA grant program as they are for the Pre-Disaster Mitigation (PDM) grant program.

It is recommended that FEMA request the Authorized Governor's Representative or other official to **provide to FEMA in writing** the names of the individuals within their organization to whom access should be provided—particularly Sign/Submit privilege—as that gives a user the ability to provide his/her electronic signature on behalf of the Applicant organization.

A user with the Assistance Officer, PDM Coordinator, Headquarters PDM Coordinator, or FMA Coordinator role(s) in the eGrants Internal System can manage registrations for the FEMA Region(s) and grant program(s) for which they have access in eGrants.

# Pending Registrations

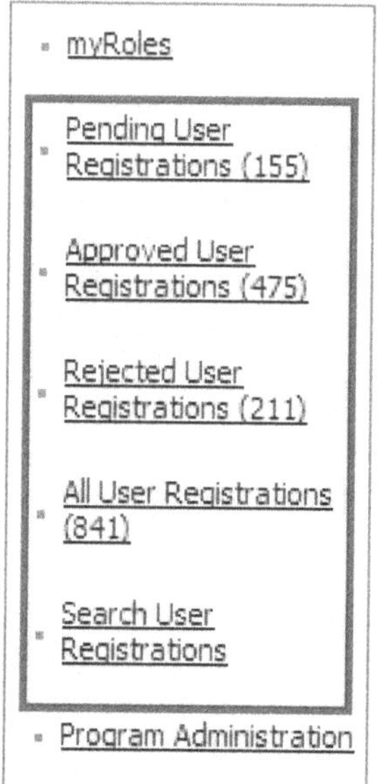


The numbers of pending, approved, and rejected user registrations are displayed with the associated link in the left sidebar menu of the eGrants Homepage.

You can also search user registrations to quickly locate a pending, approved, or rejected registration.

At the request of the Applicant, you can reassign applications from one eGrants External System user to another approved user from the same Applicant organization. For example, this function may be needed if an eGrants External System user retires or is out of the office and the Applicant needs access to that user's applications. The reassignment of applications is permanent but will **not** impact the original user's access. Only rejecting a user will ensure that he or she no longer has access to the applications.

# User Registrations

There are three types of user registrations in eGrants:

1. **Pending registrations:** User registrations that have not been processed for any HMA grant program.
2. **Approved registrations:** User registrations that have been processed for at least one HMA grant program. These registrations can be viewed in order to add privileges, remove privileges, or reject the user, as needed.
3. **Rejected registrations:** User registrations that have been rejected for all HMA grant programs. These registrations can be viewed and privileges added, if necessary.

# Viewing a Pending User Registration

You will need to manage the user registration requests for the eGrants External System that have been submitted by Applicants. In order to view the registration links, you must have the appropriate role to manage registrations. To respond to registration requests in a reasonable amount of time, it is recommended that you check your pending registrations regularly.

Alex will demonstrate how to view a pending user registration.

Scroll down to view slideshow captions.

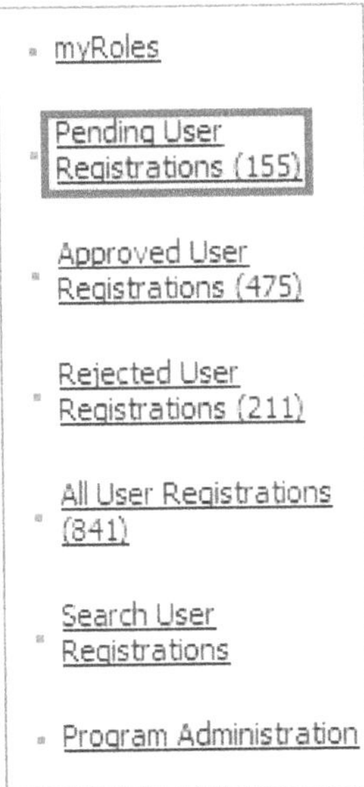

You should check the pending registrations regularly so we can process them in a timely fashion. Select the **Pending User Registrations** link from your Inbox screen.

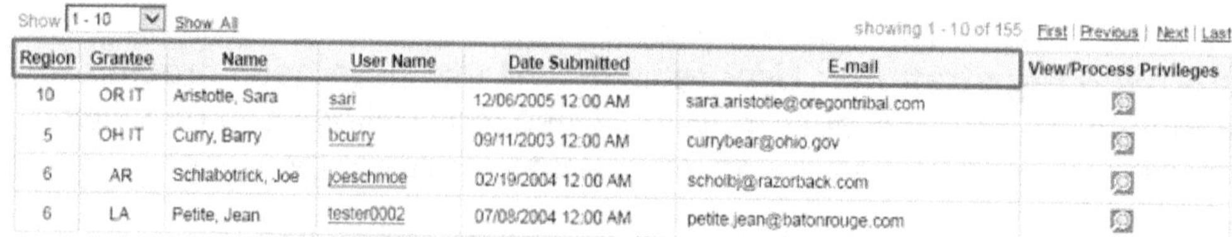

The Pending User Registrations screen displays. It lists the FEMA Region; Grantee (that is, the Applicant's state, territory, or tribe code); the registrant's name and FEIMS user name, the date the registration was submitted, and the registrant's e-mail address.

There are many functions that are common on various Internal System screens. This includes how search results and lists are displayed and sorted. The default is to display 10 items at a time. If you want to display a different group of 10 registrations, select the group you wish to view from the **Show** drop-down menu. You can also use the **First, Previous, Next,** and **Last** links to navigate among groups of 10 registrations. (This screen only displays the Next and Last links.)

Let's display all the pending registrations by selecting the **Show All** link.

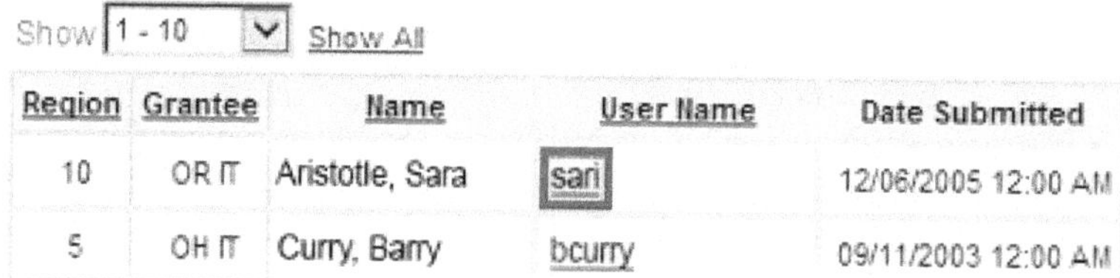

The Pending User Registrations screen appears. Before approving or rejecting any user registration, it is necessary to review the information provided by the user to ensure it is complete. Select the **User Name** link to display the user's registration information.

## User Registration: Aristotle, Sara (sari)

| Personal Information | | Contact Information | |
|---|---|---|---|
| Title: | Ms | Contact/Business Phone: | 5555550000 |
| First Name: | Sara | Home Phone: | |
| Last Name: | Aristotle | Mobile Phone/Pager: | |
| Organization: | Klamath | E-mail: | sari@oregontribe.com |
| **Address** | | **Shipping Address** | |
| Street: | | Street: | |
| City: | Chiloquin | City: | |
| State: | OR | State: | |
| ZIP: | 97624 | ZIP: | |

| Print | Close |
|---|---|

The User Registration screen appears. This screen displays the personal information, contact information, address, and shipping address that the Applicant entered into the eGrants External System. Select the **Print** button to print the registration information. When you have finished, select the **Close** button to close the window.

# Approving a Registration

You can process user registrations only for the grant program(s) for which you have an assigned eGrants role(s). For example, if a user has only the PDM Coordinator role, the FMA checkboxes will be grayed out, because the PDM Coordinator cannot approve registrations for the FMA grant program.
You will be able to reject all access to or approve registrations for the FMA or PDM grant programs, depending on your eGrants roles.
Alex will demonstrate how to approve a user's registration.
Scroll down to see slideshow captions.

**Search User Results**

The following user registrations were retrieved from the FEMA Access Management System (FAMS). Click on the User Name to view more information about

| Region | Grantee | Name | User Name | Date Submitted | E-mail | Status | View/Process Privileges | Reassign Applications |
|---|---|---|---|---|---|---|---|---|
| 1 | CT | Smith, John | smith_o_ct | 01/28/2006 12:00 AM | j.smith@wdo.org | Approved | | |
| 8 | LA | Smith, John | fams_ug | 06/02/2009 12:00 AM | noresponse@dhs.gov | Pending | | |

From the Pending User Registrations screen, select the icon in the **View/Process Privileges** column of the registration you wish to process.

### View/Process Privileges: Aristotle, Sara (sari)

| All User Access | Program | Application | Award Package | Quarterly Report Package | Financial Status Report | Performance Report |
|---|---|---|---|---|---|---|
| ☑ Reject | FMA/SRL/RFC | ☐ View<br>☐ Create/Edit<br>☐ Sign/Submit | ☐ View<br>☐ Create/Edit<br>☐ Sign/Submit | ☐ View<br>☐ Create/Edit<br>☐ Sign/Submit | ☐ View<br>☐ Create/Edit<br>☐ Sign/Submit | ☐ View<br>☐ Create/Edit<br>☐ Sign/Submit |
| | PDM-C | ☐ View<br>☐ Create/Edit<br>☐ Sign/Submit | ☐ View<br>☐ Create/Edit<br>☐ Sign/Submit | ☐ View<br>☐ Create/Edit<br>☐ Sign/Submit | ☐ View<br>☐ Create/Edit<br>☐ Sign/Submit | ☐ View<br>☐ Create/Edit<br>☐ Sign/Submit |

[ Process ]    [ Cancel ]

The View/Process Privileges screen appears. From here, you can select the privileges and access levels for the registrant. You don't have the PDM Coordinator role, so the access levels for the PDM-C program are grayed out. Since you have the FMA Coordinator role, you can approve or reject access to the FMA program. If we wanted to reject this user's access, we would select the **Reject** checkbox in the All User Access column.

### View/Process Privileges: Aristotle, Sara (sari)

| All User Access | Program | Application | Award Package | Quarterly Report Package | Financial Status Report | Performance Report |
|---|---|---|---|---|---|---|
| ☐ Reject | FMA/SRL/RFC | ☑ View<br>☑ Create/Edit<br>☐ Sign/Submit | ☐ View<br>☐ Create/Edit<br>☐ Sign/Submit | ☐ View<br>☐ Create/Edit<br>☐ Sign/Submit | ☐ View<br>☐ Create/Edit<br>☐ Sign/Submit | ☐ View<br>☐ Create/Edit<br>☐ Sign/Submit |
| | PDM-C | ☐ View<br>☐ Create/Edit<br>☐ Sign/Submit | ☐ View<br>☐ Create/Edit<br>☐ Sign/Submit | ☐ View<br>☐ Create/Edit<br>☐ Sign/Submit | ☐ View<br>☐ Create/Edit<br>☐ Sign/Submit | ☐ View<br>☐ Create/Edit<br>☐ Sign/Submit |

[ Process ]    [ Cancel ]

To provide this user with Create/Edit access for FMA applications, you need to select the **View** and **Create/Edit** checkboxes in the FMA Application section. If you needed to provide Sign/Submit access to this user, you would need to select the View and Create/Edit levels as well. When you are done, select the **Process** button.

### Confirmation

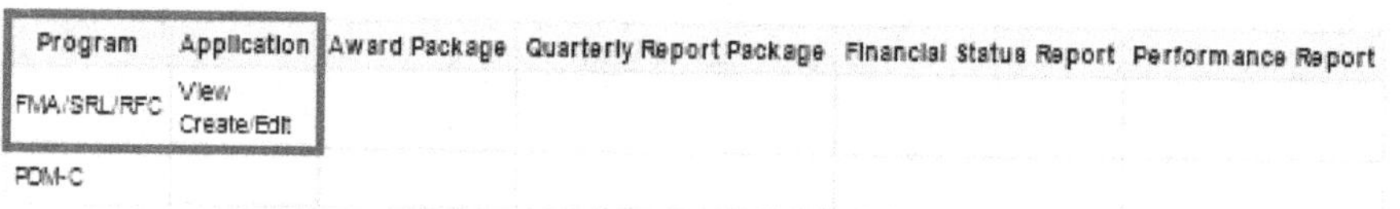

The user registration for Smith, John (connstategrant02) was successfully processed with the following privileges:

| Program | Application | Award Package | Quarterly Report Package | Financial Status Report | Performance Report |
|---|---|---|---|---|---|
| FMA/SRL/RFC | View<br>Create/Edit | | | | |
| PDM-C | | | | | |

E-mails are automatically sent to Grantee users when access is approved. E-mails are not sent when access is rejected.

Once the user registration is processed, you will get a **Confirmation** screen that lists the user's privileges, if any, and indicates whether an e-mail was sent to the user. This page is generated automatically by eGrants. You can select any of the links on the sidebar menu to continue checking pending registrations, or you can select the **Return to Inbox** link to return to the eGrants Homepage.

# Registration Confirmation Email

For approved registrations, an email will be sent to the Applicant user to notify him or her of his or her approved eGrants privileges. The e-mail message is generated automatically by eGrants.
No notification will be sent to a rejected user. If a user registration is rejected, you may contact the registrant to provide an explanation, as needed.

# Search User Registrations

Alex will demonstrate how to search for user registrations among all of the eGrants registrations, whether pending, approved, or rejected.
Scroll down to see slideshow captions.

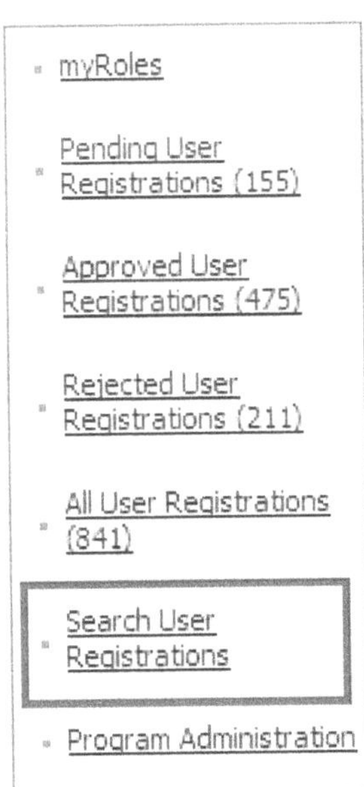


From the eGrants Internal Homepage, select the **Search User Registrations** link.

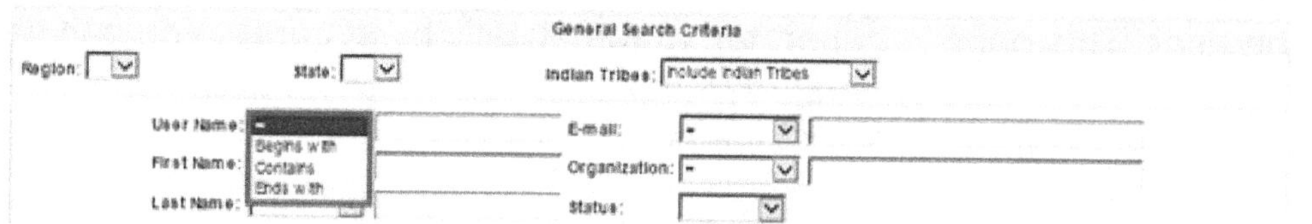


The Search User Registrations screen displays. General search criteria include Region; State; Indian Tribe; User Name; First Name; Last Name; E-mail; Organization; and Status of the registration. Not all of the search criteria fields are required. Start by selecting the **User Name** drop-down menu. This menu has four options: "Equals," "Begins with," "Contains," or "Ends with".

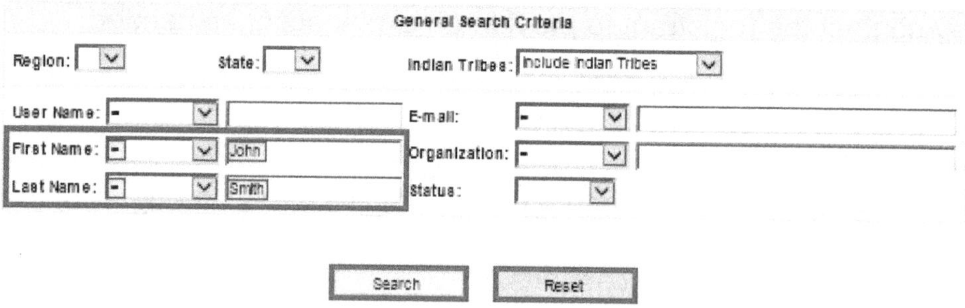


Let's search for John Smith. Type "John" in the First Name field with "=", then type "Smith" in the **Last Name** field with "=". At the bottom of the screen are two buttons. The **Reset** button will clear or reset the information you have entered. Select the **Search** button to start the search.

Search User Results

The following user registrations were retrieved from the FEMA Access Management System (FAMS). Click on the User Name to view more information about a specific user.

Show 1 - 10 ☑ Show All                                                     showing 1 - 10 of 17 Next | Last

| Region | Grantee | Name | User Name | Date Submitted | E-mail | Status | View/Process Privileges | Reassign Applications |
|--------|---------|------|-----------|----------------|--------|--------|------------------------|----------------------|
| 4 | SC | Smith, Jon | marks99 | 04/09/2007 12:00 AM | jon.smith@abc.gov | Approved | | |
| 1 | CT | Smith, John | smith_g_ct | 01/28/2005 12:00 AM | jsmith@cdo.org | Approved | | |
| 6 | LA | Smith, John | fama_us | 06/02/2009 12:00 AM | smith.j.l@state.gov | Pending | | |
| 7 | MO IT | Smith, Bill | maroon | 01/06/2004 12:00 AM | w.smith@commonwealth.gov | Approved | | |

The Search User Results screen displays. This screen shows the results of the user registration search and allows you to view user registration information, the **View/Process Privileges** icon, and the **Reassign Applications** icon. The registration information includes the FEMA Region, Grantee (or the Applicant's state, territory, or tribe abbreviation), the registrant's name and FEIMS user name, the date the registration was submitted, and the registrant's e-mail and registration status.

### Search User Results

The following user registrations were retrieved from the FEMA Access Management System (FAMS). Click on the User Name to view more information about

| Region | Grantee | Name | User Name | Date Submitted | E-mail | Status | View/Process Privileges | Reassign Applications |
|---|---|---|---|---|---|---|---|---|
| 1 | CT | Smith, John | smith_g_ct | 01/25/2005 12:00 AM | jsmith@wdc.org | Approved | | |
| 6 | LA | Smith, John | fams_uq | 06/02/2009 12:00 AM | noresponse@dhs.gov | Pending | | |

You may update privileges for previously approved or rejected registrations as well as process registrations that are pending. Selecting the icon in the **View/Process Privileges** column allows you to manage privileges for a user.

# Update User Privileges

You may update privileges for previously approved or rejected registrations. An Applicant may request that a user's privileges be modified. You may reassign an approved or rejected user's applications to another approved user in the same Applicant organization. It is best to document these requests in writing. Selecting the View/Process Privileges icon in the View/Process Privileges column allows you to manage privileges for a user.

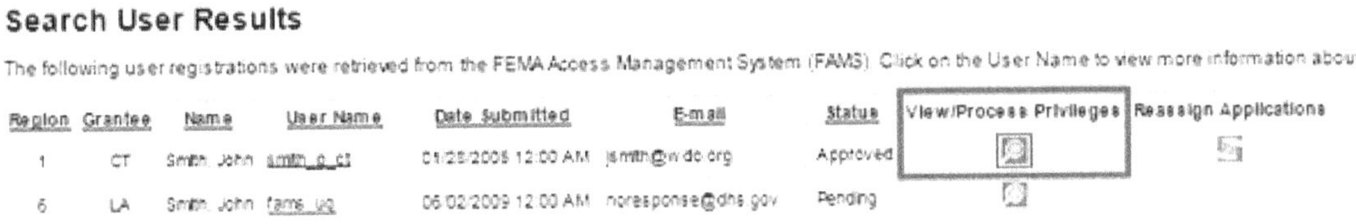

### Search User Results

The following user registrations were retrieved from the FEMA Access Management System (FAMS). Click on the User Name to view more information about

| Region | Grantee | Name | User Name | Date Submitted | E-mail | Status | View/Process Privileges | Reassign Applications |
|---|---|---|---|---|---|---|---|---|
| 1 | CT | Smith, John | smith_g_ct | 01/25/2005 12:00 AM | jsmith@wdc.org | Approved | | |
| 6 | LA | Smith, John | fams_uq | 06/02/2009 12:00 AM | noresponse@dhs.gov | Pending | | |

Select this link for the full text of the image.

# Reassign Applications

Occasionally, you may receive a request from an Applicant to reassign an approved or rejected user's applications to another approved user within the Applicant's organization. This situation may arise when an eGrants External System user retires or is out of the office and has not shared access to his or her applications with others.

The selected user will have access to all of the original user's submitted and un-submitted applications. However, the selected user will have only the privileges and level of access for applications, federal awards, and quarterly reports (i.e., View, Create/Edit, and Sign/Submit) received when his or her registration was processed. For example, you may reassign applications from one user in an Applicant organization with Sign/Submit privileges to another user with Create/Edit privileges for applications. The selected user will be able to access all of the original user's applications but will be able only to edit them, but not sign or submit them.

Reassigning applications is permanent. The only way to remove access to the applications from the selected user is to reject the selected user's registration, which will remove all access from the eGrants External System.

Reassigning applications to another user does **not** disallow the original user's access to them. For users who will no longer require access to eGrants, you may want to reject their registration.

# Reassign Applications (continued)

You will not be able to reassign applications from one user to another if they do not have privileges for the same programs, i.e., FMA or PDM. For example, if a user has privileges for **only** FMA, then you may not reassign his or her applications to a user with privileges for only PDM. If a user has privileges for FMA **and** PDM, then you may reassign their applications only to another user who has privileges for **both** programs.

Alex will demonstrate how to reassign an application to another user.

Scroll down to see slideshow captions.

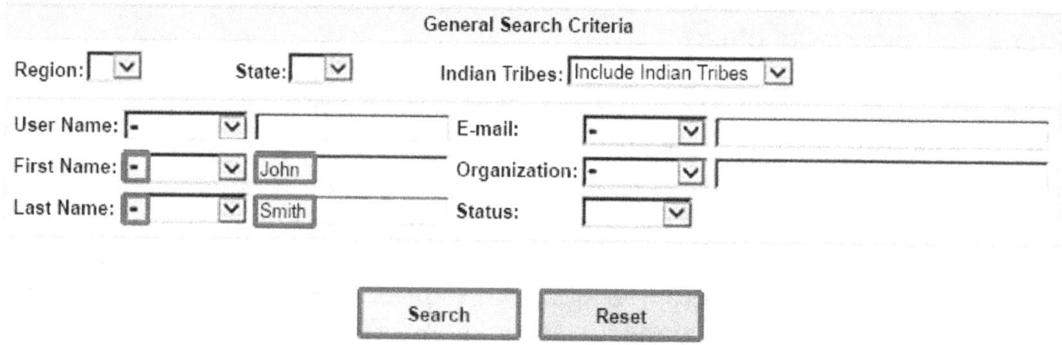

**Approved User Registrations**

The following user registrations were retrieved from the FEMA Access Management System (FAMS). Click on the User Name to view more information about a specific user.

Show 61 - 70 Show All

showing 61 - 70 of 476 First | Previous | Next | Last

| Region | Grantee | Name | User Name | Date Submitted | E-mail | View/Process Privileges | Reassign Applications |
|---|---|---|---|---|---|---|---|
| 1 | CT | Smith, John | connstategrant01 | 07/22/2003 12:00 AM | jspractice@fema.gov | | |
| 1 | CT | Smith, John | connstategrant02 | 07/22/2003 12:00 AM | jspractice@fema.gov | | |
| 1 | CT | smithson, john | connstategrant03 | 07/22/2003 12:00 AM | jsmpractice@fema.gov | | |

Let's reassign applications for user "connstategrant02." Select the **Reassign Applications** icon next to user "connstategrant02."

| | | | |
|---|---|---|---|
| **General Search Criteria** | | | |

Region: [ ]    State: [ ]    Indian Tribes: [Include Indian Tribes]

User Name: [-] [ ]    E-mail: [-] [ ]

First Name: [-] [John]    Organization: [-] [ ]

Last Name: [-] [Smith]    Status: [ ]

[ Search ]    [ Reset ]

Type "connstategrant01" in the **Username** field. Then select the **Search** button.

# Search User Results: Reassign Applications

Select user(s) from the table below by checking the box under the Select column heading. Click the Reassign button to reassign all of the applications that can be accessed by **Smith, John (connstategrant01)**to the selected user(s). Please note that reassigning applications will still allow Smith, John (connstategrant01) access to those applications; this procedure simply allows other users to access those applications.

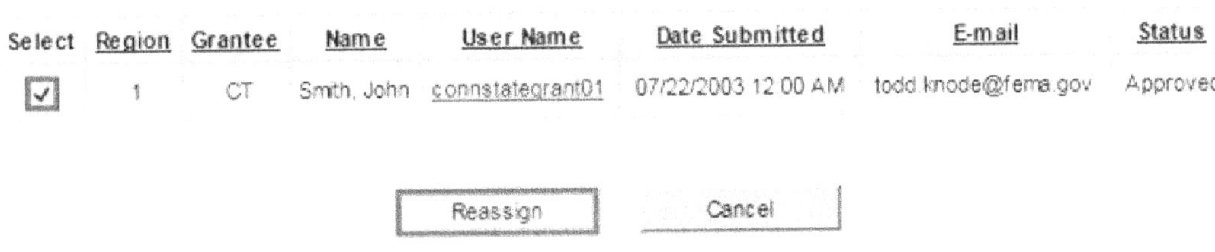

| Select | Region | Grantee | Name | User Name | Date Submitted | E-mail | Status |
|---|---|---|---|---|---|---|---|
| ✓ | 1 | CT | Smith, John | connstategrant01 | 07/22/2003 12:00 AM | todd.knode@fema.gov | Approved |

Check the **Select** box next to username "connstategrant01." Then select the **Reassign** button.

## Confirmation

The applications assigned to Smith, John (**connstategrant02**) have also been assigned to the following user(s):

| Name | User Name |
|---|---|
| Smith, John | connstategrant01 |

Return to Home

A **Confirmation** message appears indicating that you have successfully reassigned applications to another user. The original user will still retain access privileges to the applications. Select the **Return to Home** link to navigate to the eGrants Homepage.

# Lesson 4 Summary

In this lesson, you learned about the processes for:

- Managing user registrations for the eGrants External System
- Searching user registrations
- Reassigning applications to another eGrants External System user

The key points from this lesson are:

- You can approve Applicant privileges for applications, subapplications, award packages, and Financial and Performance Quarterly Reports. In addition, the levels of access that can be provided for each of these functions are View, Create/Edit, Sign/Submit—or a combination of these.
- For approved registrations, the Applicant user will be notified of his/her approved eGrants privileges automatically via e-mail.
  Registrations which are denied will also generate a notification e-mail.
- You can search pending, approved, or rejected user registrations from Applicants in the Region(s) for which you have eGrants roles to manage them.
- At the request of the Applicant, you can reassign applications from one eGrants External System Applicant user to another approved user within the same Applicant organization.
- Reassigning applications is permanent.

# Lesson 5 Overview

This lesson describes in detail the Pre-Award Eligibility Workflows for the Flood Mitigation Assistance (FMA) and Pre-Disaster Mitigation (PDM) grant programs. At the end of this lesson, you should be able to identify:

- The Pre-Award Eligibility Workflow queues
- The possible outcomes of a Pre-Award Eligibility queue review

# eGrants User Scenario

Listen to Alex
Audio transcript

**Team Leader:** Alex Salazar, FMA Program Coordinator

**Your Role:** New FMA Program Analyst

**Office:** FEMA Regional Office

**Challenge:** You need to understand how subapplications are processed through the FMA and PDM workflow queues.

**To Date:** You have learned how to provide and update eGrants access privileges for an eGrants External System user.

**The Next Step:** Alex will describe the FMA and PDM workflows and highlight their differences.

Hi, this is Alex again. Mitigation grant program subapplications must pass through several reviews before being awarded. While the FMA and PDM subapplications are much the same, the review process, or workflow, for PDM subapplications is a bit different because of the competitive nature of the grant program. I will explain the Pre-Award Eligibility Workflows for both programs and highlight their differences.

# Pre-Award Eligibility Workflow Queues

The eGrants Internal System allows FEMA to electronically manage the processes of reviewing subapplications submitted to FEMA, preparing and amending award packages, and monitoring federal award implementation.

The Pre-Award Eligibility Workflow is the process of reviewing the submitted subapplications. The Pre-Award Eligibility Workflow begins with the Receipt and Delegate queue and then the Initial Review queue. From there, it branches into three concurrent queues: Cost Review, Planning Review, and Cost Effectiveness/Engineering Review. The Cost Effectiveness/Engineering Review queue is only used for project subapplications.

After these three reviews are completed, PDM subapplications follow a different workflow than FMA subapplications. FMA subapplications proceed directly to the Pre-Award Review and Environmental/Historic Preservation (EHP) Review, which can be performed concurrently. However, under the competitive PDM grant program, subapplications go through the PDM National Review Process, which is comprised of the National Technical Review queue (for project subapplications) and then the Subgrant Selection (for Award) queue (for all subapplications). After the PDM National Review Process, PDM subapplications proceed to the Pre-Award Review queue and, for project subapplications, the EHP Review queue.

After the EHP Review is completed, the Pre-Award Review can be completed; therefore, the Pre-Award Review is the last queue in the Pre-Award Eligibility Workflow.

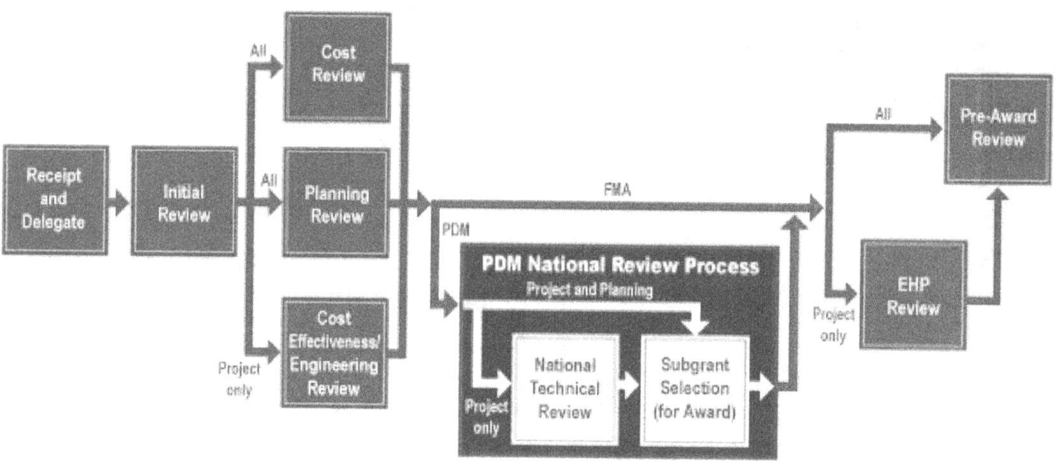


Select this link for the full text of the image.

# Receipt and Delegate Queue

This is the first queue in the Pre-Award Eligibility Workflow. During this queue, FEMA acknowledges the receipt of the application and assigns a grant program reviewer for each subsequent review queue.

# Initial Review Queue

This queue is used for planning and project subapplications. During this queue, a reviewer must complete a checklist of items before the subapplication can be forwarded to the next queue.

# Concurrent Workflow Queues

The following three queues may be completed concurrently:

- **Cost Review**—This queue is required for all subapplication types: project, planning, technical assistance, and management costs. During this queue, the breakdown of each cost is reviewed, as well as some overall information about the proposed costs from the subapplication.
- **Planning Review**—This queue is required for project and planning subapplications and documents the status of the Subapplicant's and Applicant's mitigation plans and the subapplication's consistency with the existing plans.
- **Cost-Effectiveness/Engineering Review**—This queue is required for project subapplications only. The Cost-Effectiveness/Engineering Review queue documents the results of the Cost-Effectiveness Review (usually a review of the Benefit-Cost Analysis (BCA)) and the Engineering Feasibility Review.

# PDM-Specific Workflow Queues

Since it is competitive, PDM planning and project subapplications undergo additional evaluation in the PDM National Review Process Workflow. (The PDM workflow queues are discussed in detail in Lesson 7). This workflow consists of two queues:

- **National Technical Review**—This queue is where the results of a FEMA Benefit-Cost Analysis and an Engineering Feasibility determination are recorded. The actual technical review process takes place outside of eGrants.
- **Subgrant Selection (for Award)**—This queue is where eligible planning and project subapplications are selected for further review based on the total funding available based on the PDM Congressional allocation.

# The Final Workflow Queues

The last two queues can be performed concurrently:

- **Environmental/Historic Preservation (EHP) Review**—This queue is required only for project subapplications. Project subapplications are automatically forwarded to the Environmental & Historic Preservation Management Information System (EMIS), which is outside of the eGrants Internal System. The EHP Review results are entered into the eGrants Internal System when complete.
- **Pre-Award Review**—This queue documents the pre-award requirements for all subapplication types: planning, projects, technical assistance, and management costs. Conditional awards are also documented in this queue, when applicable.

Although these two queues may be performed concurrently, the EHP Review must happen first because the Pre-Award Review documents any EHP Review findings and requirements. The Pre-Award Review is the last queue in the Pre-Award Eligibility Workflow.

# Disapproving Queues

Most of the workflow queues include the option for a FEMA Reviewer to select whether he or she approves or disapproves the queue for the subapplication. For other queues, the processing of the subapplication is halted if a queue is disapproved, and the subapplication will not be selected for funding.

If any of the queues that are marked with an **X** on the workflow diagram below are disapproved, the subapplication will not be processed any further.

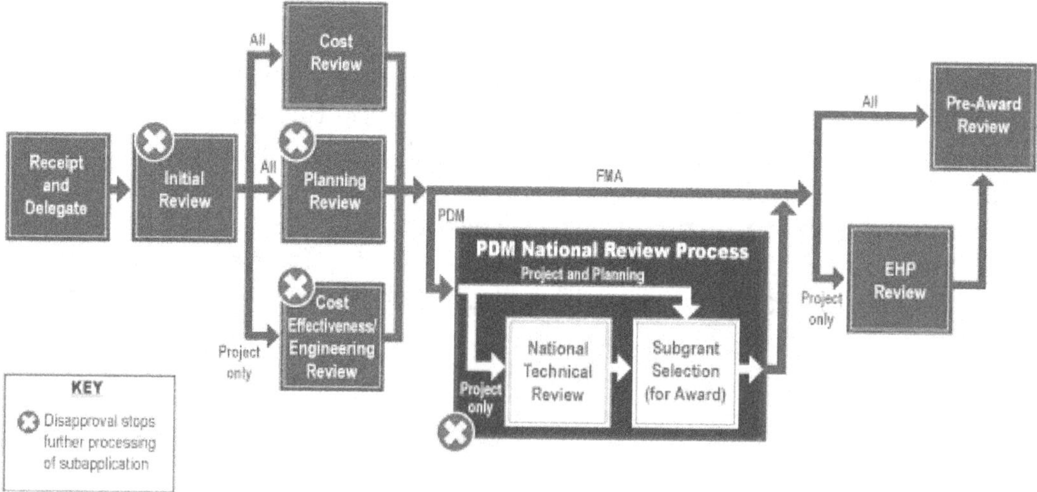

Select this link for the full text of the image.

# Requesting Revisions

It may be determined that additional or corrected information is required to continue to process a subapplication. For FMA applications and subapplications, a FEMA Reviewer may request that the Applicant revise the application or subapplication section(s), then resubmit it for further review. The Revise button at the bottom of queue screens allows revisions to be requested. Revisions can also be requested "out of queue," or after a queue has been completed. Revision requests will be discussed in detail in Lesson 8.

Since PDM is a competitive grant program, revision requests can be made only **before** the application deadline and **after** the National Review Process. This is necessary to avoid improving a subapplication's chances of being selected and creating an unfair advantage.

# Reworking Queues

During the Pre-Award Review queue, a reviewer may not be satisfied with or agree with the results of a prior queue review. For FMA subapplications, the reviewer has the ability to send the subapplication back to a previous queue for rework. The Rework button appears at the bottom of the Pre-Award Review queue screen.

Not all queues are available for rework. The diagram below indicates that a reviewer in the Pre-Award Review queue can send a subapplication back to the Cost Review, Planning Review, or Cost Effectiveness/Engineering Review queues for rework. Once the subapplication has been reworked in a previous queue(s), the subapplication will appear in the Inbox, and users with the roles to complete the queue may check out the subapplication and rework the queue. Reworking queues is discussed in detail in Lesson 8.

PDM subapplications in the Pre-Award Review queue cannot be sent back for rework. The National Review Process, which occurs outside the eGrants system would have already been completed. The results of the National Review Process are final and its queues cannot be repeated. So, neither those queues nor any of the prior queues can be reworked for a PDM subapplication.

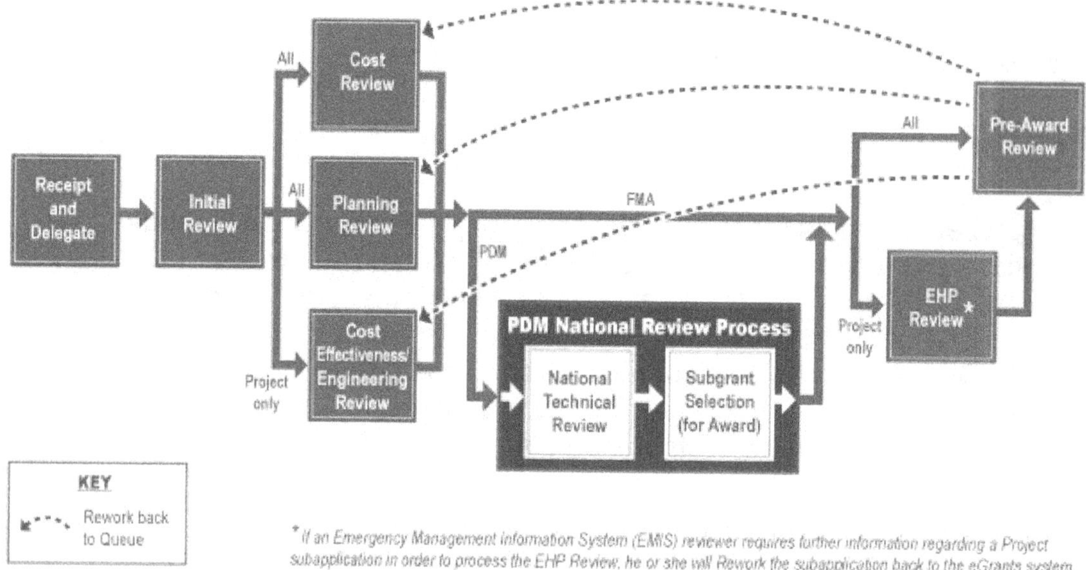



<u>Select this link for the full text of the image.</u>

# Lesson 5 Summary

In this lesson, you learned about the:

- Pre-Award Eligibility Workflow processes

Some key points from this lesson:

- The PDM Pre-Award Eligibility Workflow differs from the FMA Pre-Award Eligibility Workflow in that PDM planning and project subapplications go through the National Review Process.
- The queues through which a subapplication is processed depend on whether it is a project, planning, technical assistance, or management costs subapplication.
- FMA subapplications can be reworked, but only from the Pre-Award Review queue.
- PDM subapplications cannot be reworked because the results of the National Review Process are final and cannot be repeated.
- Disapproving certain queues will stop further processing of the subapplication in the workflow.

# Lesson 6 Overview

This lesson describes the processes and functionalities of each queue in the Pre-Award Eligibility Workflow.

At the end of this lesson, you should be able to identify:

- The steps to the Check-Out/Check-In process
- The key features of the Inbox and All Grants screens
- The purpose of the Pre-Award Eligibility Workflow queues
- The key features of Pre-Award Eligibility queue screens

# eGrants User Scenario

**Team Leader:** Alex Salazar, Flood Mitigation Assistance (FMA) Program Coordinator

**Your Role:** New FMA Program Analyst

**Office:** FEMA Regional Office

**Challenge:** Subapplications are ready to be processed in the different workflow queues.

**To Date:** You have learned about the FMA and PDM Pre-Award Eligibility Workflows.

Listen to Alex
Audio transcript

**The Next Step:** Alex will show you how to check out and review applications and subapplications.

Hello, this is Alex. Last time we met, you learned about the FMA and PDM Pre-Award Eligibility Workflows. Now, I would like you to learn how to check out and check in subapplications and how to process each queue in the FMA Workflow.

# Checking Out Queues

In order to process a queue for an application or a subapplication, you must check out the queue. While you have a queue checked out, other users can view it, but cannot modify it.

If a user who has checked out a queue is not able to forward it, then a user with the Grants Administrator role can use the Check In Tool to make the queue available for other users to work on. (The Check In Tool will be covered later in this lesson.)

Application numbers use the following format: Federal Award Program Prefix (FMA or PDM) – FEMA Region – State, Territorial, or Tribal Code – Fiscal Year. For example, a Flood Mitigation Assistance application submitted in fiscal year 2017 by an Applicant in FEMA Region IV, State of Kentucky, would appear as: FMA-04-KY-2017. Subapplications add codes for the subapplication type (PL for planning, PJ for projects, MC for management costs, and TA for technical assistance) after the program and have a numerical suffix (e.g., -001, -002, etc.) based on the when the subapplication was added to the application. For example, an FMA management costs subapplication submitted in 2017 by a user in FEMA Region IV, State of Massachusetts, that was the second subapplication added to the application, would appear as: FMA-MC-01-MA-2017-002.

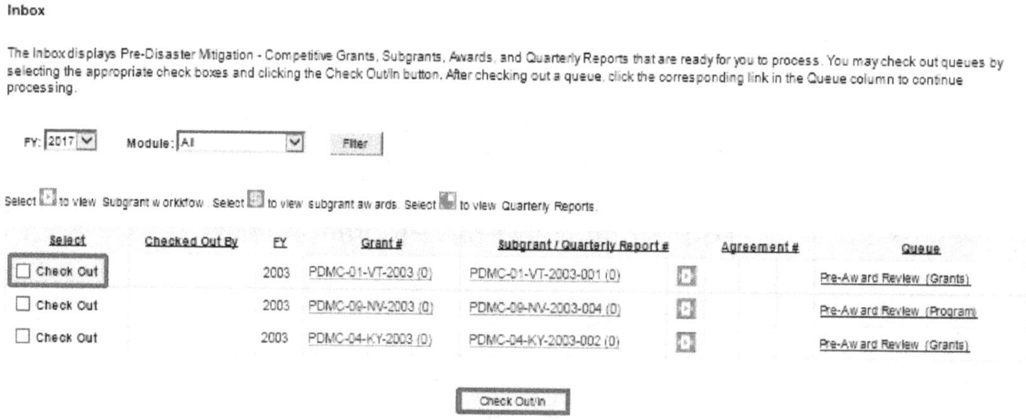

Inbox

The Inbox displays Pre-Disaster Mitigation - Competitive Grants, Subgrants, Awards, and Quarterly Reports that are ready for you to process. You may check out queues by selecting the appropriate check boxes and clicking the Check Out/In button. After checking out a queue, click the corresponding link in the Queue column to continue processing.

FY: 2017    Module: All    Filter

Select to view Subgrant workflow. Select to view subgrant awards. Select to view Quarterly Reports.

| Select | Checked Out By | FY | Grant # | Subgrant / Quarterly Report # | Agreement # | Queue |
|---|---|---|---|---|---|---|
| ☐ Check Out | | 2003 | PDMC-01-VT-2003 (0) | PDMC-01-VT-2003-001 (0) | | Pre-Award Review (Grants) |
| ☐ Check Out | | 2003 | PDMC-09-NV-2003 (0) | PDMC-09-NV-2003-004 (0) | | Pre-Award Review (Program) |
| ☐ Check Out | | 2003 | PDMC-04-KY-2003 (0) | PDMC-04-KY-2003-002 (0) | | Pre-Award Review (Grants) |

Check Out/In

Any queues that are available for check out will have a **Check Out** box in the Select column.

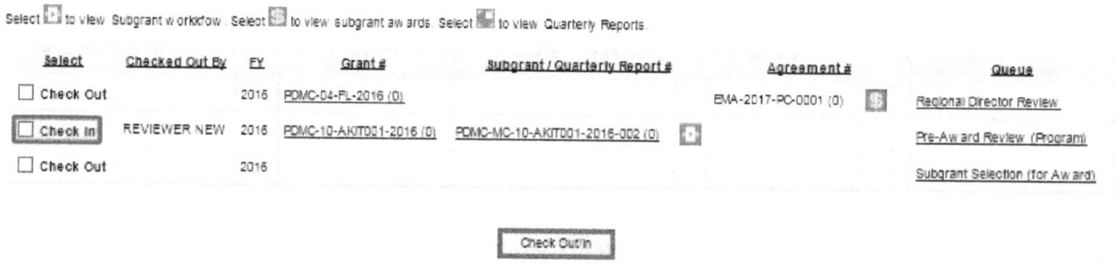

Select to view Subgrant workflow. Select to view subgrant awards. Select to view Quarterly Reports.

| Select | Checked Out By | FY | Grant # | Subgrant / Quarterly Report # | Agreement # | Queue |
|---|---|---|---|---|---|---|
| ☐ Check Out | | 2016 | PDMC-04-FL-2016 (0) | | EMA-2017-PC-0001 (0) | Regional Director Review |
| ☐ Check In | REVIEWER NEW | 2016 | PDMC-10-AKIT001-2016 (0) | PDMC-MC-10-AKIT001-2016-002 (0) | | Pre-Award Review (Program) |
| ☐ Check Out | | 2016 | | | | Subgrant Selection (for Award) |

Check Out/In

Queues that are already checked out by you will have a **Check In** box in the Select column. We will discuss the Check In functionality later in this lesson.

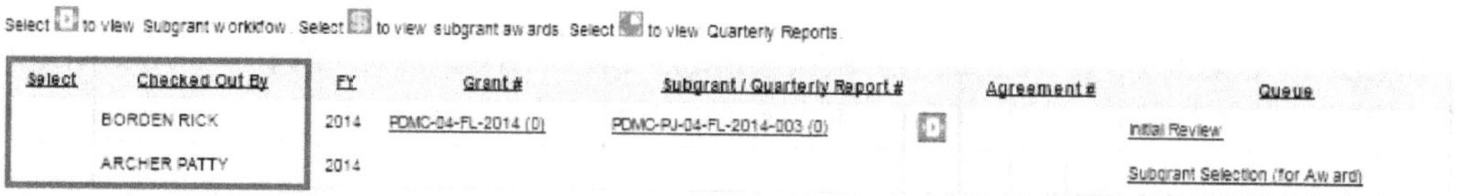

Select to view Subgrant workflow. Select to view subgrant awards. Select to view Quarterly Reports.

| Select | Checked Out By | FY | Grant # | Subgrant / Quarterly Report # | Agreement # | Queue |
|---|---|---|---|---|---|---|
| | BORDEN RICK | 2014 | PDMC-04-FL-2014 (0) | PDMC-PJ-04-FL-2014-003 (0) | | Initial Review |
| | ARCHER PATTY | 2014 | | | | Subgrant Selection (for Award) |

Queues that are already checked out by other users will not have anything in the **Select** column, and the user's name will appear in the **Checked Out By** column.

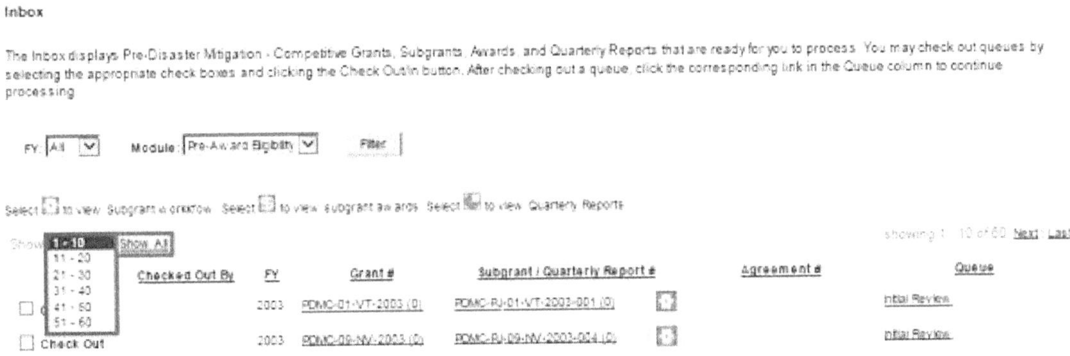

The Inbox defaults to display up to the first 10 entries in the current fiscal year. There are several ways to filter, sort, and view the available queues. You can filter the queues that show up in the list by selecting a **Fiscal Year** and/or by a **Workflow.**

You can sort by any of the columns in the list by selecting a **column title.**

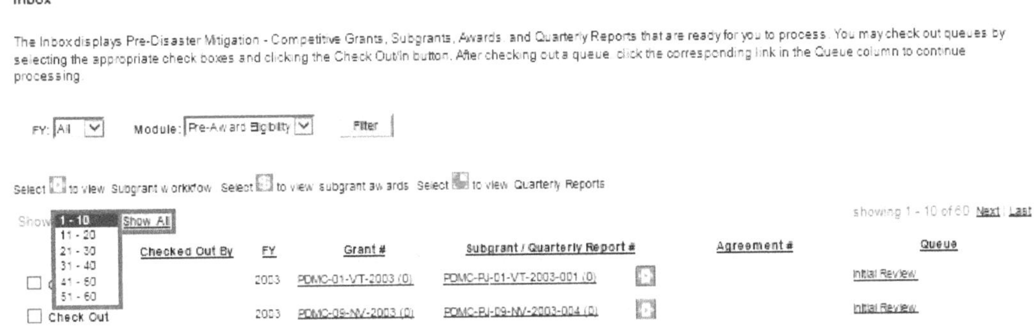

Or you can also view all the available applications by selecting the **Show** drop-down menu or the **Show All** link.

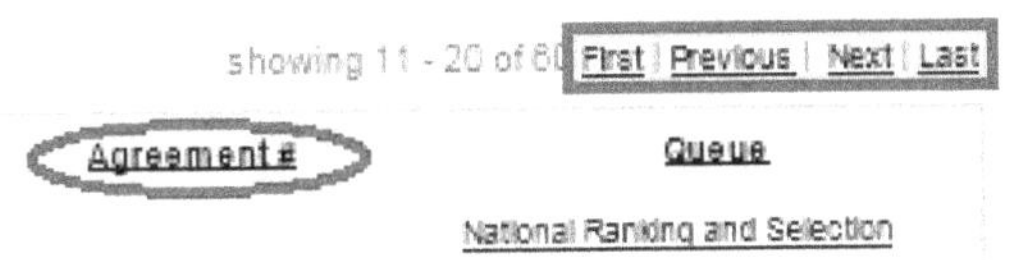

The **First, Previous, Next,** and **Last** links may be used to navigate among groups of 10 Inbox entries. The underlined **column title** links may be used to sort the applications displayed on the screen. For example, you may sort subapplications by "Agreement #" by selecting the sortable column title link.

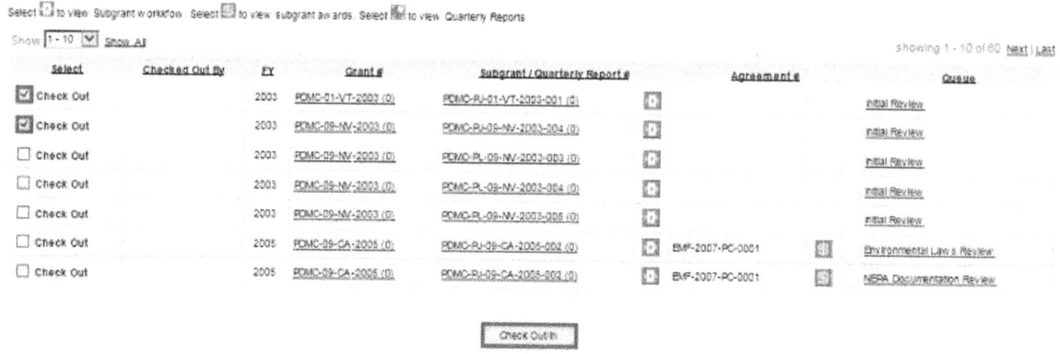

To check out a queue, find the application that you wish to work on and select the Check Out box in the **Select** column. You can check out more than one queue at a time by selecting multiple Check Out boxes. Select the **Check Out** boxes for the first two applications: PDMC-01-VT-2003 and PDMC-09-NV-2003. Then, select the **Check Out/In** button at the bottom of the screen.

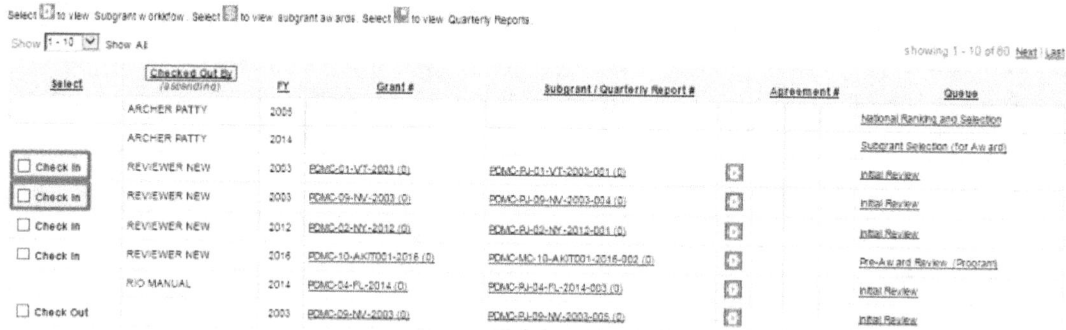

The queues that you checked out for the two applications are now displayed with a **Check In** box in the Select column and your name in the **Checked Out By** column.

# Checking In Queues

After you have checked out a queue, you can either complete it and forward it to the next queue, or you can check it back in. Forwarding a queue will automatically generate the next queue in the workflow process. You would need to check in a queue only if it is determined that someone else will need to process it instead of you. Since other users cannot edit a queue while it is checked out by you, you would need to check it back in.

If you have checked out a queue and are not able to forward it or check it back in, then a user with Grants Administrator role can use the Check In Tool to make the queue available for other users to work on. (The Check In Tool will be covered next.)

Alex will show you how to check in an application.

Scroll down to see slideshow captions.

Any application queue(s) that you currently have checked out will have a **Check In** box in the Select column and your name in the **Checked Out By** column. I have filtered and sorted the Inbox by users' last names in the Checked Out By column.

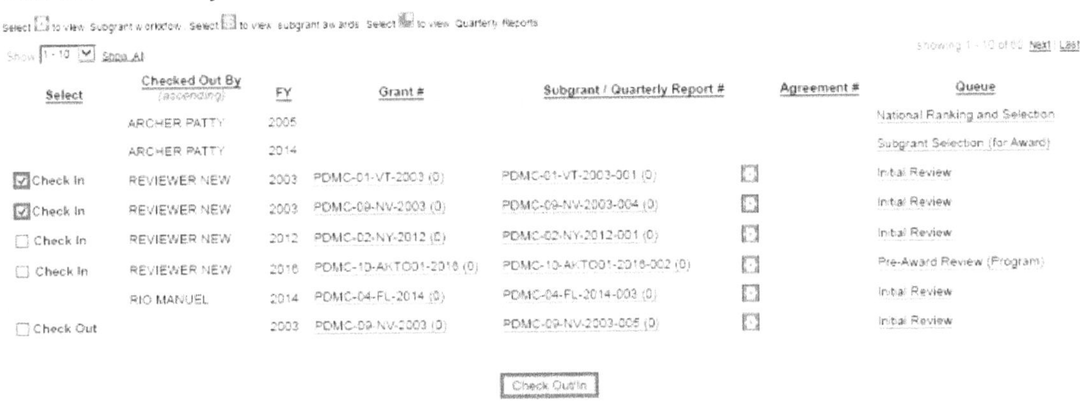

Select the **Check In** box for the queue(s) you wish to check in. You can check in more than one queue at a time by selecting multiple Check In boxes. Then, select the **Check Out/In** button.

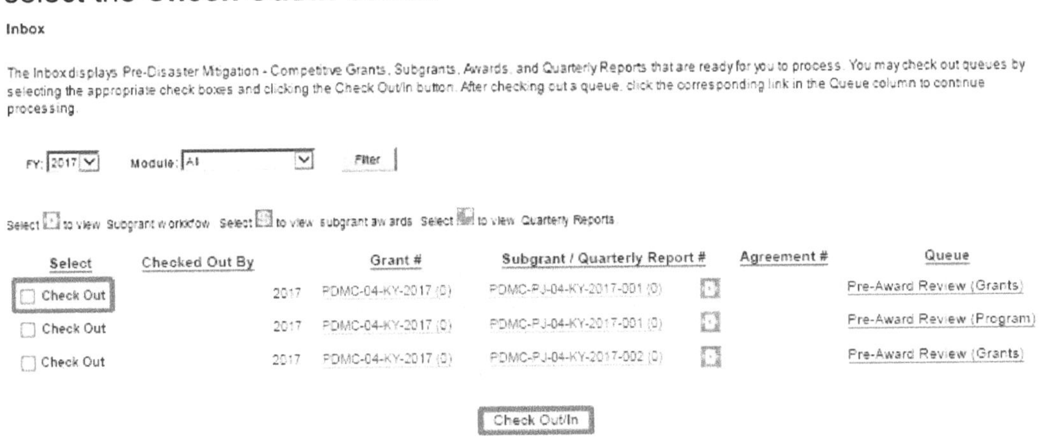

The queue(s) will now have **Check Out** boxes in the Select column.

# Check In Tool

The Check In Tool is available only to users with the Grants Administrator role to use to check in application queue(s) that are checked out. For example, using this tool may be necessary if a user who has checked out a queue is not available to forward it. The Check In Tool is used to check in a queue so that another reviewer can work on it.

Alex will show you how he would use the Check In Tool.

Scroll down to see slideshow captions.

- myRoles

- Inbox
- All Grants

√ (Selected) Check In Tool

- Closeout

A Grant Administrator can access the Check In Tool by selecting the **Check In Tool** link from the sidebar menu on the All Grants or Inbox screens.

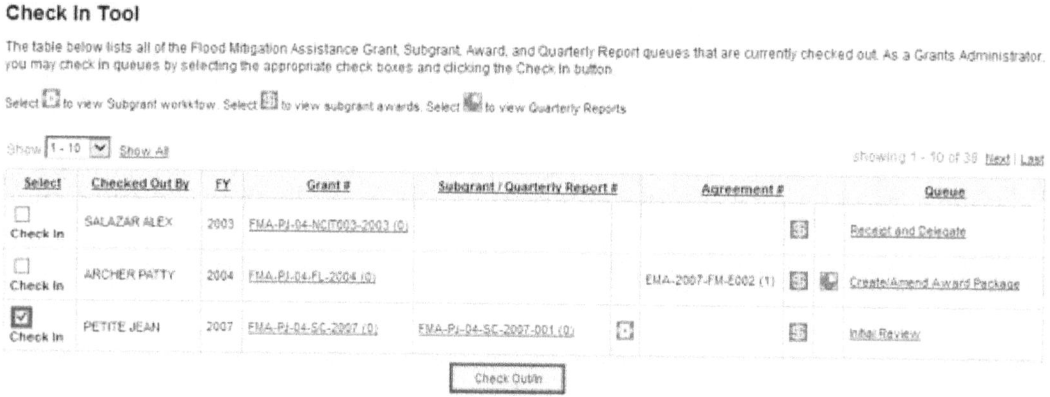

**Check In Tool**

The table below lists all of the Flood Mitigation Assistance Grant, Subgrant, Award, and Quarterly Report queues that are currently checked out. As a Grants Administrator, you may check in queues by selecting the appropriate check boxes and clicking the Check In button.

Select [ ] to view Subgrant workflow. Select [ ] to view subgrant awards. Select [ ] to view Quarterly Reports.

Show 1 - 10 [v]  Show All

showing 1 - 10 of 39 Next | Last

| Select | Checked Out By | FY | Grant # | Subgrant / Quarterly Report # | | Agreement # | | | Queue |
|---|---|---|---|---|---|---|---|---|---|
| [ ] Check In | SALAZAR ALEX | 2003 | FMA-PJ-04-NCIT003-2003 (0) | | | | | | Receipt and Delegate |
| [ ] Check In | ARCHER PATTY | 2004 | FMA-PJ-04-FL-2004 (0) | | | EMA-2007-FM-E002 (1) | | | Create/Amend Award Package |
| [x] Check In | PETITE JEAN | 2007 | FMA-PJ-04-SC-2007 (0) | FMA-PJ-04-SC-2007-001 (0) | | | | | Initial Review |

Check Out/In

You can see that the Check In Tool screen displays all of the queues currently checked out. These include queues that I've checked out, as well as queues that are checked out by other users. Jean Petite is on vacation and we need to forward application number FMA-PL-09-CA-2005 to the next queue. So, I will check the box in the **Select** column for that application and then select the **Check In** button at the bottom of the screen.

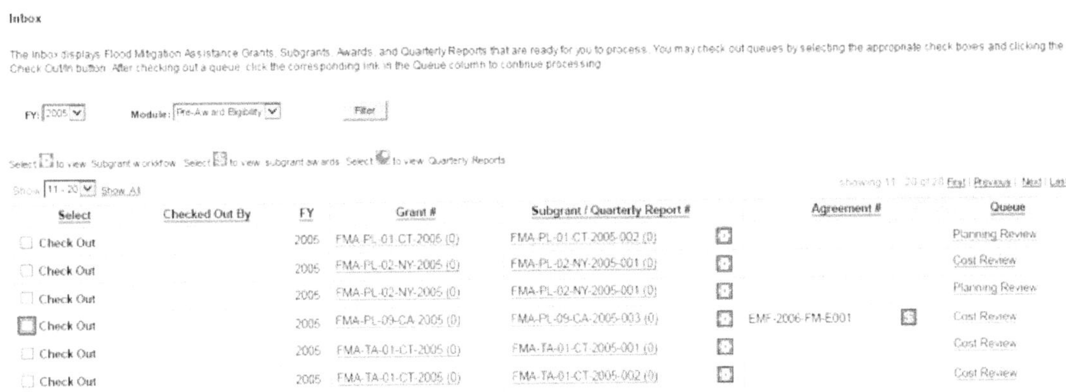

The selected queue(s) will now appear in the Inbox available for you or other users to check out.

# Inbox Screen

Each mitigation grant program has its own Inbox that can be accessed by selecting the FMA or PDM program link or icon from the eGrants Homepage. The Inbox displays the pending workflow queue for each application. For example, the Receipt and Delegate queue will be the first queue available in the Inbox for any application that an Applicant has submitted to FEMA.
Alex will point out the various elements of the Inbox screen.
Scroll down to see slideshow captions.

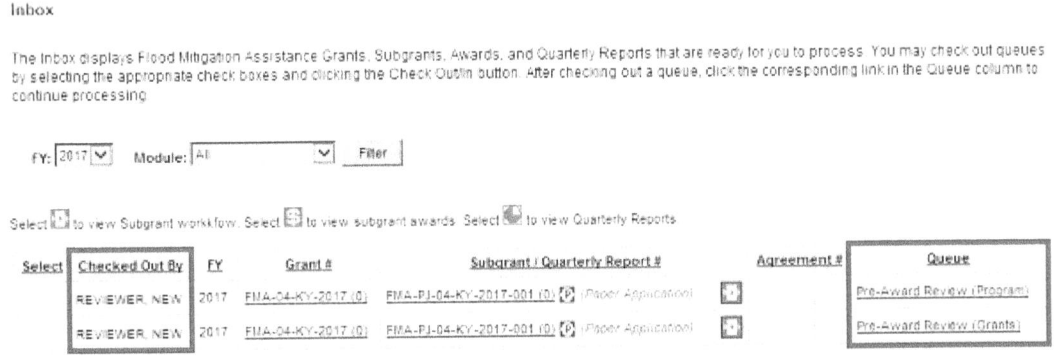

The Inbox screen displays the pending queue(s) for each application available for you to work on, based on your eGrants roles, and shows whether the **queue(s)** are already **Checked Out** by another user for processing.

To switch to the Inbox for another HMA grant program, select the **eGrants Home** link in the upper right-hand corner on the screen.

In the upper left-hand corner of the Inbox is the **Reports** tab. The Reports tab displays a list of available reports for the grant program. Reports will be covered in Lesson 9.

To the right of the Reports tab is the **Search** tab. The Search tab allows you to perform a search of all applications, subapplications, award packages, or quarterly reports available to you based on your eGrants roles. The Search function will be discussed later in this lesson.

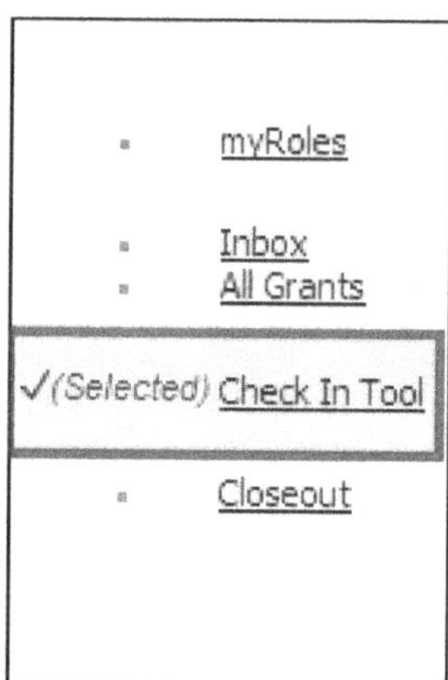


If you need to work on a queue that is checked out by another user, it can be checked in by a user with Grants Administrator role using the **Check In Tool** link on the sidebar menu on the left side of the screen.

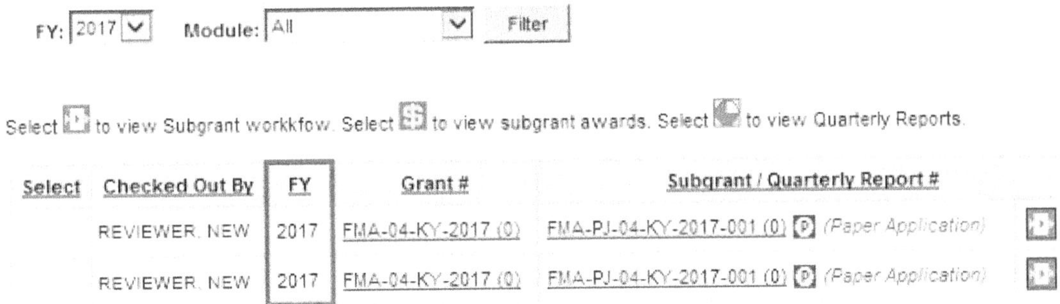

The federal fiscal year that the Applicant submitted the application is displayed in the **FY Column.**

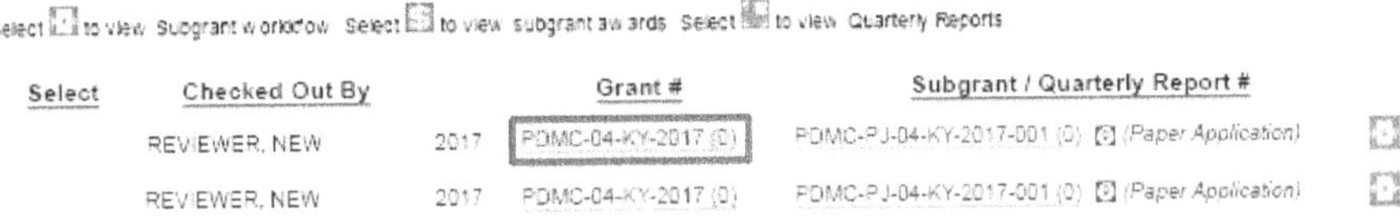

Application numbers are displayed in the Grant # column. They use the following **format:** *Federal Award Program Prefix (FMA or PDM) – FEMA Region – State, Territorial, or Tribal Code – Fiscal Year.* For example, a Flood Mitigation Assistance application submitted in fiscal year 2017 by an Applicant in FEMA Region IV, in the State of Kentucky, would appear as: FMA-04-KY-2017. Select an application number link in the **Grant #** column to open the application in a new window.

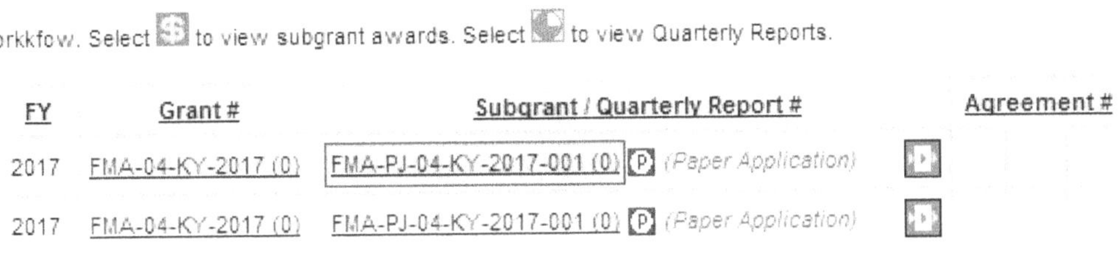

If a queue pertains to a subapplication, the **subapplication number** is displayed in the Subgrant/Quarterly Report # column. Subapplication numbers use the following **format:** *Federal Award Program Prefix (FMA or PDM) – Subapplication Type – FEMA Region – State, Territorial, or Tribal Code – Fiscal Year – Subapplication Number.* For example, an FMA project subapplication submitted in 2017 by a user in FEMA Region IV, in Kentucky, would appear as: FMA-PJ-04-KY-2017-001. Select a subapplication number in the **Subgrant/Quarterly Report #** column to open the subapplication in a new window.

Select to view Subgrant workkfow.

There are several icons that may appear in the Inbox screen. The **Subgrant (Pre-Award Eligibility) Workflow** icon looks like a right-facing arrowhead. Selecting this icon will open the Pre-Award Eligibility screen for the subapplication. We will talk about the Pre-Award Eligibility screen later in this lesson.

Select **$** to view subgrant awards.

The **Awards** icon looks like a dollar sign. Selecting this icon will allow you to view the awards packages for an application.

Select to view Quarterly Reports.

The **Quarterly Reports** icon looks like a pie graph. This icon will allow you to view the quarterly reports submitted by a Recipient for a federal award. Quarterly reports are covered in Lesson 10.

# All Grants Screen

The All Grants screen can be accessed by selecting the **All Grants** link in the sidebar menu of the Inbox or from any Pre-Award Eligibility Workflow screen. All the applications and subapplications available to you based on your eGrants roles—regardless of where they are in the Pre-Award Eligibility, Awards, and Quarterly Reports Workflows or whether you can work on them— are available from the All Grants screen.
Alex will explain the features of the All Grants screen.
Scroll down to see slideshow captions.

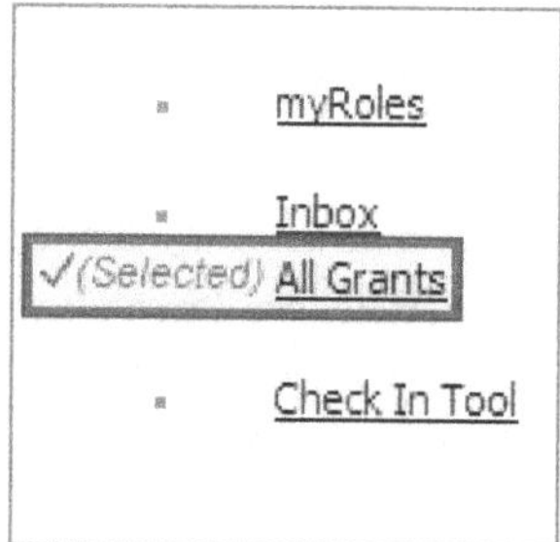


To access the All Grants screen, select the **All Grants** link from the sidebar menu on the Inbox screen.

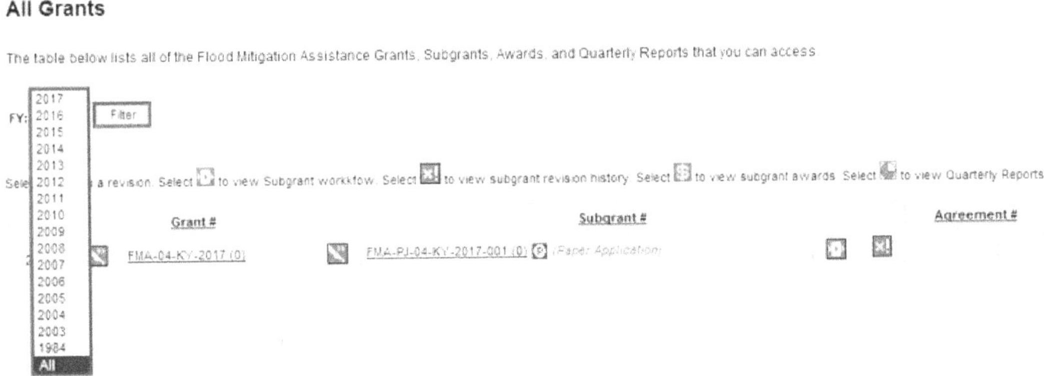

The All Grants screen displays all the applications and subapplications in the eGrants Internal System. For each, you can see the fiscal year it was created in the **FY** column, its application number link in the **Grant #** column, subapplication number link(s) in the **Subgrant #** column, and subaward agreement number link(s) in the **Agreement #** column.

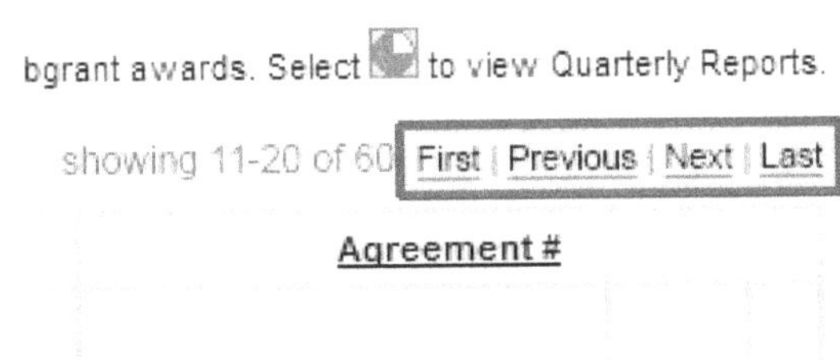

The first 10 applications are displayed for the current fiscal year. To customize the view of the screen, you can select a specific fiscal year, or "All" from the **FY** drop-down menu, then select the **Filter** button.

You can also use the **First, Previous, Next,** and **Last** links to navigate through groups of 10 applications.

You can sort the list of applications displayed on the screen by selecting a **column header.**

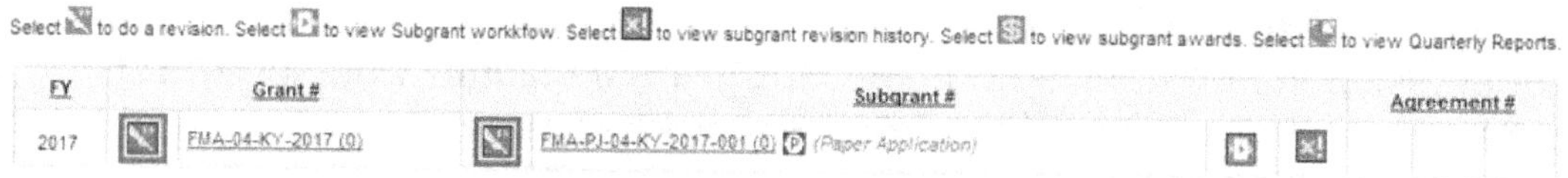

To view or print the application or subapplication, select the application number link in the **Grant #** column or the subapplication number link in the **Subgrant #** column.

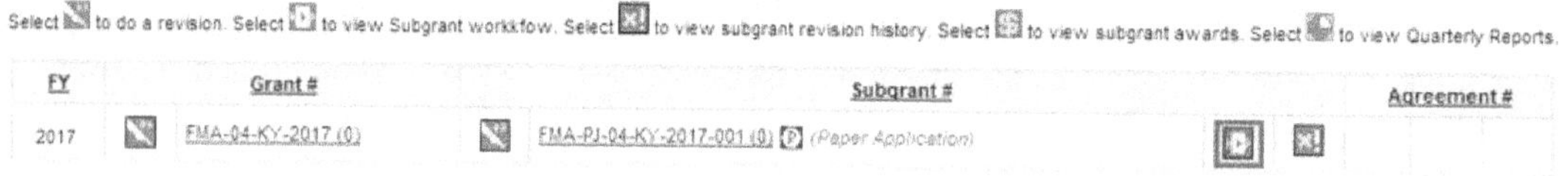

For the FMA program, you can make an out-of-queue revision request to the Applicant for an application or subapplication by selecting the corresponding **Revision Request** icon which is located to left of the application or the subapplication numbers. The Revision Request icon will not be displayed for a subapplication if an out-of-queue revision has already been requested. (Out-of-queue revisions will be discussed in Lesson 8.)

Selecting the **Subgrant (Pre-Award Eligibility) Workflow** icon will open the Pre-Award Eligibility screen. We will talk about the Pre-Award Eligibility screen next.

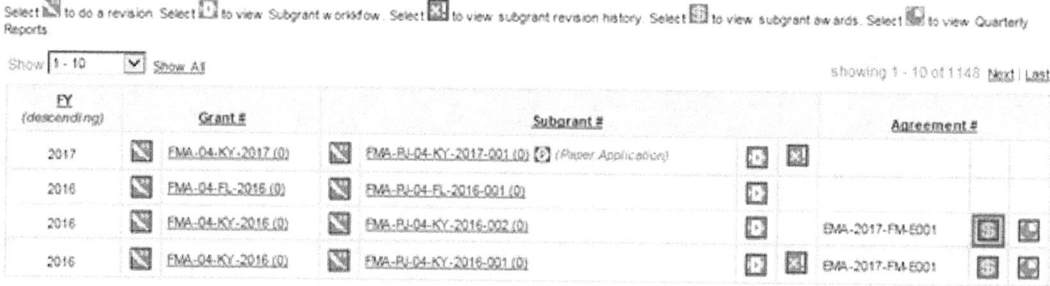

Selecting the **Awards** icon will allow you to view the award package for a particular subapplication.

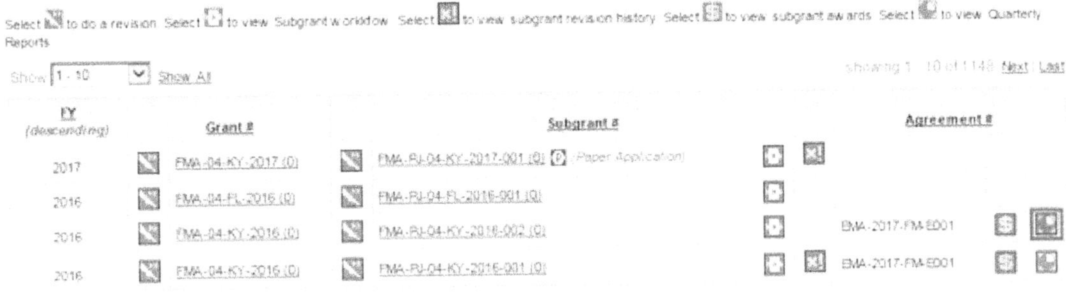

Selecting the **Quarterly Reports** icon will allow you to view the quarterly reports for a federal award. (Quarterly reports are discussed in Lesson 10.)

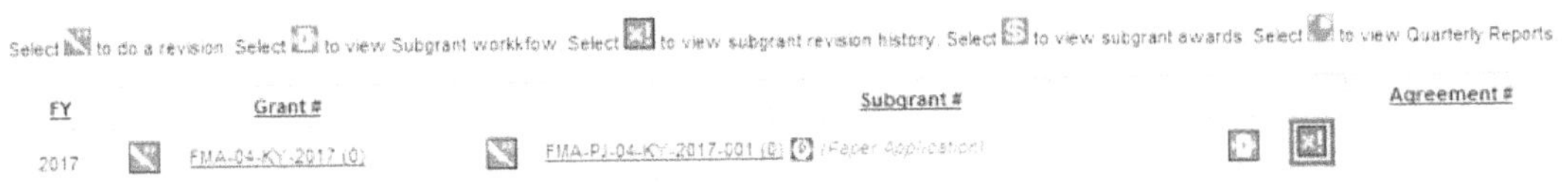

Select the **Revision History** icon to open the Revision History screen for a subapplication.

# Pre-Award Eligibility Screen

The Pre-Award Eligibility screen is a reference for you as you process subapplications through the Pre-Award Eligibility Workflow. It provides an overview of a particular subapplication's workflow path. It shows you where a subapplication is in the workflow, who has completed or is in the process of completing each queue, whether the queue was approved, the subapplication's status in each queue, and the date of that status.
Alex will describe the features of the Pre-Award Eligibility screen.
Scroll down to see slideshow captions.

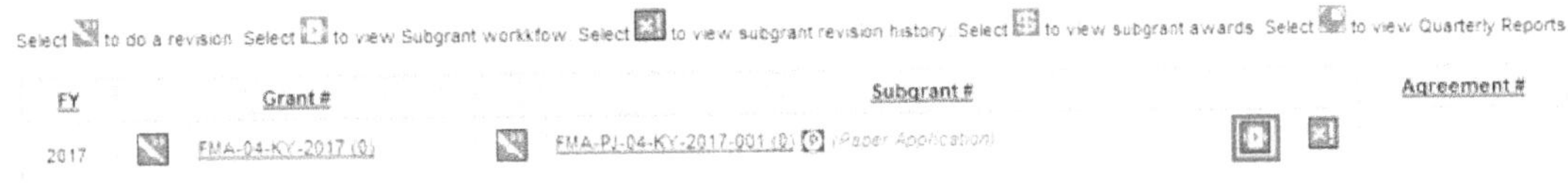

To view the Pre-Award Eligibility screen for a subapplication, select the **Subgrant (Pre-Award Eligibility) Workflow** icon beside the subapplication number link in the Subgrant # column on the Inbox screen.

## Pre-Award Eligibility

P FMA-PJ-04-KY-2017-001 (0): River City Floodplain Acquisition Project – Phase 1

| Queue | Approved | User | Status | Status Date |
|---|---|---|---|---|
| Receipt and Delegate | Yes | PARK, YEONG | Completed | 04/11/2017 07:46 PM |
| Initial Review | Yes | PARK, YEONG | Completed | 04/11/2017 07:55 PM |
| Subgrant Selection (for Award) | Yes | PARK, YEONG | Completed | 04/11/2017 08:10 AM |
| EHP Queues | Pending | | Not Ready | 04/11/2017 08:10 PM |
| Pre-Award Review (Grants) | Pending | SALMAN, MIRYAM | Pending | 04/11/2017 08:10 PM |
| Pre-Award Review (Program) | Pending | SALMAN, MIRYAM | Pending | 04/11/2017 08:10 PM |

Remove

Select one of the Workflow queue links in the **Queue** column to open a queue screen for the subapplication.

# Planning Review [Read-Only]

FMA-PJ-09-NV-2005-001 (0): Project Application #1

However, if you do not have a queue checked out, then the queue screen will be displayed as Read-Only

## Pre-Award Eligibility

FMA-PJ-06-TX-2010-007 (0): City of El Campo Flood Mitigation Assistance Project

| Queue | Approved | User | Status | Status Date |
|---|---|---|---|---|
| Receipt and Delegate | Yes | BAUMGARTNER, KELLY | Completed | 09/29/2010 02:42 PM |
| Initial Review | Yes | BAUMGARTNER, KELLY | Completed | 02/22/2011 07:41 PM |
| Cost Review | Pending | | Pending | 02/22/2011 07:41 PM |
| Cost-Effectiveness Review | Pending | | Pending | 02/22/2011 07:41 PM |
| Planning Review | Pending | | Revision Requested | 02/22/2011 07:41 PM |
| Pre-Award Review (Grants) | Pending | | Not Ready | 02/22/2011 07:41 PM |
| Pre-Award Review (Program) | Pending | | Not Ready | 02/22/2011 07:41 PM |

The status column indicates: **Completed:** Queue is completed; **Pending:** Queue needs to be completed; **Not Ready:** Subapplication cannot move to this queue until a prior queue is completed; or **Revision Requested:** Reviewer requested a revision for a subapplication section; **Rework Requested:** FMA Reviewer requested a queue be reworked.<

- myRoles

## Pre-Award Eligibility

FMA-PJ-04-KY-2017-001 (0): River City Floodplain Acquisition Project — Phase 1

In the upper left-hand corner, the **myGrants, Pre-Award Eligibility, Awards, Quarterly Reports, Reports,** and **Search** tabs are available.

Since the Pre-Award Eligibility screen is specific to a subapplication, there are additional tabs for Awards and Quarterly Reports that will open the award packages and quarterly reports for the federal award associated with the subapplication. Select the **Awards** tab to open the award package for with the subapplication displayed on the Pre-Award Eligibility screen.

Select the **Quarterly Reports** tab to open the quarterly reports for the federal award associated with the subapplication displayed on the Pre-Award Eligibility screen.



To return to the Inbox, select the **myGrants** tab.

# Sorting and Filtering Queues

There are several ways to filter, sort, and view the available queues in the Inbox.
Alex will demonstrate how to use Inbox screen features to filter and sort queues.
Scroll down to see slideshow captions.

Inbox

The Inbox displays Flood Mitigation Assistance Grants, Subgrants, Awards, and
Check Out/In button. After checking out a queue, click the corresponding link in the

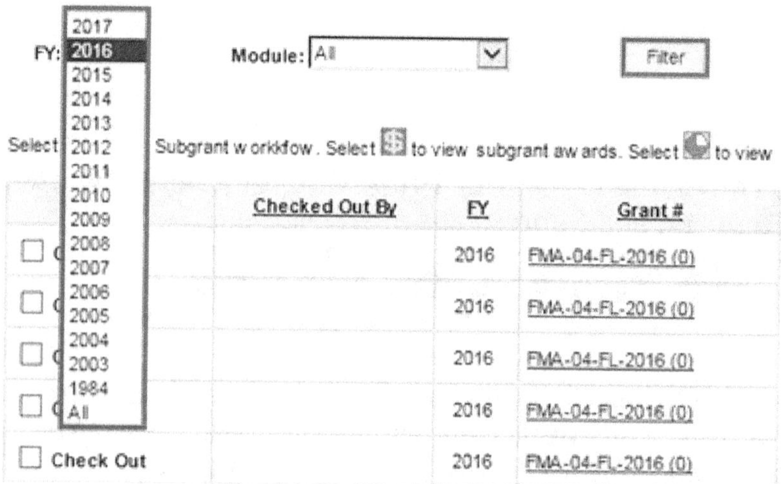



There are several screen features that allow you to view groups of queues.
You can filter the queues that show up in the list by **Fiscal Year** by selecting a
year from the **FY** drop-down menu and then selecting the **Filter** button.

Inbox

The Inbox displays Flood Mitigation Assistance Grants, Subgrants, Awards, and Quarterly Reports that are ready for you to process.
Check Out/In button. After checking out a queue, click the corresponding link in the Queue column to continue processing.

You can also filter the list by workflow by selecting Pre-Award Eligibility,
Awards, or Quarterly Reports from the **Module** drop-down menu, then
selecting the **Filter** button.

Inbox

The Inbox displays Flood Mitigation Assistance Grants, Subgrants, Awards, and
appropriate check boxes and clicking the Check Out/In button. After checking out

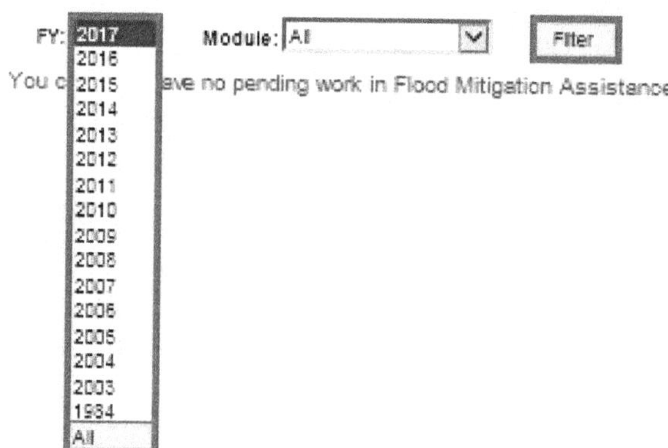

The Inbox defaults to display up to the first 10 entries. Select the **All** option in the Module drop-down menu to view all of the subapplications in your Inbox. You can also select the **All Grants** link on the sidebar menu.

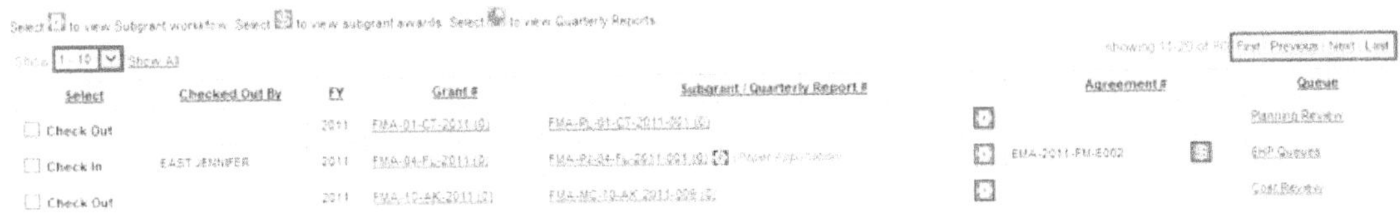

Selecting the **Show** drop-down menu allows you to select additional subapplications in groups of 10. The **First, Previous, Next,** and **Last** links may be used to navigate among groups of 10 subapplications.

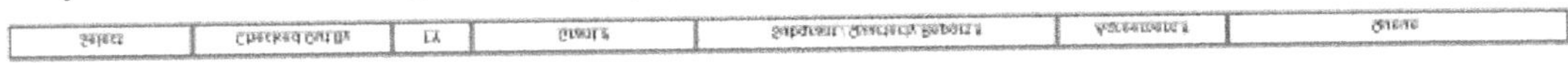

You can also choose to sort the results displayed on the screen by selecting any of the **column headers.**

# Receipt and Delegate Queue

The Receipt and Delegate queue is the first step in the Pre-Award Eligibility Workflow. This queue is performed for the application as a whole, including all subapplications attached to the application. The main purpose of this queue is to acknowledge receipt of the application and to alert eGrants Internal System users that the associated subapplication(s) have been assigned to them for processing in the next queue in the Workflow.

Alex will show you how to complete the Receipt and Delegate queue.

Scroll down to see slideshow captions.

The Receipt and Delegate queue is completed for the application, while the other queues in the Pre-Award Eligibility Workflow are completed for each subapplication.

**Note**

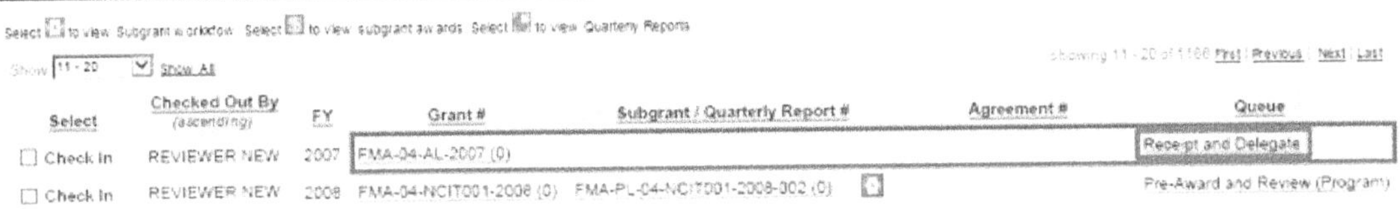

Check out the Receipt and Delegate queue for the application that you wish to work on. We have checked out and are going to review application number FMA-04-AL-2007. Select the **Receipt and Delegate** link in the Queue column for this application.

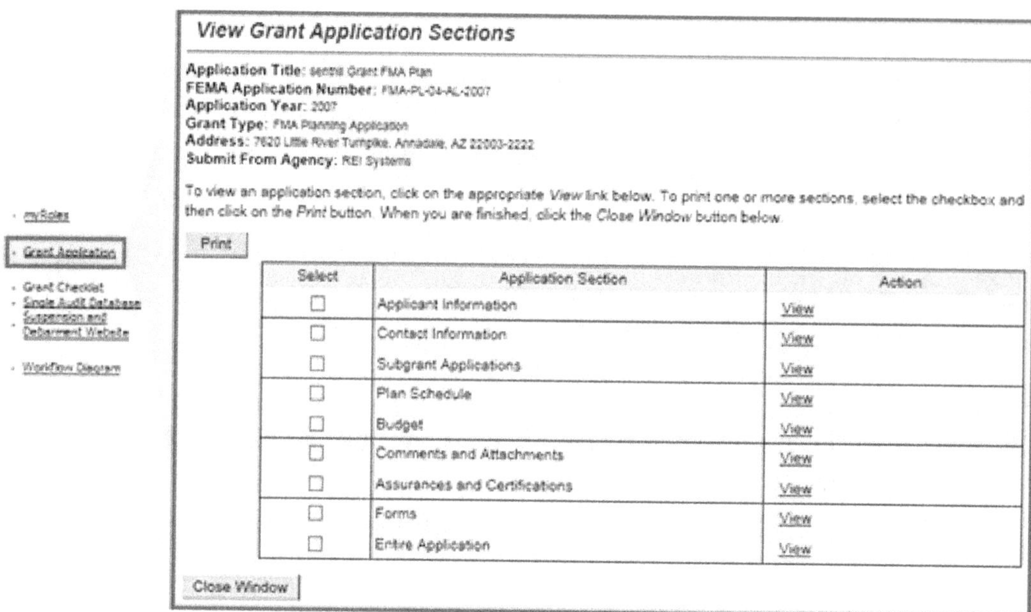

On the sidebar menu, the **Grant Application** link will open the View Grant Application Sections screen in a new window so that you can view the relevant application section while you complete this queue.

### Receipt and Delegate

FMA-PL-04-AL-2007 (0): senthil Grant FMA Plan

By forwarding the above referenced grant application, FEMA acknowledges receipt of the application and delegates program administra[...] below.

* Please select an FMA Coordinator:

User: REVIEWER, NEW     Status: Pending     Date: 11/09/2005 02:42 PM

To delegate the application to a reviewer, you need to select the appropriate **FMA Coordinator user** from the drop-down menu on the Receipt and Delegate screen. I will select Rick Borden. You may have noticed the **red asterisk** before the prompt. All required fields in eGrants are marked with that red asterisk.

### Receipt and Delegate

FMA-PL-04-AL-2007 (0): senthil Grant FMA Plan

By forwarding the above referenced grant application, FEMA acknowledges receipt of the application and delegates program administration to the person listed below.

* Please select an FMA Coordinator:     BORDEN, RICK ▾     Revision History

User: REVIEWER, NEW     Status: Pending     Date: 11/09/2005 02:42 PM

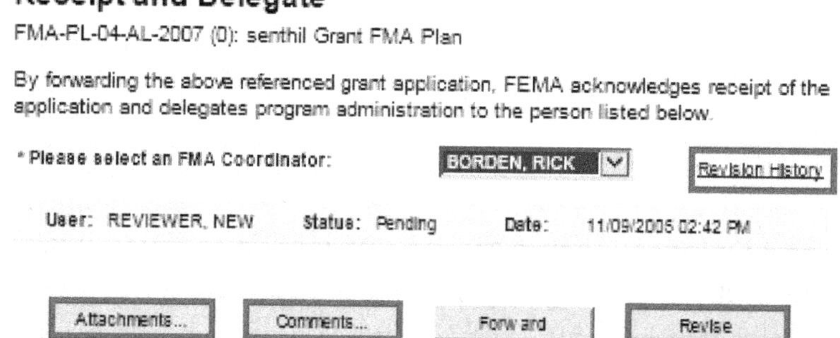

In this queue, you can view the **Revision History** (that is, the record of revisions requested for the subapplication), add or edit **attachments** or **comments,** and/or request the Applicant to **Revise** an application section by selecting the appropriate link or button. I will explain these more in detail a little bit later. Keep in mind that for PDM subapplications, the Revise button will be inactive after the application deadline since it is a competitive program.

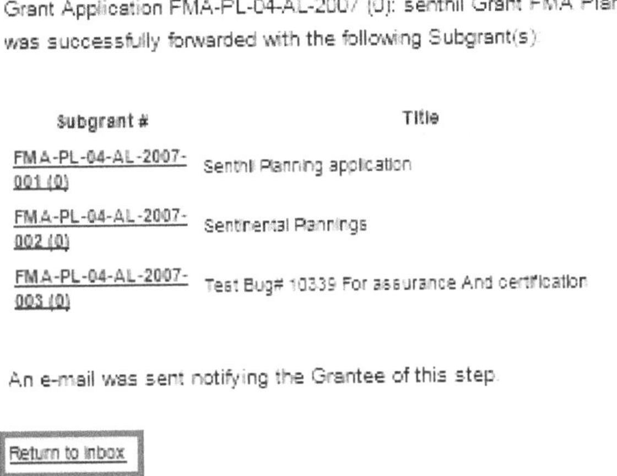


Then, select the **Forward** button to complete this queue.

## Confirmation



You will receive a **Confirmation** that you have successfully forwarded the subapplications to the next queue and that the Applicant will be notified via e-mail using the e-mail address or addresses in the Contact Information section of the application. Those e-mail addresses will be used for all notifications regarding the application and attached subapplications, including revision requests. Select the **Return to Inbox** link to process another application.

# Initial Review Queue

The Initial Review queue is completed for project and planning subapplications only. The Initial Review queue is used to review the eligibility of the Applicant and Subapplicant, the alignment of the Scope of Work and the mitigation activity selected, the eligibility of the mitigation activity, the completeness of the subapplication, and its documentation. Depending on the results of the Initial Review, the queue may be approved or disapproved. If the queue is disapproved, the subapplication will be removed from subsequent queues in the Workflow.

If it is determined that the results of the Initial Review queue are incorrect, a Headquarters PDM or FMA Coordinator can reset or restore the queue to be reprocessed. (The Restore function is covered later in this lesson. The Reset function is covered in Lesson 8.)

Alex will show you how to complete the Initial Review queue.

Scroll down to see slideshow captions.

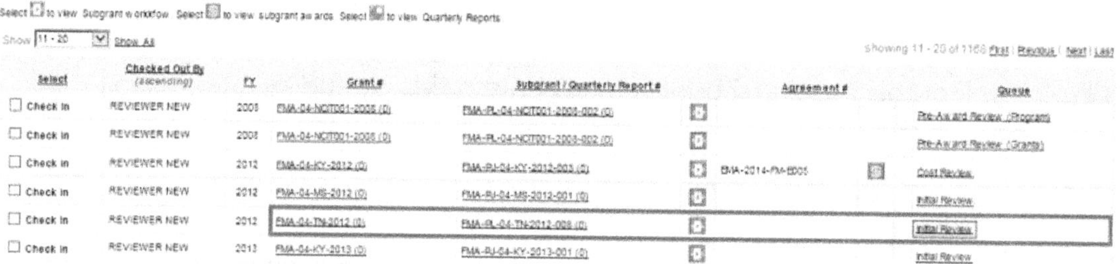

We are going to review subapplication number FMA-PL-04-TN-2012-008. So, select the **Initial Review** link in the Queue column for that subapplication.

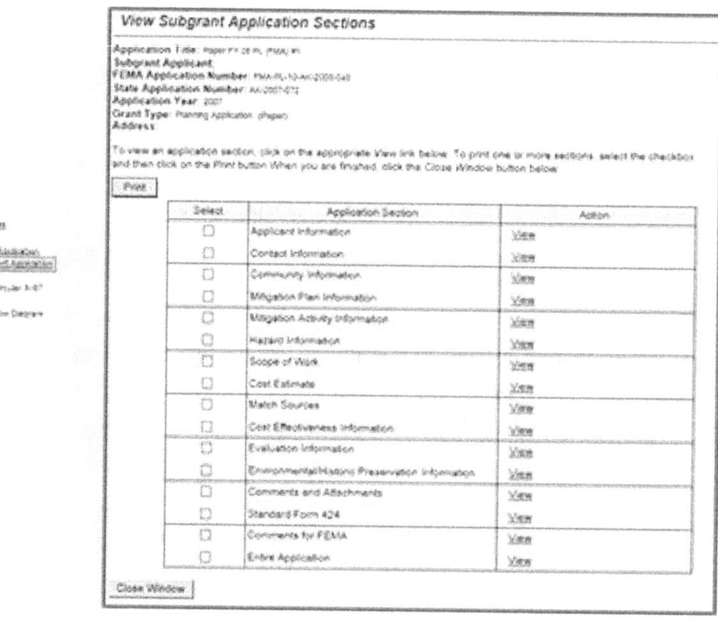

On the sidebar menu, the **Subgrant Application** link will open the View Subgrant Application Sections screen in a new window so that you can view the relevant subapplication section while you complete this queue.

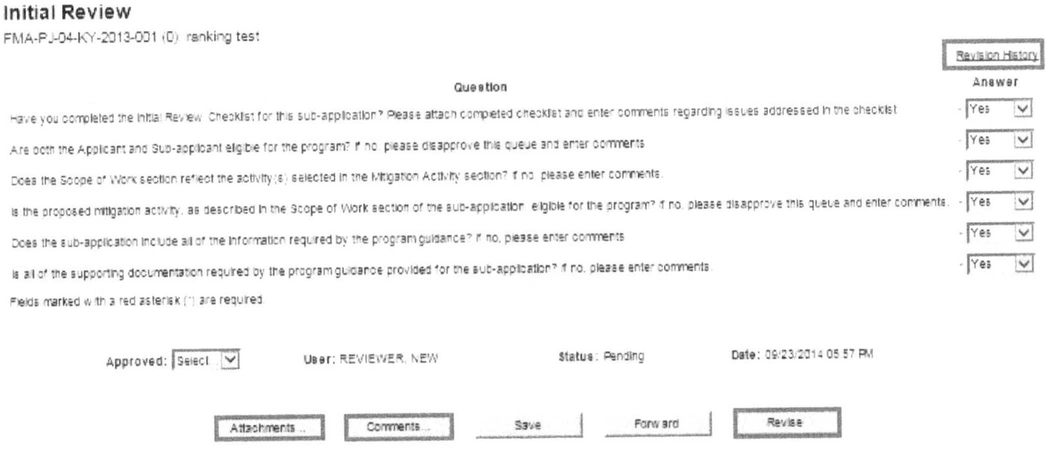

In order to complete the Initial Review queue, you will need to answer each of the required questions on the screen by selecting **Yes** or **No** from the drop-down menu. For this subapplication, we can answer **Yes** to all of the questions. When all of the questions have been answered, select the **Save** button.

From this queue, you can view the **Revision History** (that is, the record of revisions requested for the subapplication), add or edit **attachments** and **comments,** and/or request that the Applicant **Revise** a subapplication section by selecting the appropriate link or button. I will explain these functionalities in the next lesson. For PDM subapplications, the Revise button will be inactive after the application deadline since it is a competitive program.

Based on the answers to the questions above, you will select either **Yes** or **No** in the Approved drop-down menu. If you answer "No" to any of the key questions, you are required to disapprove this queue. If this queue is disapproved, you must provide comments, and the subapplication is removed from subsequent queues in the workflow. We will discuss the Comments functionality later in this lesson. For this subapplication, you can approve this queue by selecting **Yes** for all the questions. Then select the **Forward** button to move the subapplication onto the next queue.

### Confirmation



You will receive a **Confirmation** that you have completed the queue. Then, select the **Return to Inbox** link to continue processing queues for this program.

# Remove Functionality

The Remove functionality is used to remove a subapplication from all further processing in the Pre-Award Eligibility Workflow process, including any concurrent queues. A subapplication may need to be removed if the Applicant has withdrawn it from its application, if the subapplication is not determined to be eligible during the Initial Review queue, or if you need to stop a project subapplication from being forwarded to the Environmental/Historic Preservation queue.

The ability to remove a subapplication depends on your role in eGrants, the type of subapplication, and the current queue of the subapplication. Users with the Headquarters PDM Coordinator or Headquarters FMA Coordinator eGrants role may remove subapplications from the Pre-Award Eligibility screen as necessary. Users without this role will not see the Remove button on the Pre-Award Eligibility screen. If you determine that a subapplication needs to be removed, please contact the eGrants Help Desk at MTeGrants@fema.dhs.gov or 1-855-228-3362.

Alex will demonstrate how to remove a subapplication from the Pre-Award Eligibility Workflow process.

Scroll down to see slideshow captions.

To remove a subapplication from further processing, select the **Subgrant (Pre-Award Eligibility) Workflow** icon to the right of the subapplication number on the Inbox screen.

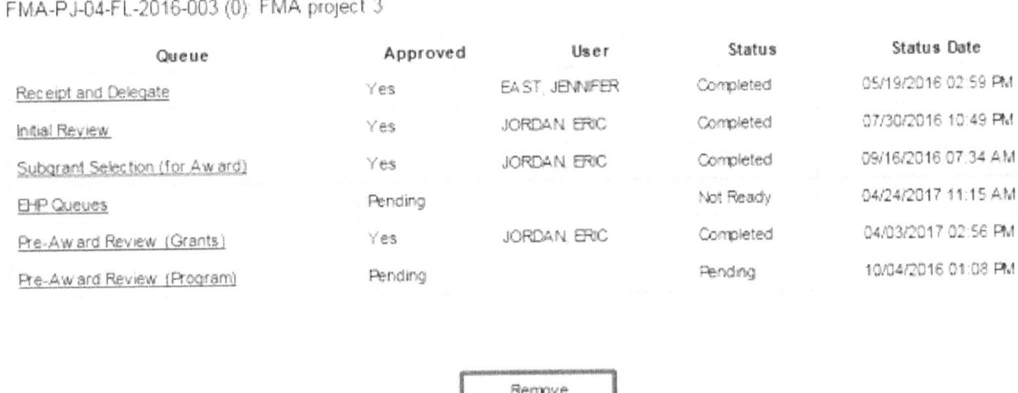

When the Pre-Award Eligibility screen displays, select the **Remove** button. Doing so removes a subapplication from all further processing in the Pre-Award Eligibility Workflow process, including any concurrent queues.

# Confirm Subgrant Removal

FMA-PJ-04-FL-2016-003 (0): FMA project 3 Conditions

Click on the **Continue** button to remove this subgrant from processing in the following queue(s):

| Queue |
| --- |
| Pre-Award Review (Program) |

Click on the **Cancel** button to return to Pre-Award Eligiblity.

You will be prompted to confirm the removal. For this subapplication, select the **Continue** button.

## Confirmation

The Queue was successfully processed for Subgrant Application FMA-PJ-04-FL-2016-003 (0): FMA project 3

Return to Inbox

A **Confirmation** screen appears and indicates the subapplication has been removed. Select the **Return to Inbox** link to return to the Inbox. Once you remove a subapplication, it is no longer in the Inbox.

# Restore Functionality

The Restore functionality is used to restore a subapplication that was removed or not approved to allow it to continue in the Pre-Award Eligibility Workflow process.

If it is determined that the results of a queue are incorrect, and a subapplication should not have been removed from processing or not approved, a Headquarters PDM or Headquarters FMA Coordinator can restore the subapplication so it can be reprocessed. If you find that a subapplication needs to be restored, please contact the eGrants Help Desk at MTeGrants@fema.dhs.gov or 1-855-228-3362.

After a subapplication queue is restored, the previous queue's status will change from "Completed" to "Pending," and the queue can be checked out from the Inbox by a user with the necessary role to complete it. The subapplication's status will change from "Disapproved" to "Pending." There will be no record of the reason for the restore, nor any notification to users regarding the restore action. Data originally entered for the restored queue, including any comments or attachments, will be retained. The user who checks out the restored queue will be able to edit any of the queue responses. However, any comments and/or attachments will only be editable by the user who entered them.

Alex will demonstrate how to restore a subapplication to the Inbox.

Scroll down to see slideshow captions.

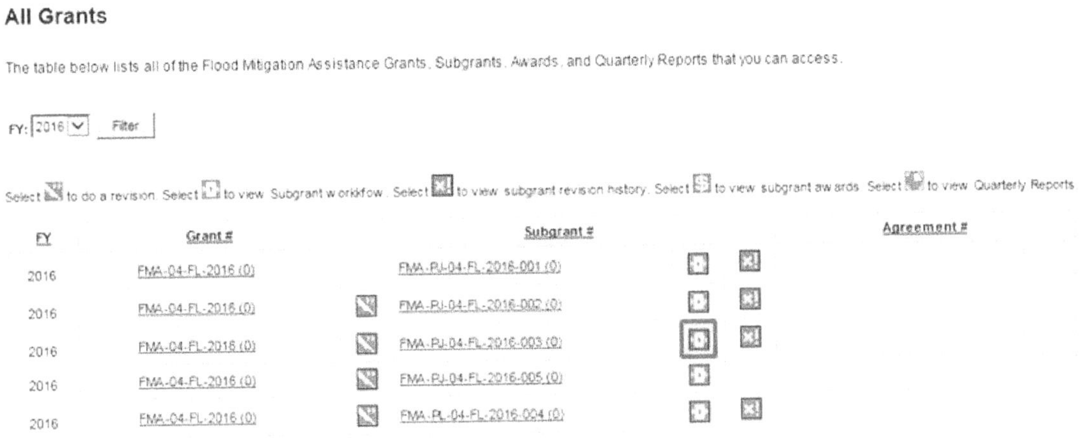

**All Grants**

The table below lists all of the Flood Mitigation Assistance Grants, Subgrants, Awards, and Quarterly Reports that you can access.

FY: 2016 ⌄  Filter

Select ⬚ to do a revision. Select ⬚ to view Subgrant workflow. Select ⬚ to view subgrant revision history. Select ⬚ to view subgrant awards. Select ⬚ to view Quarterly Reports.

| FY | Grant # | | Subgrant # | | Agreement # |
|---|---|---|---|---|---|
| 2016 | FMA-04-FL-2016 (0) | | FMA-PJ-04-FL-2016-001 (0) | | |
| 2016 | FMA-04-FL-2016 (0) | | FMA-PJ-04-FL-2016-002 (0) | | |
| 2016 | FMA-04-FL-2016 (0) | | FMA-PJ-04-FL-2016-003 (0) | | |
| 2016 | FMA-04-FL-2016 (0) | | FMA-PJ-04-FL-2016-005 (0) | | |
| 2016 | FMA-04-FL-2016 (0) | | FMA-PL-04-FL-2016-004 (0) | | |

To restore a subapplication that was removed from processing or not approved, select the **Subgrant (Pre-Award Eligibility) Workflow** icon on the All Grants screen.

## Pre-Award Eligibility

FMA-PJ-04-FL-2016-003 (0): FMA project 3

| Queue | Approved | User | Status | Status Date |
|---|---|---|---|---|
| Receipt and Delegate | Yes | EAST, JENNIFER | Completed | 05/19/2016 02:59 PM |
| Initial Review | Yes | JORDAN, ERIC | Completed | 07/30/2016 10:49 PM |
| Subgrant Selection (for Award) | Yes | JORDAN, ERIC | Completed | 09/16/2016 07:34 AM |
| Pre-Award Review (Grants) | Yes | JORDAN, ERIC | Completed | 04/03/2017 02:56 PM |
| Pre-Award Review (Program) | No | EAST, JENNIFER | Completed | 06/20/2017 06:53 PM |

Restore

Users with the Headquarters PDM Coordinator or Headquarters FMA Coordinator eGrants role may restore subapplications from the Pre-Award

Eligibility screen. Users without this role will not see the Restore button on the Pre-Award Eligibility screen. Select the **Restore** button.

## Confirm Subgrant Restore

FMA-PJ-04-FL-2016-003 (0): FMA project 3 Conditions

| Queue |
| --- |
| Pre-Award Review (Program) |

Click on the Cancel button to return to Pre-Award Eligiblity.

| Continue | | Cancel |
| --- | --- | --- |

You will be prompted to confirm the restoration. Select the **Continue** button.

## Confirmation

The Queue was successfully processed for Subgrant Application FMA-PJ-04-FL-2016-003 (0): FMA project 3

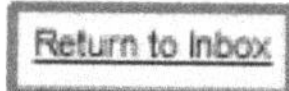

Return to Inbox

The Confirmation screen appears with a message that the subapplication has been restored to the Inbox. Select the **Return to Inbox** link. Once restored, the subapplication will be available in the Inbox for a user with the appropriate role to check out and review.

# Attachments

The Attachments functionality allows you to view, add, or delete files attached to a queue for a subapplication. This functionality is available in every workflow queue.
All users are able to add attachments to any queue for any subapplication to which they have access. You do not need to have the queue checked out in order to view the Attachments screen.
Alex will explain the features on the Attachments screen.
Scroll down to see slideshow captions.

## Cost Review

FMA-PJ-04-KY-2012-003 (0): KY FMA Project 3

| Subgrant Budget Class | Item Name | Office | Eligible |
|---|---|---|---|
| Personnel | Test Material 1 | Applicant | NA |
|  |  | Program | ☐ |
| Supplies | New Item | Applicant | NA |
|  |  | Program | ☐ |

Proposed Total Cost (A):       $:

Proposed Federal Share % (B):       75.000

Proposed Federal Share (C = A * B):       $:

Proposed Non Federal Share (A - C):

Approved: [Select ▼]       User: EAST, JENNI

[ Attachments ]       [ Comments... ]

To access the Attachments screen, select the **Attachments** button at the bottom of any queue screen.

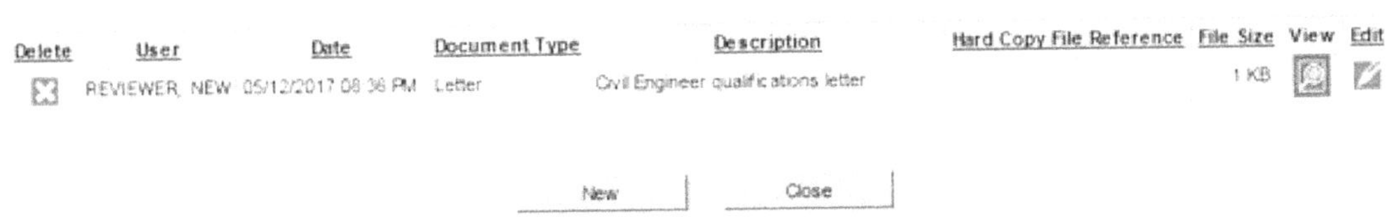

### Attachments: Planning Review

FMA-PL-01-CT-2005-001 (0): New Warks World Aid

| Delete | User | Date | Document Type | Description | Hard Copy File Reference | File Size | View | Edit |
|---|---|---|---|---|---|---|---|---|
| ☒ | REVIEWER, NEW | 05/12/2017 08:36 PM | Letter | Civil Engineer qualifications letter |  | 1 KB |  |  |

[ New ]       [ Close ]

The Attachments screen is displayed for the subapplication you are processing in the queue. You can view existing attachments by selecting the **View** icon.

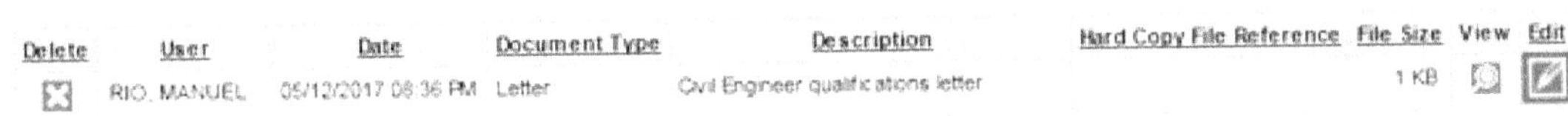

### Attachments: Planning Review

FMA-PL-01-CT-2005-001 (0): New Warks World Aid

| Delete | User | Date | Document Type | Description | Hard Copy File Reference | File Size | View | Edit |
|---|---|---|---|---|---|---|---|---|
| ☒ | RIO, MANUEL | 05/12/2017 08:36 PM | Letter | Civil Engineer qualifications letter |  | 1 KB |  |  |

Select the **Edit** icon to edit an attachment you have included with a subapplication.

### Attachments: Planning Review

FMA-PL-01-CT-2005-001 (0): New Warks World Aid

| Delete | User | Date | Document Type | Description | Hard Copy File Reference | File Size | View | Edit |
|---|---|---|---|---|---|---|---|---|
| ☒ | RIO MANUEL | 05/12/2017 08:36 PM | Letter | Civil Engineer qualifications letter |  | 1 KB |  |  |

You can delete any attachment you have included by selecting the **Delete** icon.

### Attachments: Planning Review

FMA-PL-01-CT-2005-001 (0): New Warks World Aid

| Delete | User | Date | Document Type | Description |
|---|---|---|---|---|
| ☒ | RIO, MANUEL | 05/12/2017 08:36 PM | Letter | Civil Engineer qualifications letter |

New     Close

Select the **Close** button to return to the previous screen.

# Adding an Attachment

Alex will show you how to add an attachment to a subapplication in a queue. Scroll down to see slideshow captions

### Attachments: Planning Review

FMA-PL-01-CT-2005-001 (0): New Warks World Aid

| Delete | User | Date | Document Type | Description |
|---|---|---|---|---|
| ☒ | RIO, MANUEL | 05/12/2017 08:36 PM | Letter | Civil Engineer qualifications letter |

New     Close

In order to add a new attachment to a queue, select the **New** button on the bottom-center of the Attachments screen.

## New Attachment: Planning Review

FMA-PL-01-CT-2005-001 (0): New Warks World Aid

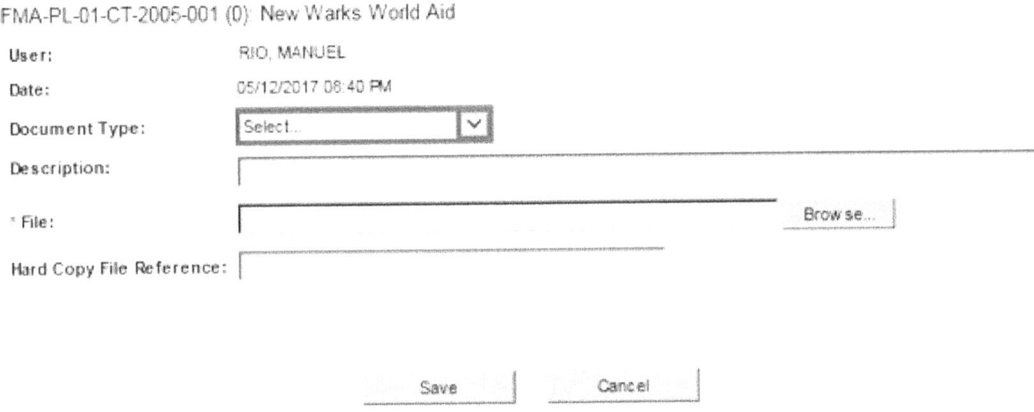

The New Attachment screen opens in a new window. Select the **Document Type** drop-down menu.

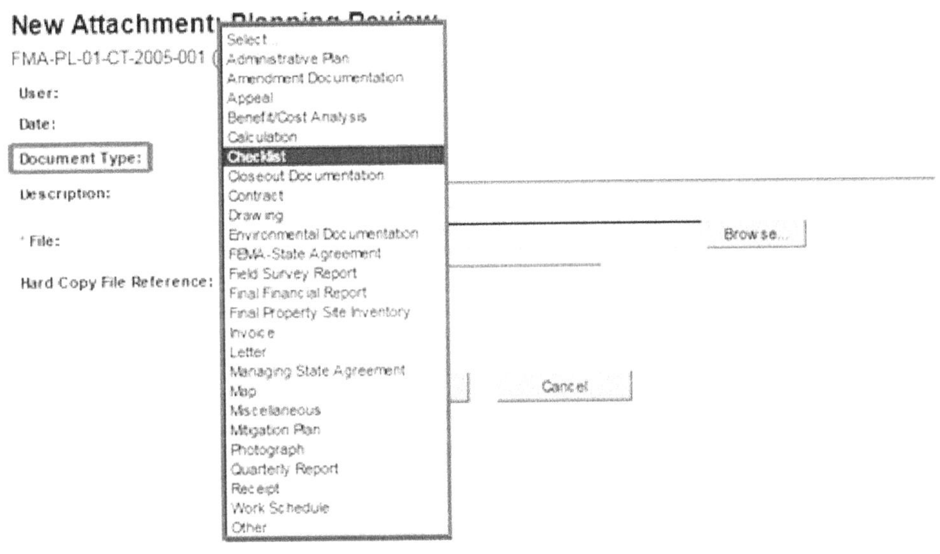

The Document Type drop-down menu lists 25 options. For this application, you will want to select the **Checklist** item.

## New Attachment: Planning Review

FMA-PL-01-CT-2005-001 (0): New Warks World Aid

| | |
|---|---|
| User: | REVIEWER, NEW |
| Date: | 05/12/2017 08:40 PM |
| Document Type: | Checklist |
| Description: | Planning Review Checklist |
| * File: | |
| Hard Copy File Reference: | |

Enter a description of the attached document in the **Description** field. Type "Planning Review Checklist" in the text field.

**New Attachment: Planning Review**

FMA-PL-01-CT-2005-001 (0): New Warks World Aid

| | |
|---|---|
| **User:** | REVIEWER, NEW |
| **Date:** | 05/12/2017 08:40 PM |
| **Document Type:** | Checklist |
| **Description:** | Planning Review Checklist |
| *** File:** | Browse... |
| **Hard Copy File Reference:** | |

Select the **Browse** button to search your computer files for the document you wish to upload as an attachment.

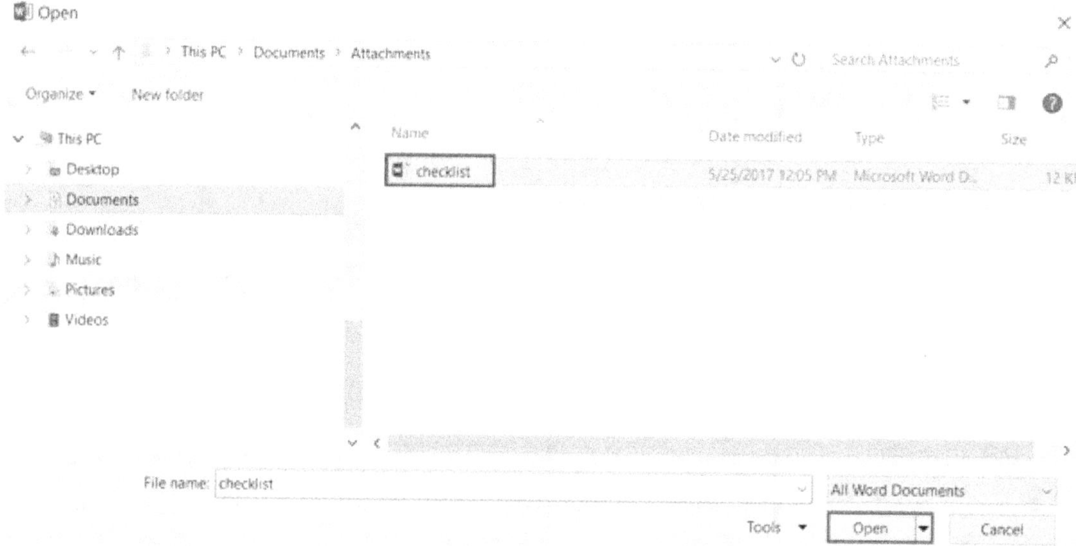


On your computer, locate the file you wish to attach and select it. You want to attach the file named **Checklist.docx.** Then, select the **Open** button.

**New Attachment: Planning Review**

FMA-PL-01-CT-2005-001 (0): New Warks World Aid

| | |
|---|---|
| **User:** | REVIEWER, NEW |
| **Date:** | 05/12/2017 08:40 PM |
| **Document Type:** | Checklist |
| **Description:** | Planning Review Checklist |
| *** File:** | C:\Users\nreviewer\Documents\Checklist.docx    Browse... |
| **Hard Copy File Reference:** | |

The **file name** appears in the File text field.

**New Attachment: Planning Review**

FMA-PL-01-CT-2005-001 (0): New Warks World Aid

| | |
|---|---|
| User: | REVIEWER, NEW |
| Date: | 05/12/2017 08:40 PM |
| Document Type: | Checklist |
| Description: | Planning Review Checklist |
| * File: | C:\Users\nreviewer\Documents\Checklist.rtf  Browse... |
| Hard Copy File Reference: | |

Save        Cancel

Enter a **Hard Copy File Reference** if needed. If you made an error, you can select the **Cancel** button to cancel the action. We have identified the correct document, so you can select the **Save** button to save the attachment to the queue.

**Attachments: Planning Review**

FMA-PL-01-CT-2005-001 (0): New Warks World Aid

| Delete | User | Date | Document Type | Description | Hard Copy File Reference | File Size | View | Edit |
|---|---|---|---|---|---|---|---|---|
| ☒ | REVIEWER, NEW | 05/12/2017 08:47 PM | Checklist | Planning Review Checklist | | 1 KB | | |
| ☒ | REVIEWER, NEW | 05/12/2017 08:36 PM | Letter | Civil Engineer qualifications letter | | 1 KB | | |

New        Close

The attachment you added should show up in the list of attachments. Select the **Close** button to return to the queue.

# Cost Review Queue

The Cost Review queue is required for all subapplication types: project, planning, technical assistance, and management costs. The Cost Review queue displays a breakdown of each line item cost, as well as some overall information about the proposed costs from the subapplication.

The Cost Review, Planning Review, and Cost-Effectiveness/Engineering Review queues are concurrent workflow queues. This means that these three queues can be processed simultaneously by separate users, as necessary. The subapplication will not be forwarded to the subsequent queue in the workflow until all of the appropriate concurrent queues are complete.

If it is determined that a mistake was made in the Cost Review queue, either the queue can be reset by an Headquarters PDM Coordinator, or it can be reworked from the Pre-Award Eligibility queue for FMA subapplications. (The Rework and Reset functionalities are discussed in Lesson 8.)

# Cost Review Queue (continued)

Alex will show you how to complete the Cost Review queue.
Scroll down to see slideshow captions.

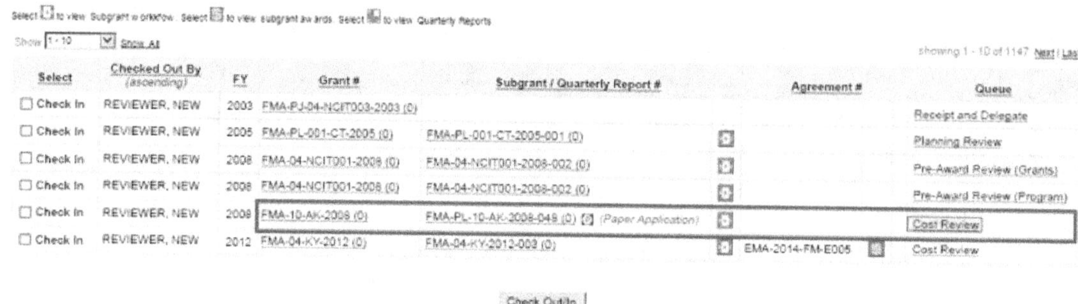

Check out the Cost Review queue for the subapplication that you wish to work on. We are going to review subapplication number FMA-PL-10-AK-2008-048. Select the **Cost Review** link in the Queue column for this subapplication.

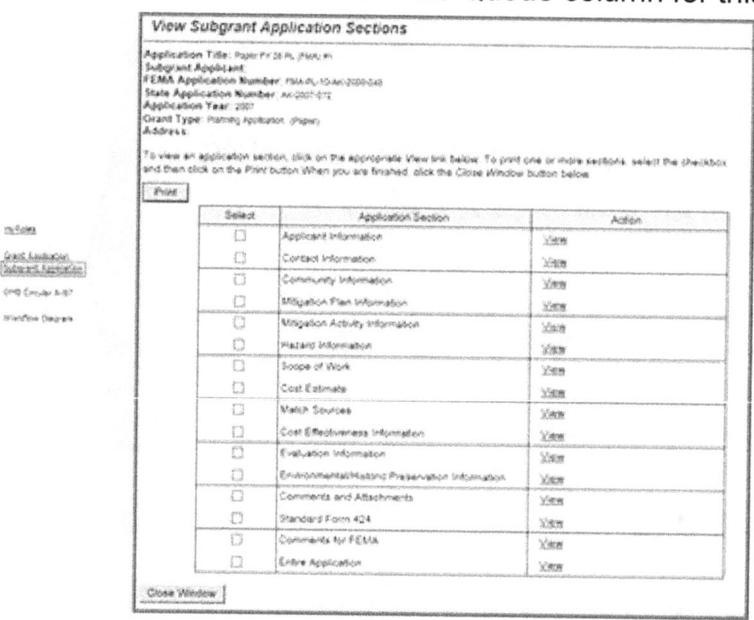

On the Cost Review screen sidebar menu, selecting the **Subgrant Application** link will open the View Subgrant Application Sections screen in a new window so that you can view the relevant subapplication section while you complete this queue.

### Cost Review

FMA-PL-10-AK-2008-048 (0): Paper FY 08 PL (FMA) #1

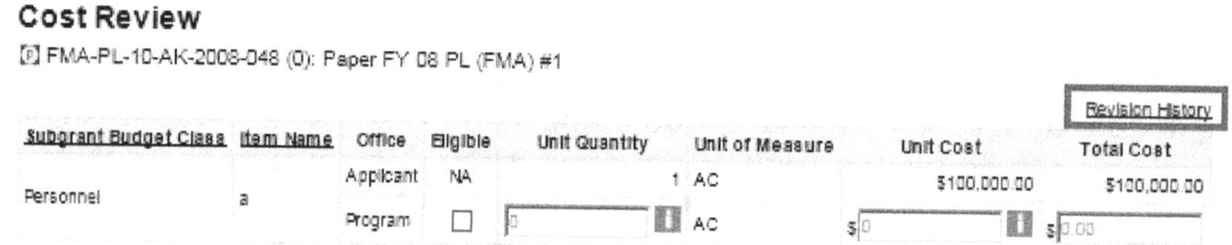

From this queue, you can view the **Revision History** by selecting this link. We will talk about Revision History in Lesson 8. <

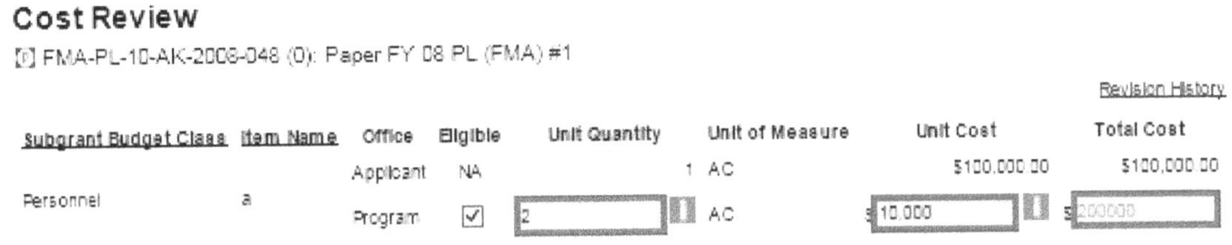

After reviewing the subapplication, select the Subgrant Budget Class items that you believe represent eligible costs for this activity by selecting the box in the **Eligible** column. We can see one of the activities that is listed in the Cost Estimate section for this subapplication. This Personnel costs activity is eligible, so we will select the **checkbox** for it.

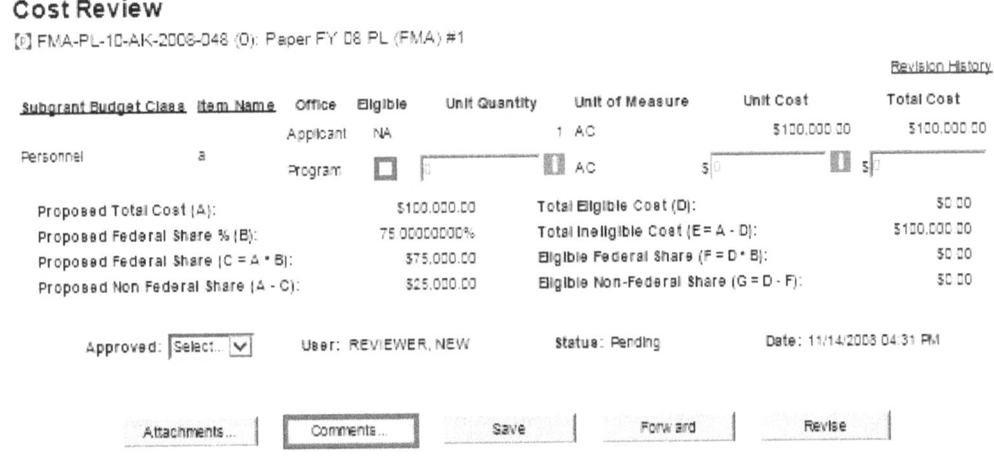

You can change the **Unit Quantity** and **Unit Cost** of each Subgrant Budget Class item by modifying the associated fields after you have selected the checkbox in the Eligible column for that activity. The **Total Cost** field is automatically updated. Any changes to the unit quantity or unit cost will require the subapplication being sent back to the Applicant for revisions. For PDM subapplications, you may **not** modify any cost line items due to the competitive nature of the program.

If you determine that a Subgrant Budget Class item is ineligible, you should document that by entering a comment using the **Comments** button.

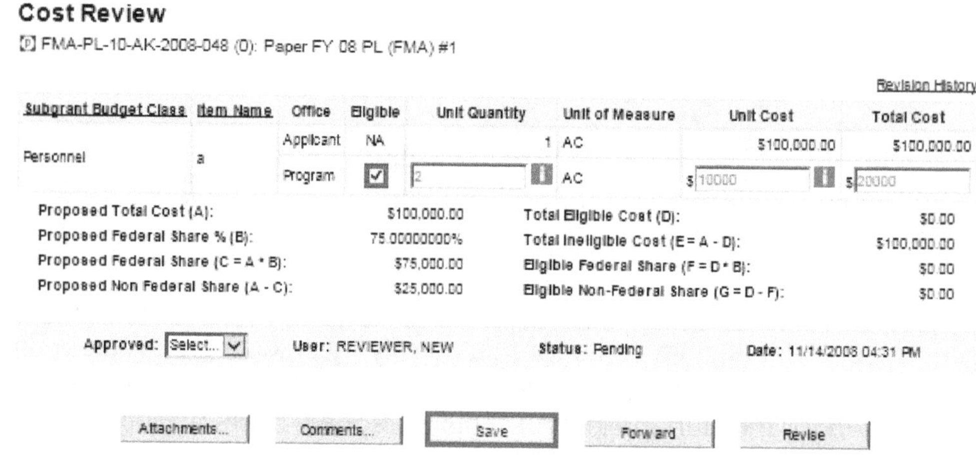

Once all of the eligible line items are selected, select the **Save** button to save your selections.

Once saved, the updated **Total Eligible Costs,** which reflect the total eligible line items, are displayed on the lower right side of the Cost Review screen. The **Proposed Costs** are displayed on the lower left side for comparison.

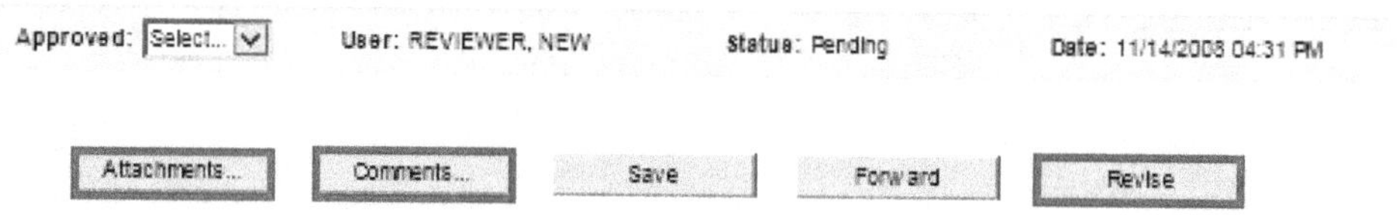

From the Cost Review queue, you can also add or edit **Attachments** or **Comments,** and request that the Applicant **Revise** the Cost Estimate section of the subapplication by selecting the appropriate link or button. For PDM subapplications, the Revise button will be inactive> after the application deadline since it is a competitive program.

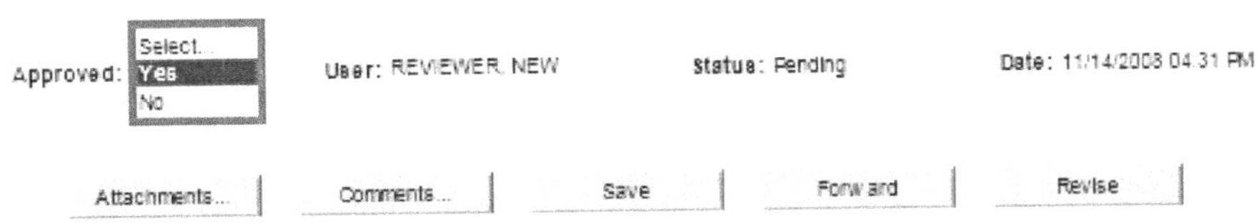

When you have completed your eligibility review of the cost line items and edited the unit quantity and unit cost for each, as necessary, select **Yes** or **No** from the Approved drop-down menu. If you disapprove this queue, comments are required, but disapproving the queue will **not** remove the subapplication from further processing in the workflow. For this subapplication, we will approve this queue by selecting **Yes.**

Then, select the **Forward** button to complete this queue.

### Confirmation

The Queue was successfully processed for Subgrant Application ⓘ FMA-PL-10-AK-2008-048 (0): Paper FY 08 PL (FMA) #1

Return to Inbox

You will receive **Confirmation** that you have completed the queue. Select the **Return to Inbox** link to continue processing queues for this program.

# Comments

The Comments functionality allows you to view, edit, add, or delete comments associated with a queue for a subapplication. The Comments button is available on every Workflow queue screen. However, for PDM National Review queues, you will need to select the Comments icon for the desired subapplication to access the Comments functionality.
Any user can add comments to any queue for a subapplication to which he or she has access. However, you can view the comments without having to check out the queue.

Remember, you must provide comments for a disapproved queue before forwarding to the next queue.

Alex will show you how to add a comment to a subapplication in a queue.
Scroll down to see slideshow captions

**Initial Review**

FMA-PJ-04-KY-2012-010 (0) test revision



| Question | Answer |
|---|---|
| Have you completed the Initial Review Checklist for this sub-application? Please attach completed checklist and enter comments regarding issues addressed in the checklist. | Select... |
| Are both the Applicant and Sub-applicant eligible for the program? If no, please disapprove this queue and enter comments. | Select... |
| Does the Scope of Work section reflect the activity(s) selected in the Mitigation Activity section? If no, please enter comments. | Select... |
| Is the proposed mitigation activity, as described in the Scope of Work section of the sub-application, eligible for the program? If no, please disapprove this queue and enter comments. | Select... |
| Does the sub-application include all of the information required by the program guidance? If no, please enter comments. | Select... |
| Is all of the supporting documentation required by the program guidance provided for the sub-application? If no, please enter comments. | Select... |

Fields marked with a red asterisk (*) are required.

Approved: Select...    **User:** REVIEWER, NEW    **Status:** Pending    **Date:** 02/04/2015 08:20 PM

Attachments... | Comments... | Save | Forward | Revise

For this subapplication, we will add a comment to the Initial Review queue. Select the **Comments** button at the bottom of the screen.

## Comments: Initial Review

FMA-PJ-04-KY-2012-010 (0): test revision

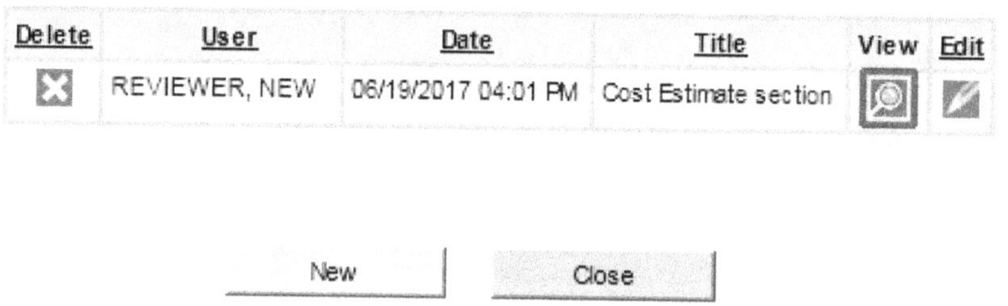

| Delete | User | Date | Title | View | Edit |
|---|---|---|---|---|---|
| ✖ | REVIEWER, NEW | 06/19/2017 04:01 PM | Cost Estimate section | 🔍 | ✎ |

New | Close

The Comments screen will open in a new window. If there is an existing comment, you will see it listed here. You can view the comment by selecting the **View** icon.

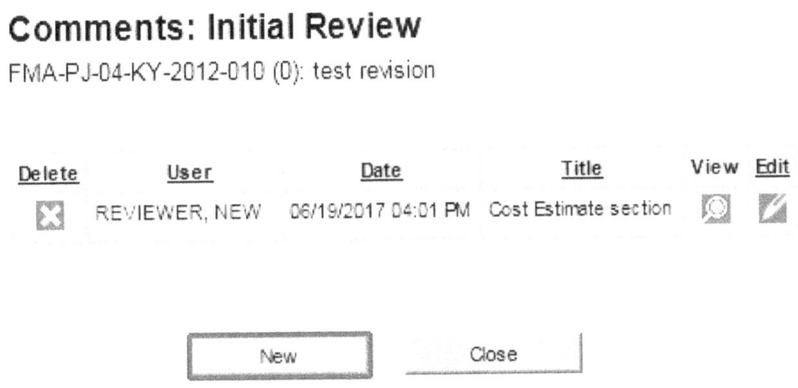

# Comments: Initial Review

FMA-PJ-04-KY-2012-010 (0): test revision

| Delete | User | Date | Title | View | Edit |
|---|---|---|---|---|---|
| ☒ | REVIEWER, NEW | 06/19/2017 04:01 PM | Cost Estimate section | | |

New     Close

In order to add a new comment, select the **New** button.

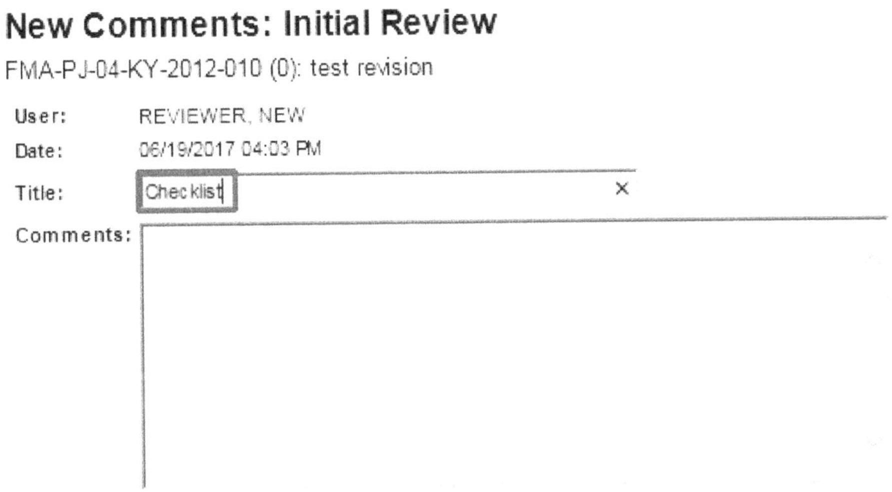

## New Comments: Initial Review

FMA-PJ-04-KY-2012-010 (0): test revision

User:     REVIEWER, NEW

Date:     06/19/2017 04:03 PM

Title:     Checklist     ×

Comments:

The New Comments screen appears in a new window. Enter a title in the **Title** field. For this subapplication, we will use the title "Checklist."

**New Comments: Initial Review**

FMA-PJ-04-KY-2012-010 (0): test revision

| | |
|---|---|
| User: | REVIEWER, NEW |
| Date: | 06/19/2017 04:03 PM |
| Title: | Checklist |
| Comments: | This is a comment regarding the checklist that was submitted. It needs to be reviewed. |

Save    Cancel

Enter the comment in the **Comments** field. For this subapplication we will enter the comment, "This is a comment regarding the checklist that was submitted. It needs to be reviewed." Select the **Save** button to save the comment and return to the queue.

## Comments: Initial Review

FMA-PJ-04-KY-2012-010 (0): test revision

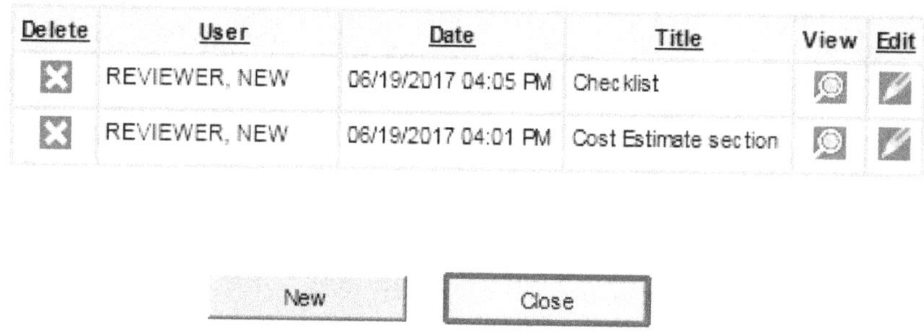

| Delete | User | Date | Title | View | Edit |
|---|---|---|---|---|---|
| ✖ | REVIEWER, NEW | 06/19/2017 04:05 PM | Checklist | | |
| ✖ | REVIEWER, NEW | 06/19/2017 04:01 PM | Cost Estimate section | | |

New    Close

The new comment appears on the list of comments for the queue. Select the **Close** button to return to the queue.

# Planning Review Queue

The Planning Review queue documents the status of the Subapplicant's and Applicant's mitigation plans and the subapplication's consistency with those existing plans. This queue is required for project and planning subapplications.

The Planning Review, Cost Review, and Cost-Effectiveness/Engineering Review queues are concurrent workflow queues. This means that the queues can be processed simultaneously by separate users, as necessary. The subapplication will not be forwarded to the subsequent queue in the Workflow until all of the appropriate concurrent queues are complete.

If it is determined that the outcome of this Planning Review queue is incorrect, the queue can be reset by a Headquarters PDM Coordinator for PDM subapplications, or it can be reworked from the Pre-Award Eligibility queue for FMA subapplications. (The Rework and Reset functionalities will be discussed in Lesson 8.)

# Planning Review Queue (continued)

Alex will demonstrate how to complete the Planning Review queue.
Scroll down to see slideshow captions.

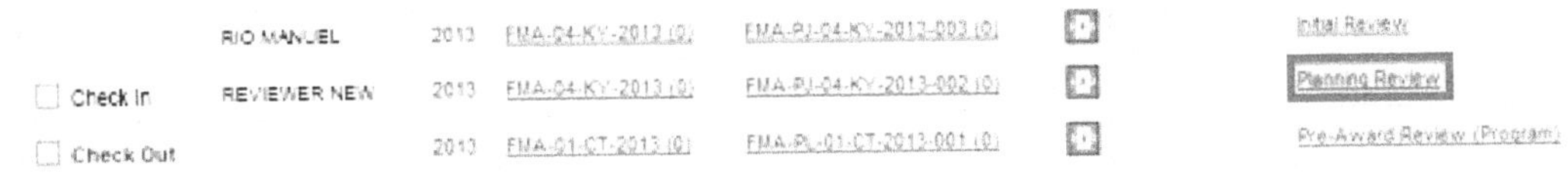


Check out the Planning Review queue for the subapplication that you wish to work on. In this case, we are going to review Subapplication number FMA-PJ-04-KY-2013-002. Select the **Planning Review** link for this subapplication.

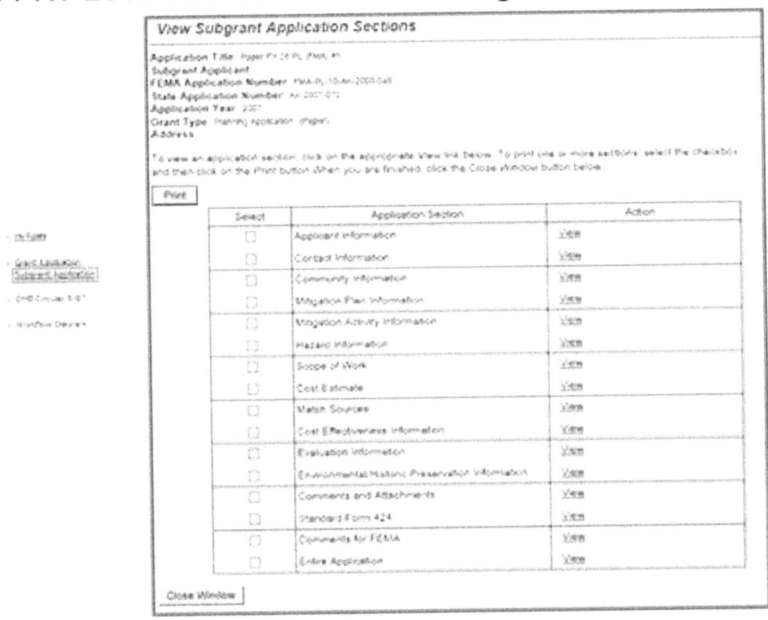

The **Subgrant Application** link on the Inbox sidebar menu will open the View Subgrant Application Sections screen in a new window so that you can review the subapplication while you complete the queue.

From this queue, you can view the **Revision History** of the subapplication. I will explain more about Revision History later in the course.

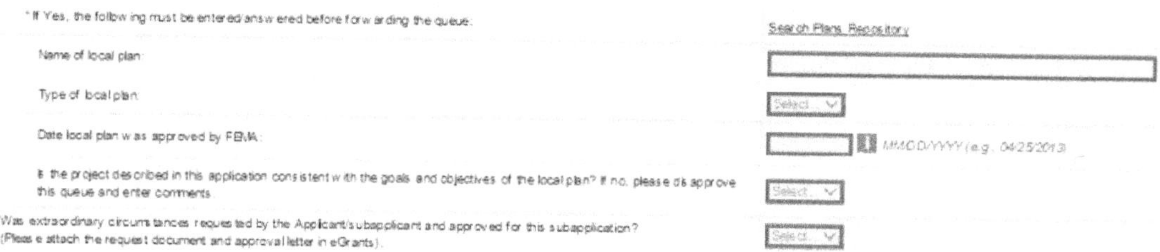


Select either the "Yes" or "No" option to answer the questions asking whether the Subapplicant and Applicant have FEMA-approved mitigation plans. The questions with **red asterisks** are required. Select the "Yes" option for both questions because both the Subapplicant and Applicant have FEMA-approved mitigation plans.



When you indicate that there is a FEMA-approved mitigation plan, you must provide the plan information. You can either enter the information by typing in the required fields, or by selecting the **Search Plans Repository** link to search for the plan information. Once you select a plan from the repository, eGrants will auto-populate the mitigation plan information fields.

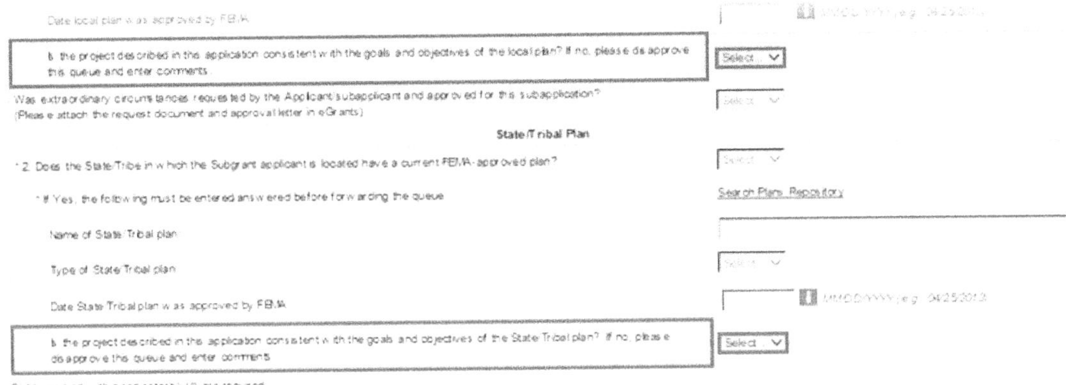

In addition, if there is an approved plan, you must respond to the question about the proposed activity's consistency with the FEMA-approved plan. Project subapplications have an additional question about whether the proposed project is consistent with the goals and objectives of the local mitigation plan.

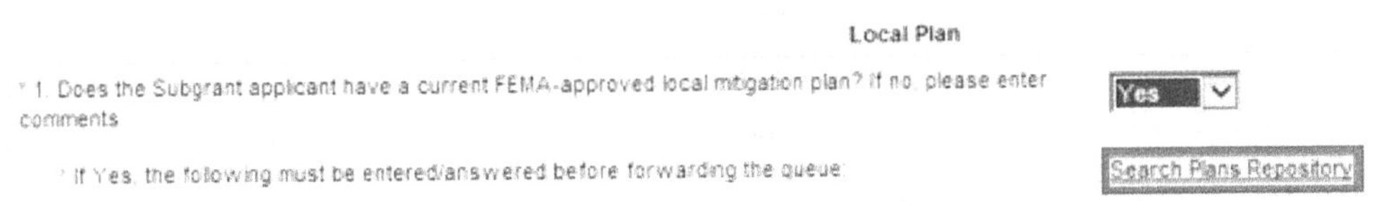

Let's search for the FEMA-approved mitigation plan for this community. Select the **Search Plans Repository** link.

### Plans Repository Search

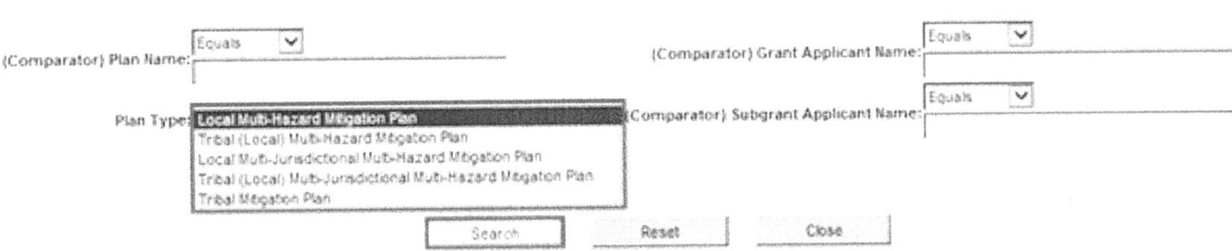

The Plans Repository Search window displays. You can search by **Plan Name, Plan Type, Grant Applicant Name** and **Subgrant Applicant Name.** The criteria available for each search are "Equals", "Begins with", "Contains", and "Ends with."

The **Plan Type** drop-down menu will display different options for mitigation plan types, depending on whether you are searching for an Applicant's plan or a Subapplicant's plan. When searching for a Subapplicant's plan, the Plan Type drop-down menu displays five options. Select the "Local Multi-Hazard Mitigation Plan" option. If you want to clear the plan information results, select the Reset button. The Close button will return you to the previous screen. Select the **Search** button to begin the search.

The Search Results screen displays the results of the search. Select the radio button in the **Select** column for the appropriate plan. Then select the **Return** button to select the plan and return to the Planning Review queue. If the plan you have selected has expired, you will receive a warning message.

The plan information is auto-filled into the text fields. When all questions have been completed, select the **Save** button.

From this queue, you can also add or edit **Attachments** or **Comments,** and request that the Applicant **Revise** the Mitigation Plan section of the subapplication by selecting the appropriate link or button. The Revise button will be inactive for PDM subapplications after the application deadline since it is a competitive program. We will discuss Revision Requests in more detail in Lesson 8.

Now it is time to select "Yes" or "No" in the **Approved** drop-down menu. If you answer "No" to any of the key questions, you are required to disapprove this queue. If you disapprove this queue, you must provide comments, and the subapplication will be removed from subsequent queues in the Workflow. Since you have answered "Yes" to the questions, you can approve this queue. Select the **Yes** option. Then select the **Forward** button.

# Cost-Effectiveness/Engineering Review Queue

The Cost-Effectiveness/Engineering Review queue documents the review of the Benefit-Cost Analysis (BCA) and its supporting documentation for project subapplications. Only project subapplications require the Cost-Effectiveness/Engineering Review.

For PDM subapplications, this queue is called the Cost-Effectiveness Review queue and does not include the FEMA Benefits-Cost Ratio (BCR) or Engineering Feasibility fields, since those are recorded for all eligible projects during the PDM National Technical Review queue. (The National Technical Review queue will be covered in Lesson 7.)

The Cost Review, Planning Review, and Cost-Effectiveness/Engineering Review queues are concurrent workflow queues. This means that these queues can be processed simultaneously by separate users, as necessary. The subapplication will not be forwarded to the subsequent queue in the workflow until all of the appropriate concurrent queues are complete.

If it is determined that a mistake was made in the Cost-Effectiveness/Engineering Review queue, the queue can be reset by a Headquarters PDM Coordinator for PDM subapplications, or it can be reworked from the Pre-Award Eligibility queue for FMA subapplications. (The Rework and Reset functionalities will be discussed in Lesson 8.)

# Cost-Effectiveness/Engineering Review Queue (continued)

Alex will demonstrate how to complete the Cost-Effectiveness/Engineering Review queue for an FMA project subapplication.

Scroll down to see slideshow captions.

| Select | Checked Out By | FY | Grant # | Subgrant / Quarterly Report # | Agreement # | Queue |
|---|---|---|---|---|---|---|
| ☐ Check Out | | 2013 | FMA-01-CT-2013 (0) | FMA-PL-01-CT-2013-001 (0) | | Pre-Award Review (Program) |
| | PETITE JEAN | 2013 | FMA-04-KY-2013 (0) | FMA-PJ-04-KY-2013-001 (0) | | Initial Review |
| ☐ Check In | REVIEWER NEW | 2013 | FMA-04-KY-2013 (0) | FMA-PJ-04-KY-2013-002 (0) | | Cost-Effectiveness Review |
| | PETITE JEAN | 2013 | FMA-04-KY-2013 (0) | FMA-PJ-04-KY-2013-003 (0) | | Initial Review |
| | PETITE JEAN | 2013 | FMA-10-AK-2013 (0) | FMA-PJ-10-AK-2013-003 (0) | | EHP Queues |

Check out the Cost-Effectiveness Review queue for the project subapplication that you wish to work on. In this case, we are going to review subapplication number FMA-PJ-04-KY-2013-002. Then select the **Cost-Effectiveness Review** link for this subapplication.

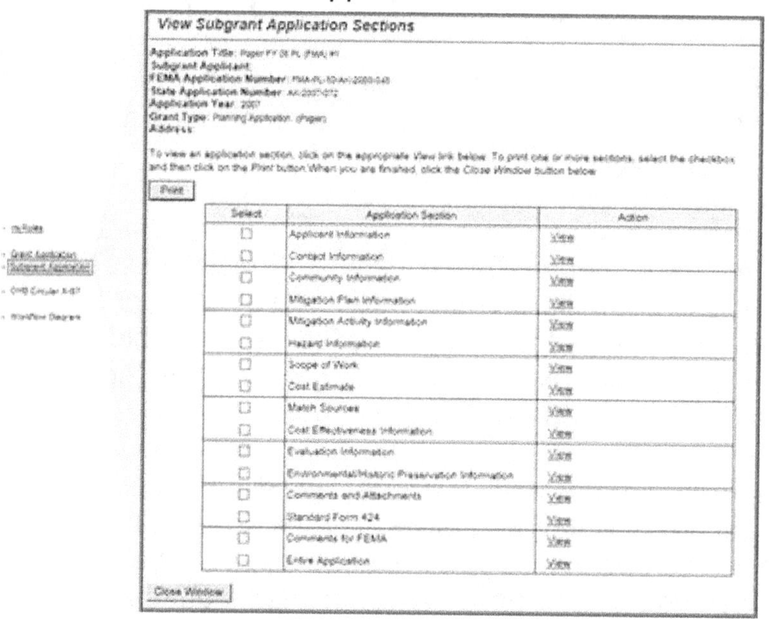

The **Subgrant Application** link on the Inbox sidebar menu will open the View Subgrant Application Sections screen in a new window so that you can review the subapplication while you complete the queue.

### Cost-Effectiveness/Engineering Review

FMA-PJ-02-NY-2005-001 (0): Project #1

Based on your review of the Benefit-Cost Analysis (BCA) for the subapplication, indicate your response to the questions by selecting "Yes" or "No" from the drop-down menu. The subapplication cannot be forwarded until all of the required questions are complete. For this subapplication, you can select the **"Yes"** option for each of the questions.

FMA-PJ-02-NY-2005-001 (0) Project #1
*(Paper Application)*

Next, you need to record the FEMA Benefit-Cost Ratio (BCR) for this project. Enter **1.0** into the BCR (FEMA) text field. The question below asks if the Greatest Savings to the Fund was used. It is appropriate to select the **"No"** option from the drop-down menu for this subapplication. Then, select the **Save** button.

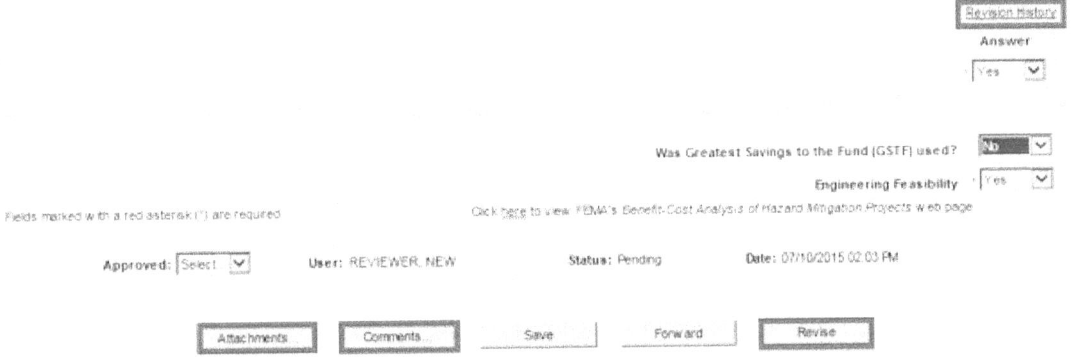

To view the subapplication's Revision History select the **Revision History** link at the top right of the screen. You can also add or edit **Attachments** and **Comments,** and request the Applicant to **Revise** the Cost-Effectiveness section of a subapplication by selecting the appropriate button at the bottom of the screen. Keep in mind that the Revise button will be inactive for PDM subapplications after the application deadline since it is a competitive program.

| Question | Answer |
| --- | --- |
| Is an electronic copy of the benefit-cost analysis (BCA) for this project attached to the application? | * Yes |
| Is the benefit-cost ratio (BCR) greater than or equal to 1.0? If no, please disapprove this queue and enter comments. | * Yes |
| Was the attached BCA performed using a FEMA-approved methodology? (If alternative non-FEMA BCA software was used, did the appropriate FEMA Regional Office and FEMA Headquarters approve the methodology prior to the applicant's submission of the project application to FEMA?) If no, please disapprove this queue and enter comments. | * Yes |
| Does the attached BCA reflect the total net present value of benefits and total project cost provided in the project application? If no, please enter comments. | * Yes |
| BCR (Applicant) | 0.0 |
| BCR (FEMA) | 1.0 |
| Was Greatest Savings to the Fund (GSTF) used? | No |
| Engineering Feasibility | * Yes |

Fields marked with a red asterisk (*) are required.     Click here to view FEMA's *Benefit-Cost Analysis of Hazard Mitigation Projects* web page.

Approved: [Select... / Yes / No]     User: REVIEWER, NEW     Status: Pending     Date: 07/10/2015 02:03 PM

To approve the queue, you would select "Yes" from the **Approved** drop-down menu. However, if you have answered "No" to any of the key questions, you are required to disapprove this queue by selecting the **"No"** option. You must also disapprove the queue if you entered a FEMA BCR that is less than 1.0 or if you selected "No" for the Engineering Feasibility prompt. If you disapprove the queue, you must provide comments, and the subapplication will be removed from subsequent queues in the workflow.

Approved: Yes     User: REVIEWER, NEW     Status: Pending     Date: 07/10/2015 02:03 PM

[ Attachments ]     [ Comments... ]     [ Save ]     [ Forward ]     [ Revise ]

For this subapplication, you can approve this queue by selecting **"Yes."** Then, select the **Forward** button to complete this queue.

## Confirmation

The Queue was successfully processed for Subgrant Application [P] FMA-PJ-02-NY-2005-001 (0): Project #1

[ Return to Inbox ]

You will receive **Confirmation** that you have completed the queue. Select the **Return to Inbox** link to continue processing queues for this program.

# PDM National Review Process

After the concurrent Cost Review, Planning Review, and Cost-Effectiveness/Engineering Review queues, the next queue in the Pre-Award Eligibility Workflow depends upon whether the subapplication is being evaluated under the PDM or FMA grant program. PDM planning and project subapplications go through the National Review Process first, while the FMA planning and project subapplications continue directly to the Pre-Award Review queue, with project subapplications moving through the concurrent Environmental/Historical Preservation (EHP) Review queue.

The PDM National Review Process (which will be discussed in detail in Lesson 7) consists of the following queues:

1.  National Technical Review
2.  Subgrant Selection (for Award)

# Environmental/Historical Preservation (EHP) Review Queues

All project subapplications must be reviewed for consistency with Environmental/Historic Preservation (EHP) requirements. This review occurs in the Environmental & Historic Preservation Management Information System (EMIS), which is outside of the eGrants system.

Due to differences in the Pre-Award Eligibility Workflow, PDM project subapplications go through the EHP Review queues immediately after the concurrent queues (Cost Review, Planning Review, and Cost-Effectiveness Review) are completed and approved. PDM project subapplications are forwarded to the EHP Review queues after the National Review Process identifies the subapplications which have been selected for further review. If a Regional Environmental Officer (REO) requires further information regarding a project subapplication in order to process the EHP Review, he or she will rework the project subapplication back to the eGrants system.

The EHP Review may be processed concurrently with the Pre-Award Review queue and may continue after any project subapplications are selected for conditional award in the Pre-Award Review queue.

# EHP Review Queues (Continued)

While an eGrants user does not complete the EHP Review queues, a reviewer may be able to view the status of the subapplication in the different EMIS queues and may have to respond to a rework request sent by an EMIS user. Alex will demonstrate how to view a Rework request, provide a response, and submit it back to the EHP Review queues.
Scroll down to see slideshow captions.

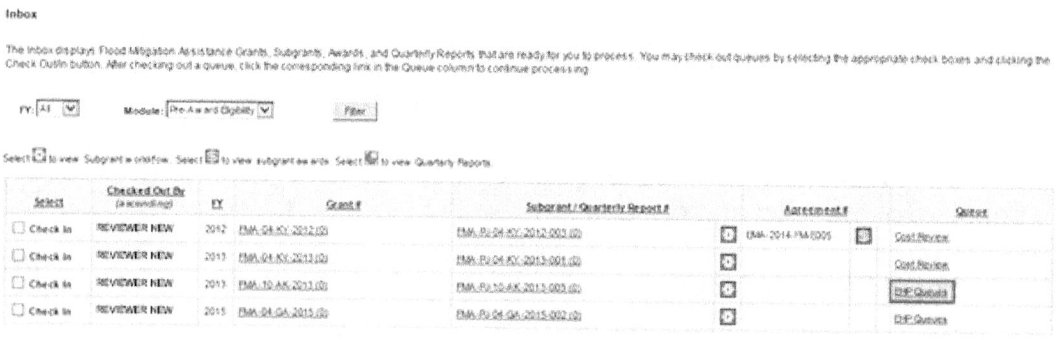

**Inbox**

The Inbox displays Flood Mitigation Assistance Grants, Subgrants, Awards, and Quarterly Reports that are ready for you to process. You may check out queues by selecting the appropriate check boxes and clicking the Check Out/In button. After checking out a queue, click the corresponding link in the Queue column to continue processing.

FY: All    Module: Pre-Award Eligibility    Filter

Select to view Subgrant workflow. Select to view subgrant awards. Select to view Quarterly Reports.

| Select | Checked Out By (ascending) | FY | Grant # | Subgrant / Quarterly Report # | Agreement # | Queue |
|---|---|---|---|---|---|---|
| Check In | REVIEWER NEW | 2012 | FMA-04-KY-2012 (0) | FMA-PJ-04-KY-2012-003 (0) | EMA-2014-FMA-0005 | Cost Review |
| Check In | REVIEWER NEW | 2013 | FMA-04-KY-2013 (0) | FMA-PJ-04-KY-2013-001 (0) | | Cost Review |
| Check In | REVIEWER NEW | 2013 | FMA-10-AK-2013 (0) | FMA-PJ-10-AK-2013-005 (0) | | EHP Queues |
| Check In | REVIEWER NEW | 2015 | FMA-04-GA-2015 (0) | FMA-PJ-04-GA-2015-002 (0) | | EHP Queues |

To view any rework requests, you must first check out the **EHP Queues** queue for the subapplication assigned to you. In this case, we are going to review subapplication number FMA-PJ-10-AK-2013-005.

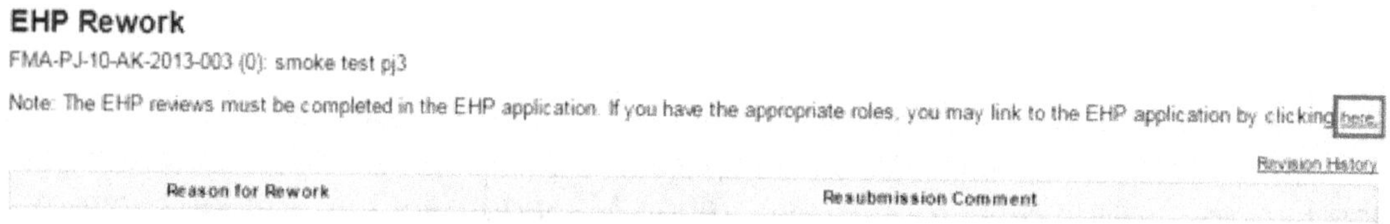

**EHP Rework**

FMA-PJ-10-AK-2013-003 (0): smoke test pj3

Note: The EHP reviews must be completed in the EHP application. If you have the appropriate roles, you may link to the EHP application by clicking here.

Revision History

| Reason for Rework | Resubmission Comment |
|---|---|
| | |

The screen that is displayed to eGrants reviewers is the EHP Rework screen. If you have Environmental/Historic Preservation review roles, you may access the Environmental & Historic Preservation Management Information System (or EMIS) and view the EHP Review Workflow queues by selecting the **here** link at the top of the screen.) We haven't been assigned that role, so we can't access those screens.

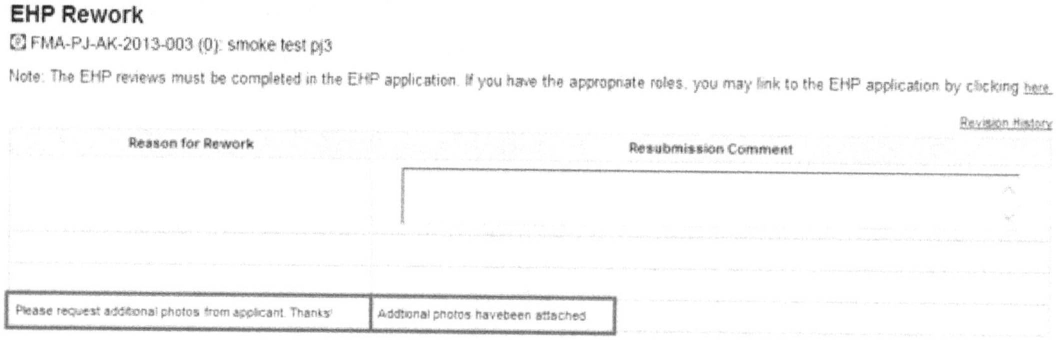

**EHP Rework**

FMA-PJ-AK-2013-003 (0): smoke test pj3

Note: The EHP reviews must be completed in the EHP application. If you have the appropriate roles, you may link to the EHP application by clicking here.

Revision History

| Reason for Rework | Resubmission Comment |
|---|---|
| | |
| Please request additional photos from applicant. Thanks! | Additional photos have been attached |

The EHP Rework screen indicates whether an EMIS user has requested a rework of a project subapplication to the eGrants system. A PDM or FMA Coordinator can view and respond to Rework Requests and resubmit the project subapplication to the EMIS system. The **Reason for Rework,** which the Regional Environmental Officer entered in EMIS when the rework was requested, and the **Resubmission Comments** from the FMA Coordinator, are displayed.

**EHP Rework**

FMA-PJ-10-AK-2013-003 (0): smoke test pj3

Note: The EHP reviews must be completed in the EHP application. If you have the appropriate roles, you may link to the EHP application by clicking here.

Revision History

| Reason for Rework | Resubmission Comment |
|---|---|
| test rework to egrants | |

Attachments...    Comments...    Resubmit    Revise

From this queue, you can view the **Revision History,** add or edit **attachments** and **comments,** and request **revisions** by selecting the appropriate link or button.

**EHP Rework**

FMA-PJ-10-AK-2013-003 (0): smoke test pj3

Note: The EHP reviews must be completed in the EHP application. If you have the appropriate roles, you may link to the EHP application by clicking here.

Revision History

| Reason for Rework | Resubmission Comment |
|---|---|
| Please attach letter from the State Historical Preservation Officer regarding this project | Letter is attached |

Attachments...    Comments...    Resubmit    Revise

In this case, the **Reason for Rework** is that the EMIS reviewer has asked for an approval letter from the State Historical Preservation officer. After obtaining the letter from the Applicant, you can enter your response in the **Resubmission Comment** text field. You can enter, "Letter is attached," and then select the **Resubmit** button.

## Confirmation

FMA-PJ-10-AK-2013-003 (0): smoke test pj3

was successfully resubmitted

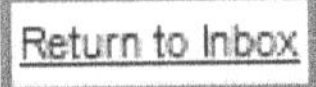


You will receive a **Confirmation** that the project subapplication has been resubmitted for EHP Review. Select the **Return to Inbox** link to continue processing queues assigned to you.

# Pre-Award Review Queue

The Pre-Award Review queue is the last step in the Pre-Award Eligibility Workflow. The purpose of the Pre-Award Review queue is to document the completion of pre-award requirements for subapplications. This is a joint queue that must be completed by both the Program Office and the Grants Management Office. Therefore, two separate queues will be displayed in the Inbox:

- Pre-Award (Program) Review
- Pre-Award (Grants) Review

Both of these queues are required for all subapplication types: planning, project, technical assistance, and management costs. Project subapplications with award conditions cannot be included in an award package until the EHP Review is complete.

During this queue, if a reviewer disagrees with the result of an earlier queue, the subapplication may be reworked to the earlier queue. (The Rework functionality will be discussed in Lesson 8.) If the outcome of the Pre-Award Review queue is determined to be incorrect, a PDM or FMA Coordinator can have the subapplication reset to the Inbox or removed, as appropriate. (The Reset functionality will also be discussed in Lesson 8.)

# Pre-Award Review Queue (continued)

Alex will demonstrate how to complete the Pre-Award Review queue.

<p<< p="">Scroll down to see slideshow captions.</p<<>

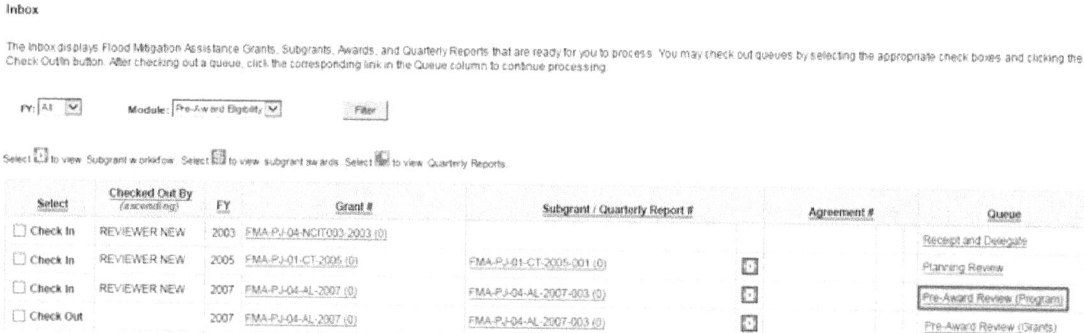



| Select | Checked Out By (ascending) | FY | Grant # | Subgrant / Quarterly Report # | Agreement # | Queue |
|---|---|---|---|---|---|---|
| Check In | REVIEWER NEW | 2003 | FMA-PJ-04-NCIT003-2003 (0) | | | Receipt and Delegate |
| Check In | REVIEWER NEW | 2005 | FMA-PJ-01-CT-2005 (0) | FMA-PJ-01-CT-2005-001 (0) | | Planning Review |
| Check In | REVIEWER NEW | 2007 | FMA-PJ-04-AL-2007 (0) | FMA-PJ-04-AL-2007-003 (0) | | Pre-Award Review (Program) |
| Check Out | | 2007 | FMA-PJ-04-AL-2007 (0) | FMA-PJ-04-AL-2007-003 (0) | | Pre-Award Review (Grants) |

Check out the Pre-Award Review (Program) queue for the subapplication that you wish to work on. In this case, we are going to complete the Pre-Award programmatic review for subapplication number FMA-PJ-04-AL-2007-003. Select the **Pre-Award Review (Program)** link for this application.

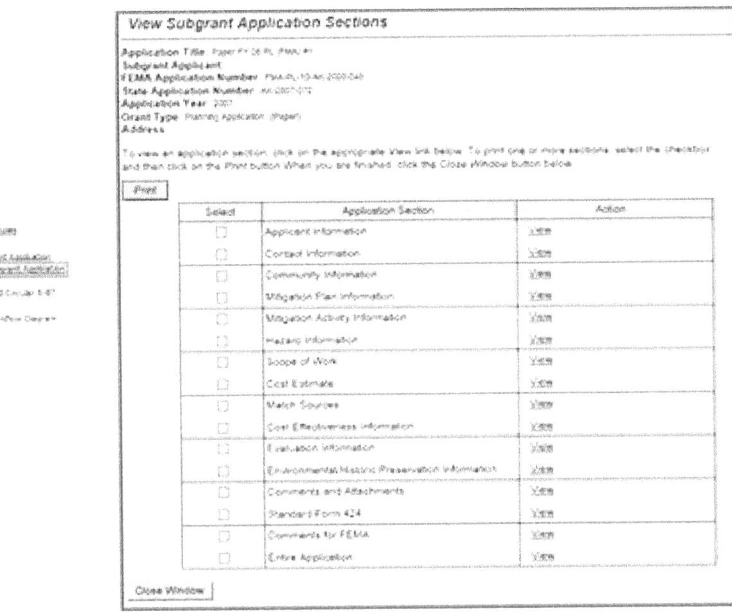

The **Subgrant Application** link on the Inbox sidebar menu will open the View Subgrant Application Sections screen in a new window so that you can review the subapplication while you complete the queue.

### Pre-Award Review

FMA-PJ-04-AL-2007-003 (0)  PJ-3 AL GaS 2007

|  |  | Rework History | Revision History |
|---|---|---|---|
| Office | Question |  | Answer |
| Program | Have you reviewed the Grant and Subgrant applications? |  | Yes |
| Program | Have you reviewed the previous queues for this Subgrant? |  | Yes |
| Program | Are the reviews complete? |  | Yes |
| Program | Are the reviews satisfactory? |  | Yes / Yes / No |
| Program | Conditional Award? |  |  |
| Grants | Did an authorized official electronically sign all of the Grant forms? |  | Yes |
| Grants | Did you review the single audit database? |  | Yes |
| Grants | Were there any audit findings that should be addressed? If so, please enter comments to this effect in the system. |  | Yes |
| Grants | Is this applicant suspended or debarred? If so, this Grant must be rejected |  | Yes |
| Grants | Did you complete the Grant Checklist? If so, please enter your comments about the following: a) Were all costs adequately described in the narrative? b) Was the source and amount of the match verified? c) Were there any other issues addressed when completing the checklist? |  | Yes |

All of the review questions are displayed on a single screen. As an FMA Coordinator, I can answer the programmatic questions based on a review of the subapplication and the review conducted in previous Workflow queues. An Assistance Officer will answer the Grants questions. For this subapplication, select the **"Yes"** option from the drop-down menu for all of the questions except **Conditional Award.** For the Conditional Award question, "No" is selected by default. Project subapplications that are conditionally awarded cannot be included in an award package until the EHP Review is complete.

Since this subaward will not need to be conditionally awarded, you can select the **"No"** option from the drop-down menu.

From this queue, view the application's Revision History by selecting the **Revision History** link.

For FMA subapplications, if I disagree with any of the prior reviews, I can select the **Rework** button to send the subapplication back to one or more of the concurrent queues: Cost Review, Planning Review, and/or Cost-Effectiveness/Engineering Review. We will discuss the Rework functionality in Lesson 8.

Once I have answered the eligibility questions, I'll select the **Save** button.

From this queue, you can also add or edit **Attachments** and **Comments,** and request the Applicant to **Revise** a subapplication section by selecting the appropriate button at the bottom of the screen. Keep in mind that the Revise button will be inactive for PDM subapplications after the application deadline since it is a competitive program.&

To approve this queue, select **"Yes"** in the **Approved** drop-down menu. You must enter comments if you disapprove the queue. If the Program Office disapproves this queue, then the subapplication cannot be processed further and will not be forwarded to the Awards Workflow. In addition, if it is a project subapplication, it will be removed automatically from the Environmental/Historic Preservation Review queue in EMIS. Once you have approved the queue, select the **Forward** button.

## Confirmation



You will receive **Confirmation** that you have completed the queue. Select the **Return to Inbox** link to continue processing queues assigned to you.

# Lesson 6 Summary

In this lesson, you learned about the:

- Check-Out/Check-In process
- Inbox (myGrants) screen
- All Grants screen
- Pre-Award Eligibility screen
- Screen features for sorting and filtering queues
- Pre-Award Eligibility Workflow queues
- Remove and Restore functionalities

Some key points from this lesson include:

- You can view the queue(s) pending completion for a subapplication in the Inbox based on your eGrants roles
- The All Grants screen displays all the applications and subapplications available to you based on your eGrants roles
- The Pre-Award Eligibility screen provides an overview of a particular subapplication's Workflow path

# Lesson 6 Summary (continued)

More key points from Lesson 6 include:

- You can sort and filter queues using Inbox screen features
- The Receipt and Delegate queue is performed for the application as a whole, including all subapplications attached to the application, and generates an automatic e-mail message to the Applicant to acknowledge the receipt of the application
- Cost Review, Planning Review, and Cost-Effectiveness queues are concurrent queues, which means that all three queues can be completed simultaneously and all applicable concurrent queues must be completed before the subapplication can be forwarded to the next queue in the Workflow
- In the PDM Workflow, the National Review Process follows the concurrent queues for planning and project subapplications, and only selected subapplications are forwarded to the Pre-Award Review queue
- In the FMA Workflow, the Pre-Award Review queue directly follows the concurrent queues.
- Removing a subapplication will remove it from further processing in the Workflow queues
- Restoring a subapplication will return it to a previously disapproved queue
- For project subapplications, the EHP Review and Pre-Award Review queues can be completed concurrently
- The Pre-Award Review queue is the last queue in the Pre-Award Eligibility Workflow

# Lesson 7 Overview

This lesson describes the Pre-Disaster Mitigation (PDM) National Review Process in detail.

At the end of this lesson, you should be able to identify:

- The purpose of the PDM National Review Process queues

# eGrants User Scenario

**Team Leader:** Alex Salazar, Flood Mitigation Assistance (FMA) Program Coordinator

**Your Role:** New FMA Program Analyst

**Office:** FEMA Regional Office

**Challenge:** PDM subapplications must be processed through the National Review Process.

**To Date:** You have learned how to complete all queues that are common to the FMA and PDM grant programs.

Listen to Alex
Audio transcript

**The Next Step:** Hope Samuels, a PDM Coordinator, will explain the PDM National Review Workflow queues to you.

Hi, its Alex. You did a great job learning how to process all the queues for an FMA application. Now, I am going to ask Hope Samuels, the FEMA Pre-Disaster Mitigation grant program coordinator, to tell you about the National Review Process queues that are unique to Pre-Disaster Mitigation applications.

# The National Review Process

As described in Lesson 6, the PDM National Review Process applies only to the PDM Pre-Award Eligibility Workflow. It is not applicable to the FMA grant program.
The National Review Process consists of the two queues shown below and is applicable only to project and planning subapplications. The National Technical Review queue is required only for project subapplications, but the Subgrant Selection for Award queue is applicable to both project and planning subapplications.

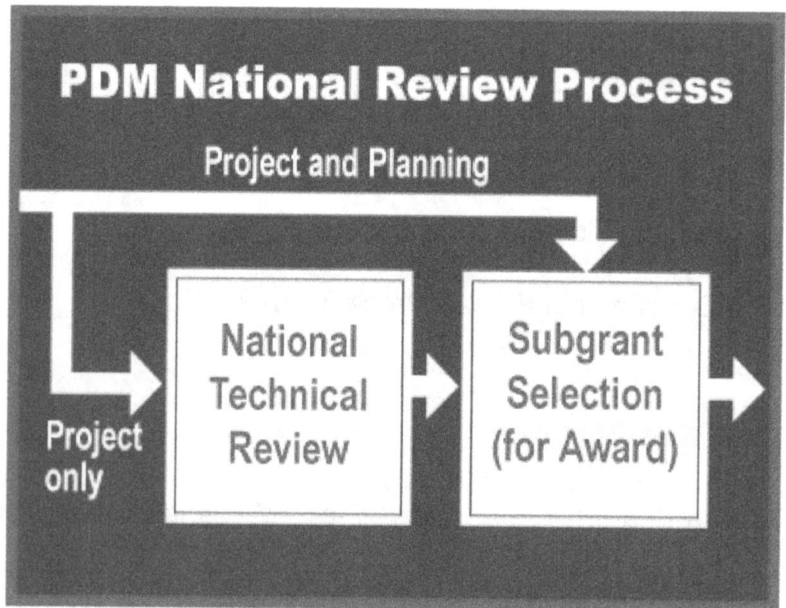



You must have the appropriate PDM role(s) to process each of these queues. Applicable roles for each queue will be discussed later in this lesson. Refer to Lesson 3 for details about requesting roles and positions.

# National Technical Review Queue

The National Technical Review process occurs outside the eGrants system and applies only to PDM Project subapplications. It consists of reviewing the Benefit-Cost Analysis (BCA) and making an Engineering Feasibility determination. The National Technical Review queue is where a FEMA Headquarters Technical Reviewer records the results of the National Technical Review.

# Subgrant Selection (for Award) Queue

In the Subgrant Selection (for Award) queue, the Headquarters PDM Coordinator selects the eligible planning and project subapplications to be considered for further review based on the total funding available for PDM federal awards. However, not all selected PDM subapplications are automatically awarded. Selected subapplications must first complete the Environmental/Historic Preservation (EHP) Review queue and the Pre-Award Review queue (as discussed in Lesson 6).

A user assigned to a role of Headquarters Contractor PDM Coordinator may select subapplications, add comments and attachments, save, and export subapplication data. However, only users with the Headquarters PDM Coordinator role may complete and forward the queue.

If it is determined that a subapplication was approved or disapproved in error, the subapplication can be reset or restored as long as the Selection (for Award) queue is still available in the Inbox. (The Restore functionality was discussed in Lesson 6, and the Reset functionality will be discussed in Lesson 8.) If a project subapplication is reset, then the subapplication will be removed from the EHP Review queue.

**Note** If a subapplication is selected for award, eGrants will automatically send an e-mail message to notify the Applicant Point(s) of Contact provided in the associated application. However, if the status of a subapplication is "Not Approved" or "Not Selected," there will be no e-mail notification.

# Subgrant Selection (for Award) Queue (continued)

Hope Samuels, the Headquarters PDM Coordinator, will demonstrate how to process the Subgrant Selection (for Award) queue.
Scroll down to see slideshow captions.

| Check Out | ALASKA ALEX | 2006 | PDM-PJ-04-CT-2006 (0) | PDM-PJ-04-CT-2006-001 (0) | | Management Workflow |
| Check In | ALASKA ALEX | 2016 | | | | Subgrant Selection (for Award) |
| Check In | ALASKA ALEX | 2015 | | | | Subgrant Selection (for Award) |

Only users with the Headquarters PDM Coordinator role or Headquarters Contractor PDM Coordinator role can check out the Subgrant Selection (for Award) queue. I select the **Subgrant Selection (for Award)** link in the Queue column on the Inbox screen.

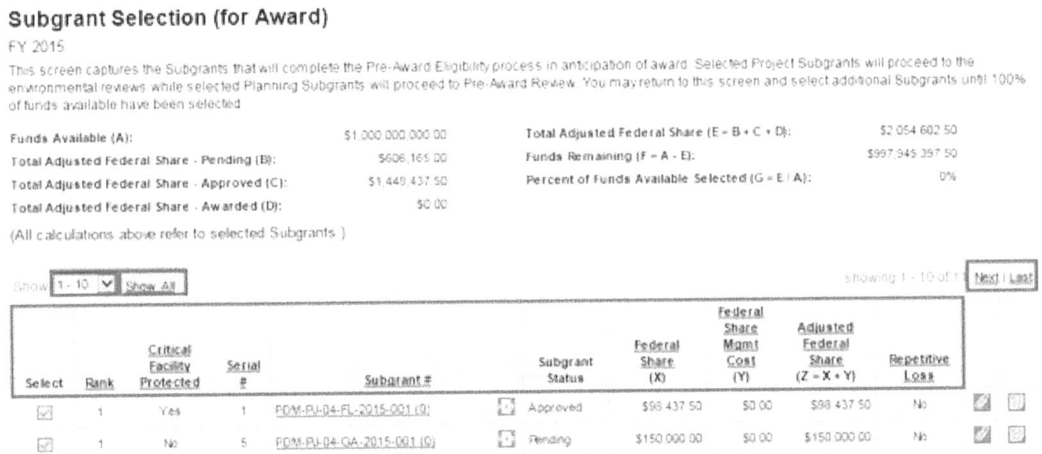

**Subgrant Selection (for Award)**

FY 2015

This screen captures the Subgrants that will complete the Pre-Award Eligibility process in anticipation of award. Selected Project Subgrants will proceed to the environmental reviews while selected Planning Subgrants will proceed to Pre-Award Review. You may return to this screen and select additional Subgrants until 100% of funds available have been selected.

| | | | |
|---|---|---|---|
| Funds Available (A): | $1,000,000,000.00 | Total Adjusted Federal Share (E = B + C + D): | $2,054,602.50 |
| Total Adjusted Federal Share - Pending (B): | $606,165.00 | Funds Remaining (F = A - E): | $997,945,397.50 |
| Total Adjusted Federal Share - Approved (C): | $1,449,437.50 | Percent of Funds Available Selected (G = E / A): | 0% |
| Total Adjusted Federal Share - Awarded (D): | $0.00 | | |

(All calculations above refer to selected Subgrants.)

Show 1 - 10   Show All     Showing 1 - 10 of 1   Next | Last

| Select | Rank | Critical Facility Protected | Serial # | Subgrant # | Subgrant Status | Federal Share (X) | Federal Share Mgmt Cost (Y) | Adjusted Federal Share (Z = X + Y) | Repetitive Loss | | |
|---|---|---|---|---|---|---|---|---|---|---|---|
| ☑ | 1 | Yes | 1 | PDM-PJ-04-FL-2015-001 (0) | Approved | $98,437.50 | $0.00 | $98,437.50 | No | | |
| ☑ | 1 | No | 5 | PDM-PJ-04-GA-2015-001 (0) | Pending | $150,000.00 | $0.00 | $150,000.00 | No | | |

The subapplications listed on the screen have been sorted by rank. The screen defaults to display up to the first 10 subapplications. As we saw earlier, there are several ways I can filter, sort, and view the subapplications. I can select the

**Show** drop-down menu, the **Show All** link, the **Next** and **Last** links, or the **column title** link in any of the column headers. Longer lists will display First, Previous, Next, and Last links.

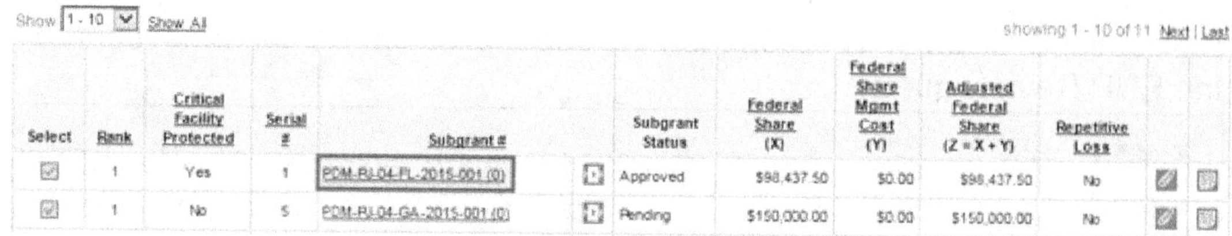

I select a subapplication number in the **Subgrant #** column to open the subapplication in a new window.

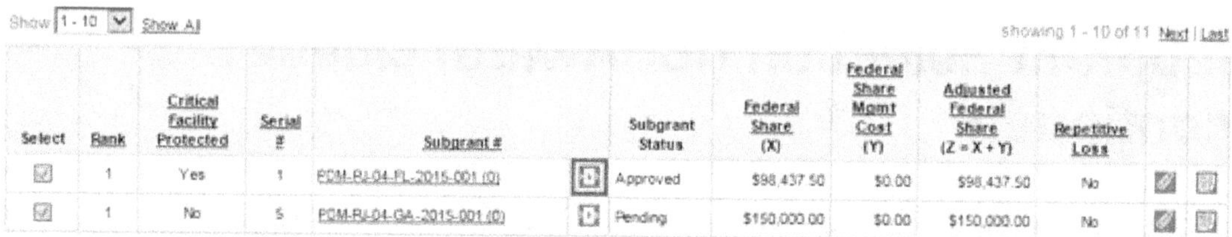

I select the **Subgrant (Pre-Award Eligibility) Workflow** icon to see the status of previous Workflow queues for the subapplication.

| Select | Rank | Critical Facility Protected | Serial # | Subgrant # | | Subgrant Status |
|---|---|---|---|---|---|---|
| ☑ | 4 | No | 2 | PDM-PJ-04-FL-2015-003 (0) | ▶ | Approved |
| ☑ | 3 | No | 3 | PDM-PJ-04-FL-2015-004 (0) | ▶ | Approved |
| ☑ | 5 | No | 4 | PDM-PJ-04-FL-2015-005 (0) | ▶ | Approved |
| ☑ | 1 | No | 5 | PDM-PJ-04-GA-2015-001 (0) | ▶ | Pending |

The **Rank** is the Applicant's rank for the subapplication in the application.

| Select | Rank | Critical Facility Protected | Serial # | Subgrant # | | Subgrant Status |
|---|---|---|---|---|---|---|
| ☑ | 4 | No | 2 | PDM-PJ-04-FL-2015-003 (0) | ▶ | Approved |
| ☑ | 3 | No | 3 | PDM-PJ-04-FL-2015-004 (0) | ▶ | Approved |
| ☑ | 5 | No | 4 | PDM-PJ-04-FL-2015-005 (0) | ▶ | Approved |
| ☑ | 1 | Yes | 5 | PDM-PJ-04-GA-2015-001 (0) | ▶ | Pending |

The **Critical Facility Protected** column indicates whether the mitigation activity proposed in the project subapplication protects a critical facility.

| Subgrant # | | Subgrant Status | Federal Share (X) | Federal Share Mgmt Cost (Y) | Adjusted Federal Share (Z = X + Y) | Repetitive Loss | | |
|---|---|---|---|---|---|---|---|---|
| PDM-PJ-04-FL-2015-003 (0) | | Approved | $450,000.00 | $45,000.00 | $495,000.00 | No | | |
| PDM-PJ-04-FL-2015-004 (0) | | Approved | $450,000.00 | $45,000.00 | $495,000.00 | No | | |
| PDM-PJ-04-FL-2015-005 (0) | | Approved | $450,000.00 | $45,000.00 | $495,000.00 | No | | |
| PDM-PJ-04-GA-2015-001 (0) | | Pending | $150,000.00 | $15,000.00 | $165,000.00 | Yes | | |

The **Federal Share Mgmt Cost** (i.e., the Federal Share for Management Costs) is calculated as 10% of the Federal Share, which is the maximum amount eligible for each federal award. The **Adjusted Federal Share** is the amount of the federal share plus the amount for the federal share for management costs.

| Subgrant # | | Subgrant Status | Federal Share (X) | Federal Share Mgmt Cost (Y) | Adjusted Federal Share (Z = X + Y) | Repetitive Loss | | |
|---|---|---|---|---|---|---|---|---|
| PDM-PJ-04-FL-2015-003 (0) | | Approved | $450,000.00 | $45,000.00 | $495,000.00 | No | | |
| PDM-PJ-04-FL-2015-004 (0) | | Approved | $450,000.00 | $45,000.00 | $495,000.00 | No | | |
| PDM-PJ-04-FL-2015-005 (0) | | Approved | $450,000.00 | $45,000.00 | $495,000.00 | No | | |
| PDM-PJ-04-GA-2015-001 (0) | | Pending | $150,000.00 | $15,000.00 | $165,000.00 | Yes | | |

**Repetitive Loss** indicates whether the Applicant indicated that the subapplication includes Repetitive Loss properties.

Show 1 - 10 ▾ Show All

| Select | Rank | Critical Facility Protected | Serial # | Subgrant # | | Subgrant Status |
|---|---|---|---|---|---|---|
| ☑ | 1 | Yes | 1 | PDM-PJ-04-FL-2015-001 (0) | | Approved |
| ☑ | 4 | No | 2 | PDM-PJ-04-FL-2015-003 (0) | | Approved |
| ☑ | 3 | No | 3 | PDM-PJ-04-FL-2015-004 (0) | | Approved |

As the Headquarters PDM Coordinator, I check the boxes in the **Select** column for the subapplications that will be considered for further review and processing in the Workflow.

| Subgrant # | | Subgrant Status | Federal Share (X) | Fede Share Mgm Cos (Y) |
|---|---|---|---|---|
| 2016-001 (0) | ▶ | Pending | $98,437.50 | |
| 2016-002 (0) | ▶ | Approved | $1,500,360.00 | |
| 2016-003 (0) | ▶ | Pending | $98,437.50 | |
| 2016-005 (0) | ▶ | Approved | $118,125.00 | |
| 2016-001 (0) | ▶ | Approved | $15,000.00 | |
| 2016-002 (0) | ▶ | Obligated | $15,000.00 | |
| 2016-004 (0) | ▶ | Pending / **Not Approved** / Not Selected | $9,375.00 | |

If it is determined that a subapplication is not eligible for a subaward, I will select the **Not Approved** status from the drop-down menu in the Subgrant Status column. This will halt further processing of the subapplication in the PDM Workflow.

| Subgrant # | | Subgrant Status | Federal Share (X) | Fede Shar Ma Cos (Y) |
|---|---|---|---|---|
| 2016-003 (0) | ▶ | Pending | $98,437.50 | |
| 2016-005 (0) | ▶ | Approved | $118,125.00 | |
| 2016-001 (0) | ▶ | Approved | $15,000.00 | |
| 2016-002 (0) | ▶ | Obligated | $15,000.00 | |
| 2016-004 (0) | ▶ | Pending / Not Approved / **Not Selected** | $9,375.00 | |

I change the status of eligible planning and project subapplications that will not be able to be funded by selecting the **"Not Selected"** option from the drop-down menu in the Subgrant Status column.

| Subgrant # | | Subgrant Status | Federal Share (X) | Federal Share Mgmt Cost (Y) | Adjusted Federal Share (Z = X + Y) | Repetitive Loss | | |
|---|---|---|---|---|---|---|---|---|
| PDM-PJ-04-FL-2015-003 (0) | ▶ | Approved | $450,000.00 | $0.00 | $450,000.00 | No | ✎ | 📋 |
| PDM-PJ-04-FL-2015-004 (0) | ▶ | Approved | $450,000.00 | $0.00 | $450,000.00 | No | ✎ | 📋 |

I add comments and attachments to each individual subapplication by selecting the **Comments** and **Attachments** icons in the columns on the far right.

**Subgrant
Status**

Approved

Approved

Approved

Approved

Pending

Pending

Once my selection is saved, the status of the selected subapplications will change from "Pending" to "Approved" in the Subgrant Status column. The status for subapplications that do not have the Select checkbox checked or display "Not Approved" or "Not Selected" will remain "Pending."

| ☑ | 2 | | 9 | PDM-PJ-04-KY-2015-002 (0) | | Pending | $71,790.00 | $0.00 | $71,790.00 | No | | |
| ☑ | 2 | | 10 | PDM-PL-04-FL-2015-002 (0) | | Pending | $9,375.00 | $0.00 | $9,375.00 | No | | |

Export

I can select the **Export** button at the bottom of the screen to export the data to a spreadsheet for analysis.

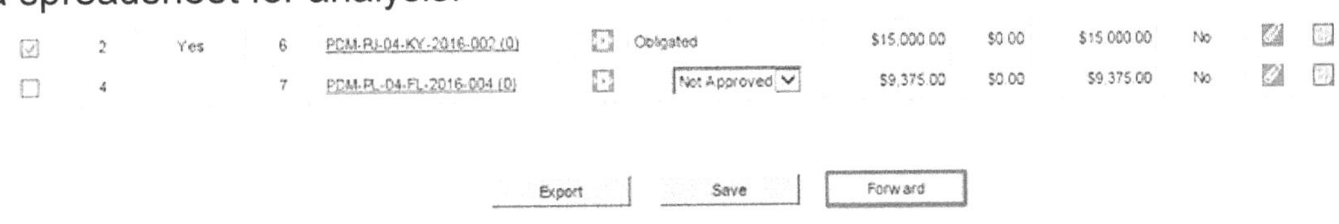


When I select the **Forward** button, the approved planning subapplications will be forwarded to the Pre-Award Review queue. Approved project subapplications will be forwarded to both the Pre-Award Review queue and the EHP queues to be processed concurrently.

# Confirmation

The Queue was successfully processed for Subgrant Application:

PDM-PJ-04-KY-2014-001 (0) POP Test 2 Application

Return to Inbox

A **Confirmation** screen appears indicating that I have completed the queue. I will select the **Return to Inbox** link to continue processing queues assigned to me.

# Funds Available

When the Subgrant Selection (for Award) queue is saved, the totals at the top of the screen will be calculated automatically based on the funds available and the total amount of the selected subapplications. The total adjusted federal share is the sum of the adjusted federal shares of selected subapplications that are pending (that is, under consideration for award), have been approved for award, and have already been awarded.

The Total Adjusted Federal Share, Funds Remaining, and Percent of Funds Available Selected are useful to ensure that the funds available are sufficient to cover the selected subapplications. However, the Headquarters PDM Coordinator may select subapplications that total more than 100% of the Funds Available when subapplications are withdrawn or are awarded for an amount less than the calculated total Federal Share.

The Subgrant Selection (for Award) queue will remain available in the PDM Inbox as long as there are any subapplications with a "Pending" status.

### Subgrant Selection (for Award)  [Read-Only]

FY 2015

This screen captures the Subgrants that will complete the Pre-Award Eligibility process in anticipation of award. Selected Project Subgrants will proceed to the environmental reviews while selected Planning Subgrants will proceed to Pre-Award Review. You may return to this screen and select additional Subgrants until 100% of funds available have been selected.

| | | | |
|---|---|---|---|
| Funds Available (A): | $1,000,000,000.00 | Total Adjusted Federal Share (E = B + C + D): | $2,054,602.50 |
| Total Adjusted Federal Share - Pending (B): | $606,165.00 | Funds Remaining (F = A - E): | $997,945,397.50 |
| Total Adjusted Federal Share - Approved (C): | $1,448,437.50 | Percent of Funds Available Selected (G = E / A): | 0% |
| Total Adjusted Federal Share - Awarded (D): | $0.00 | | |

(All calculations above refer to selected Subgrants.)

Select this link for the full text of the image.

# Lesson 7 Summary

In this lesson, you learned about the:

- PDM National Review Process

Some key points from this lesson include the following:

- During the National Technical Review, a reviewer records the FEMA Benefit-Cost Ratio and the Engineering Feasibility of PDM project subapplications.
- Subgrant Selection (for Award) is the last queue in the National Review Process Workflow and determines which planning and project subapplications will be forwarded for further review

# Lesson 8 Overview

This lesson describes the Rework, Reset, and Revise functionalities for subapplications.

At the end of this lesson, you should be able to identify the:

- The Reset, Revision, and Rework functionalities

# eGrants User Scenario

**Team Leader:** Alex Salazar, Flood Mitigation Assistance (FMA) Program Coordinator

**Your Role:** New FMA Program Analyst

**Office:** FEMA Regional Office

**Challenge:** You need to correct review errors and request additional information for a subapplication.

**To Date:** You have learned how to complete the FMA and PDM subapplication review processes.

Listen to Alex
Audio transcript

**The Next Step:** Alex will explain the Rework, Reset, and Revise functionalities.

Hello. It's your supervisor, Alex Salazar. Sometimes a reviewer will determine that additional information is needed or a correction needs to be made to an application or subapplication before it can be approved. Or, a reviewer may determine that an earlier decision about a subapplication was incorrect and the queue needs to be reworked, or an application be reset. I would like to show you how we can process these actions.

# Requests to Rework

If you are not satisfied with the results or outcome of a queue, the Rework functionality allows you to send a subapplication back to a previous queue or queues for rework so that responses can be changed. The subapplication will be returned to the Inbox, and users having the roles needed to complete the reworked queue may check it out, review the Rework History, and rework the queue.

As mentioned in Lesson 5, this functionality is available in the Pre-Award Eligibility Workflow to rework FMA subapplications from the Pre-Award Review queue. Refer to the Workflow Diagram in Lesson 5 that shows the queues that may be reworked from the Pre-Award Review queue.

The Rework functionality is also available in the Awards and Quarterly Reports Workflows for both grant programs. The Awards Workflow will be discussed in Lesson 9 and the Quarterly Reports Workflow will be discussed in Lesson 10.

# Requests to Rework (continued)

When flagged for rework, the subapplication is returned to the previous queue(s) in the Inbox for completion by users with the roles to complete the reworked queue(s). The existing responses in the reworked queue(s) are retained, but they can be edited as necessary prior to completing and forwarding the queue. In addition, any existing comments and attachments in the queue will be retained, but they can be edited or deleted at any time regardless of the queue status, as discussed in Lesson 6.

Alex will demonstrate how to request a subapplication be reworked.

Scroll down to see slideshow captions.

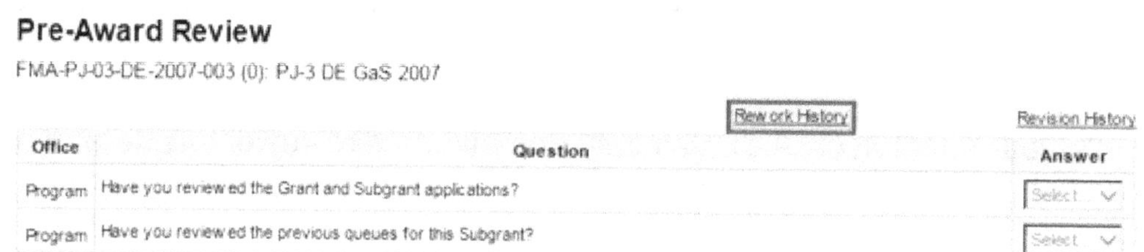

**Pre-Award Review**

FMA-PJ-03-DE-2007-003 (0): PJ-3 DE GaS 2007

| Office | Question | Rework History | Revision History |
| --- | --- | --- | --- |
| | | | Answer |
| Program | Have you reviewed the Grant and Subgrant applications? | | Select... |
| Program | Have you reviewed the previous queues for this Subgrant? | | Select... |

A Rework History link is located to the left of the Revision History link on the Pre-Award Review screen. The Rework History link opens a window that displays a record of the rework request(s) for a subapplication. To review the Rework History of this subapplication, select the **Rework History** link.

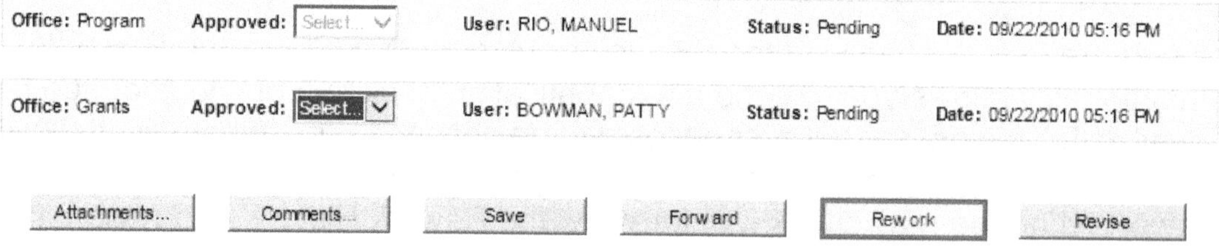

| Office: Program | Approved: Select... | User: RIO, MANUEL | Status: Pending | Date: 09/22/2010 05:16 PM |
| Office: Grants | Approved: Select... | User: BOWMAN, PATTY | Status: Pending | Date: 09/22/2010 05:16 PM |

| Attachments... | Comments... | Save | Forward | Rework | Revise |

To send a subapplication back to a previous queue to be reworked, select the **Rework** button at the bottom of the screen.

**Rework Request**

FMA-PJ-03-DE-2007-003 (0)  PJ-3 DE GaS 2007

Please select the queue(s) to be reworked and enter comments describing the reason(s) for requesting rework.

| Select | Queue | Reason(s) for Rework Request |
|---|---|---|
| ☑ | Cost Review | Please review completeness of project budget |
| ☐ | Cost-Effectiveness Review | |
| ☐ | Planning Review | |

Continue        Cancel

You can select one or more queues that require rework. For this subapplication, we will request a rework from the Pre-Award Review queue to the Cost Review queue. Select the checkbox in the **Select** column for the Cost Review section. Enter a **comment** to provide the reason for the rework request. For this subapplication, enter "Please review completeness of project budget." Then, select the **Continue** button.

## Confirmation

FMA-PJ-03-DE-2007-003 (0)  PJ-3 DE GaS 2007

was successfully returned for rework

Return to Inbox

A **Confirmation** notice appears indicating that the subapplication was reworked to the previous queue. Select the **Return to Inbox** link to process another queue.

# Requests to Reset

The Reset functionality is similar to the Rework functionality. The Reset functionality is only available to users with the Headquarters PDM Coordinator role or Headquarters FMA Coordinator role. Users with those roles may reset subapplications from the Pre-Award Eligibility screen, if necessary. Users without this role will not see the Reset button on the Pre-Award Eligibility screen. If you find that a subapplication needs to be reset, please contact the eGrants Help Desk at MTeGrants@fema.dhs.gov or 1-855-228-3362.

If necessary, a planning or project subapplication in the Cost Review, Cost-Effectiveness/Engineering, or Planning Review queues can be reset to the Initial Review queue. The Initial Review queue then will be listed in the Inbox for any user with the appropriate role to work on it. There will be no record of the reason for the reset and no notification to users regarding the reset action. Data originally entered for the Initial Review queue, including any comments or attachments, will be retained. The user who checks out the queue will be able to edit any of the data. However, any comments and attachments will only be editable by the user who entered them.

Alex will demonstrate how to reset a subapplication to the Initial Review queue.

Scroll down to see slideshow captions.

The subapplication that needs to be reset to the Initial Review queue is currently in the Cost Review queue. From the Inbox screen, select the **Subgrant (Pre-Award Eligibility) Workflow** icon.

## Pre-Award Eligibility

FMA-PJ-04-KY-2013-001 (0): ranking test

| Queue | Approved | User | Status | Status Date |
|---|---|---|---|---|
| Receipt and Delegate | Yes | RIO, MANUEL | Completed | 09/23/2014 05:57 PM |
| Initial Review | Yes | REVIEWER, NEW | Completed | 05/08/2017 09:29 PM |
| Cost Review | Pending | REVIEWER, NEW | Pending | 05/08/2017 09:29 PM |
| Cost-Effectiveness Review | Yes | REVIEWER, NEW | Completed | 05/09/2017 08:56 PM |
| Planning Review | Yes | REVIEWER, NEW | Completed | 05/09/2017 08:29 PM |
| Pre-Award Review (Grants) | Pending | | Not Ready | 05/08/2017 09:29 PM |
| Pre-Award Review (Program) | Pending | | Not Ready | 05/08/2017 09:29 PM |

Reset

Select the **Reset** button.

## Confirm Subgrant Reset

FMA-PJ-04-KY-2013-001 (0): ranking test Conditions

Click on the **Continue** button to reset this subgrant.

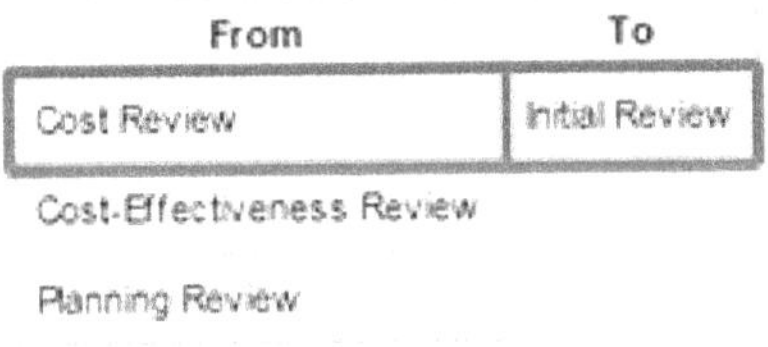

| From | To |
|---|---|
| Cost Review | Initial Review |

Cost-Effectiveness Review

Planning Review

Click on the **Cancel** button to return to Pre-Award Eligiblity.

Continue     Cancel

You will be prompted to confirm the reset. The reset will return the subapplication from the Cost Review queue to the Initial Review queue. Select the **Continue button** to reset the subapplication.

## Reset Confirmation

Subgrant Application FMA-PJ-04-KY-2013-001 (0): ranking test was successfully reset

Return to Inbox

You will receive **Confirmation** that the subapplication was reset to the Initial Review queue. Select the **Return to Inbox** link to continue processing subapplications.

# Application Revision Requests

The Revision Request functionality allows a user to request a revision from the Applicant when it is determined that additional or corrected information is required to continue to process an application.

For the FMA grant program, application revisions can be requested from the Receipt and Delegate queue, or at any other time with an out-of-queue Revision Request, unless the application has already been returned to the Applicant for revision.

Once the PDM application deadline has passed, a reviewer cannot request a revision for a PDM application until **after** the National Review Process has been completed.

Alex will demonstrate how to use the Revision Request functionality to request a revision to an application from the Receipt and Delegate queue.

Scroll down to see slideshow captions.

### Receipt and Delegate

FMA-TA-03-PA-2006 (0): SCR 615 – FMA TA

By forwarding the above referenced grant application, FEMA acknowledges receipt of the application and delegates program administration to the person listed below.

* Please select an FMA Coordinator:   Select...   ▾   Revision History

| User: REVIEWER, NEW | Status: Pending | Date: 09/21/2005 09:24 PM |

Attachments...   Comments...   Forward   Revise

Select the **Revise** button to request a revision to this application from the Receipt and Delegate screen.

**Revision Request**

FMA-03-PA-2006 (0): SCR 615 FMA PJ

Please enter general comments, select the Subgrants that need to be revised, and enter comments describing the reason(s) for requesting revision

* General Comments:

You may attach a management costs subgrant application to request up to 10% of the total plan and project subgrant applications submitted. Note that management costs must be cost shared.

* Revision Deadline Date:

| Select | Subgrant # | Reason(s) for Revision Request |
|---|---|---|
| ☐ | FMA-TA-03-PA-2006-001 (0) | |

Fields marked with a red asterisk (*) are required

Continue    Cancel

In the **General Comments** field, provide any comments you wish the Applicant to see. For this application we will enter in the comment: "You may attach a Management Costs subapplication to request up to 10% of the total of the plan and project subgrant applications submitted. Note that management costs must be cost shared."

**Revision Request**

FMA-04-KY-2017 (0): Columbia DEM Flood Mitigation Assistance Grant

Please enter general comments describing the reason(s) for requesting revision and indicate whether or not Subgrants may be added to this Grant

* General Comments:

You may attach a Management Costs subapplication to request up to 10% of the total of the Planning and Project subapplications submitted. Note that management costs must be cost-shared.

* Revision Deadline Date: 11/30/2017 ×

* Subgrants may be added: Select ∨

Fields marked with a red asterisk (*) are required

You must provide a revision deadline date in the **Revision Deadline Date** field. The date format should be two-digit month/two-digit day/four-digit year. For this application, enter a revision date of "11/30/2017." Keep in mind that the deadline you set is simply a suggested timeframe and FEMA may choose to accept revisions submitted after the revision deadline date.

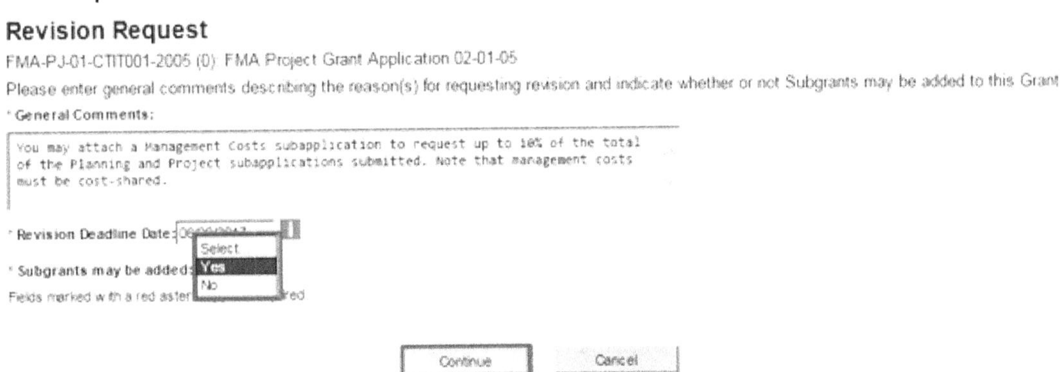

**Revision Request**

FMA-PJ-01-CTIT001-2005 (0): FMA Project Grant Application 02-01-05

Please enter general comments describing the reason(s) for requesting revision and indicate whether or not Subgrants may be added to this Grant

* General Comments:

You may attach a Management Costs subapplication to request up to 10% of the total of the Planning and Project subapplications submitted. Note that management costs must be cost-shared.

* Revision Deadline Date: 06/00/2017

* Subgrants may be added: Select / Yes / No

Fields marked with a red asterisk (*) are required

Continue    Cancel

For this type of application revision request, you may also request a revision for any subapplication attached to the application. Select the checkbox for the subapplication that needs to be revised and enter the reason for the revision requested. Select the box in the **Select** column for subapplication number FMA-TA-04-FL-2006-001 (0) and enter the **comment:** "Please update Cost Estimate section to include contracting costs." Then, select the **Continue** button to process the revision request.

**Revision Request**

FMA-03-PA-2006 (0): SCR 615 FMA PJ

Please enter general comments, select the Subgrants that need to be revised, and enter comments describing the reason(s) for requesting revision.

* General Comments:

> You may attach a Management Costs subapplication to request up to 10% of the total of the plan and project subgrant applications submitted. Note that management costs must be cost shared.

* Revision Deadline Date: 11/30/2017

| Select | Subgrant # | Reason(s) for Revision Request |
|---|---|---|
| ☑ | FMA-PJ-03-2006 (0) | Please update Cost Estimate section to include contracting costs. |

Fields marked with a red asterisk (*) are required.

Continue    Cancel

For this type of application revision request, you may also request a revision for any subapplication attached to the application. Select the checkbox for the subapplication that needs to be revised and enter the reason for the revision requested. Select the box in the **Select** column for subapplication number FMA-TA-04-FL-2006-001 (0) and enter the **comment:** "Please update Cost Estimate section to include contracting costs." Then, select the **Continue** button to process the revision request.

## Confirmation

FMA-TA-03-PA-2006 (0): SCR 615 - FMA TA

Grantee was successfully notified of revision request.

Return to Inbox

A **Confirmation** screen appears, confirming that the Applicant was notified of the revision request via e-mail. The e-mail addresses in the Contact Information section of the application are used for all e-mail notifications regarding the application and attached subapplications.

**All Grants**

The table below lists all of the Flood Mitigation Assistance Grants, Subgrants, Awards, and Quarterly Reports that you can access

FY: 2006  Filter

Select [icon] to do a revision. Select [icon] to view Subgrant workflow. Select [icon] to view subgrant revision history. Select [icon] to view subgrant awards. Select [icon] to view Quarterly Reports

Show 11 - 20  Show All                                                                 showing 11 - 20 of 23 First | Previous | Next | Last

| FY (ascending) | Grant # | Subgrant # | Agreement # |
|---|---|---|---|
| 2006 | FMA-PL-09-NV-2006 (0) | FMA-PL-09-NV-2006-002 (0) | |
| 2006 | FMA-TA-01-CTIT001-2006 (0) | FMA-TA-01-CTIT001-2006-001 (0) | |
| 2006 | FMA-TA-01-CTIT001-2006 (0) | FMA-TA-01-CTIT001-2006-002 (0) | |
| 2006 | FMA-TA-03-PA-2006 (0) | FMA-TA-03-PA-2006-001 (0) | |
| 2006 | FMA-TA-04-FL-2006 (0) | FMA-TA-04-FL-2006-001 (0) | FMA-2007-FM-5003 |

Once a revision is requested, no further processing of the application in the Workflow will be possible until the Applicant resubmits it. When the application is resubmitted, the queue will appear in the Inbox and you should check it out to ensure that your requested revisions were made. Until then, the application is available only from the All Grants screen. You may select the **Revision History** icon to view the revisions requested.

# Application Revision History

The Revision History screen shows a record of revision requests for a particular application. Users with access to the application can view the Revision History for any application without checking out the application. An application's Revision History can be accessed by either one of the following methods:

- Selecting the application number link in the Grant # column from either the All Grants screen or Inbox screen and then selecting the Revision History link
- Selecting the Revision History icon to the right of the Subgrant (Pre-Award Eligibility) Workflow icon on the All Grants screen

Alex will demonstrate how to access an application's Revision History by selecting the application number link.

Scroll down to see slideshow captions.

## Inbox

The Inbox displays Flood Mitigation Assistance Grants, Subgrants, Awards, and Quarterly Reports that
Check Out/In button. After checking out a queue, click the corresponding link in the Queue column to

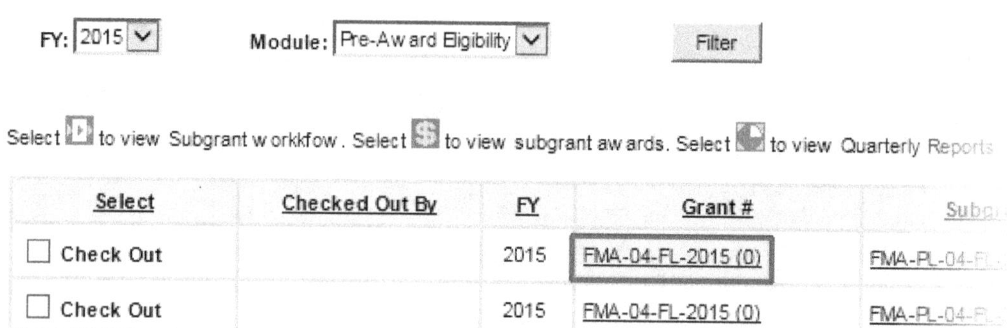

From the Inbox, select the application number link in the **Grant #** column to
review the Revision History of an application.

Click here to view the actual Grant application submitted by the Grantee.

Revision History

| Grant Information | |
|---|---|
| Grant Number: | FMA-04-FL-2015 (0) |
| Grant Title: | FY 2015 Grant Application |
| Submitted By: | femahquser1 (on 09/22/2014 05:50 PM) |
| Federal Share: | $1,457,812.50 (Proposed = $1,457,812.50) |
| Non-Federal Share: | $485,937.50 (Proposed = $485,937.50) |
| Total Estimated Cost: | $1,943,750.00 (Proposed = $1,943,750.00) |
| Duration: | 3 YEARS |
| Congressional District: | |
| Status: | Approved (as of 10/08/2015 09:46 PM) |
| Number of Subgrants: | 5 |

A new window opens displaying a summary of the application. Select the
**Revision History** link in the upper right-hand corner of the screen.

# Revision History: Grant

FMA-04-FL-2015 (0): FY 2015 Grant Application

| Revision Request # | Queue | Subgrant # | Requested By | Date Requested | Resubmitted By | Date Resubmitted |
|---|---|---|---|---|---|---|
| 3 | Grant | | ARCHER, PATTY | 02/09/2015 06:08 PM | femahquser1 | 02/09/2015 06:10 PM |
| | | General Comments | attach new PJ with new property | | | |
| | | Subgrants may be added? | Yes | | | |
| Revision Request # | Queue | Subgrant # | Requested By | Date Requested | Resubmitted By | Date Resubmitted |
| 2 | Grant | | RIO, MANUEL | 09/23/2014 04:37 PM | femahquser1 | 02/09/2015 05:31 PM |
| | | General Comments | Need more subgrants for FY15 FMA | | | |
| | | Subgrants may be added? | Yes | | | |
| Revision Request # | Queue | Subgrant # | Requested By | Date Requested | Resubmitted By | Date Resubmitted |
| 1 | Grant | | REVIEWER, NEW | 09/22/2014 06:45 PM | femahquser1 | 09/22/2014 06:52 PM |
| | | General Comments | add planning subgrant | | | |
| | | Subgrants may be added? | Yes | | | |

The Revision History: Grant screen opens in a new window. This screen provides a history of revisions requested for the application. The history includes the Application number and title, the **Revision Request #,** the **Queue** from which the revision was requested (or "Grant" if requested out-of-queue), the **Subgrant #** for any subapplication that required revision, the requester's name, and the **Date Requested.** Also included are general comments and indication whether more subapplications may be added to the application at that time. Out-of-queue revision requests will be discussed later in this lesson.


# Revision History: Grant

FMA-04-FL-2015 (0): FY 2015 Grant Application

| Revision Request # | Queue | Subgrant # | Requested By | Date Requested | Resubmitted By | Date Resubmitted |
|---|---|---|---|---|---|---|
| 3 | Grant | | ARCHER, PATTY | 02/09/2015 06:08 PM | femahquser1 | 02/09/2015 06:10 PM |
| | | General Comments | attach new PJ with new property | | | |
| | | Subgrants may be added? | Yes | | | |
| Revision Request # | Queue | Subgrant # | Requested By | Date Requested | Resubmitted By | Date Resubmitted |
| 2 | Grant | | RIO, MANUEL | 09/23/2014 04:37 PM | femahquser1 | 02/09/2015 05:31 PM |
| | | General Comments | Need more subgrants for FY15 FMA | | | |
| | | Subgrants may be added? | Yes | | | |
| Revision Request # | Queue | Subgrant # | Requested By | Date Requested | Resubmitted By | Date Resubmitted |
| 1 | Grant | | REVIEWER, NEW | 09/22/2014 06:45 PM | femahquser1 | 09/22/2014 06:52 PM |
| | | General Comments | add planning subgrant | | | |
| | | Subgrants may be added? | Yes | | | |


If the Applicant has resubmitted the application, then the Revision History: Grant screen will also display the user name of the Applicant who resubmitted it and the **Date Resubmitted.** Select the **Close** button to return to the Inbox screen.

# Subapplication Revision Request

The Subapplication Revision Request functionality allows users to request a revision from the Applicant when it is determined that additional or corrected information is required to continue to process a subapplication. Similar to application revision requests, for the FMA grant program, subapplication revision requests can be made at any time, unless the subapplication has already been returned to the Applicant for revision.

Once the PDM application deadline has passed, a reviewer cannot request a revision for a PDM subapplication until after the National Review Process has been completed.

# Subapplication Revision Requests (continued)

You can request revisions to subapplications from any of Pre-Award Eligibility queue.

Alex will demonstrate how to process a subapplication revision request from the Initial Review queue.

Scroll down to see slideshow captions.

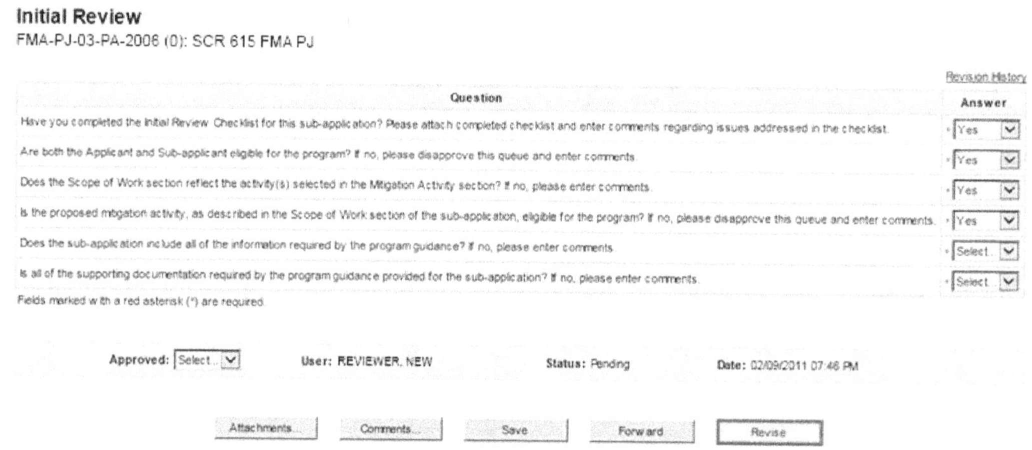



Select the **Revise** button to request the Applicant make a revision to a subapplication.

**Revision Request**

FMA-PJ-03-PA-2006 (0): SCR 615 FMA PJ

Please enter general comments, select the Subgrants that need to be revised, and enter comments describing the reason(s) for requesting revision.

* General Comments:

* Revision Deadline Date:

| Select | Subgrant # | Reason(s) for Revision Request |
|---|---|---|
| ☑ | FMA-PJ-03-PA-2006 (0) | |

Fields marked with a red asterisk (*) are required

Check the box in the **Select** column for the subapplication that needs to be revised.

**Revision Request**

FMA-PJ-03-PA-2006 (0): SCR 615 FMA PJ

Please enter general comments, select the Subgrant sections that need to be revised and enter comments describing the reason(s) for requesting revision.

* General Comments:

* Revision Deadline Date:                                                09/08/2017

The **Revision Deadline** date has already been set for an application revision request. We will not need to adjust it.

| Select | Subgrant Section | Reason(s) for Revision Request |
|---|---|---|
| ☐ | Applicant Information | |
| ☐ | Contact Information | |
| ☐ | Community | |
| ☐ | Mitigation Plan | |
| ☐ | Scope of Work | |
| ☐ | Properties | |
| ☑ | Cost Estimate | |

Next, check the box(es) in the **Select** column for the subapplication section(s) you would like to release for revision. This enables you to limit access to only those sections of the subapplications for which you are authorizing revisions. You will only need to review these revised sections as opposed to the entire subapplication. For this subapplication, select the box for the **Cost Estimate** section. Then, in the **Reason for Revision Request** text field, type the reason for requesting the revision to the cost estimate.

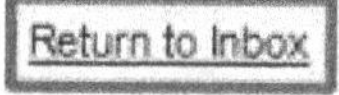

If you needed to cancel the action, you would select the Cancel button. We are ready to process the revision request for this subapplication, so select the **Continue** button.

## Confirmation

FMA-PJ-04-SC-2007-002 (0): PJ-2 SC GaS 2007

Grantee was successfully notified of revision request.

Return to Inbox

A **Confirmation** message appears that confirms that the Applicant was notified of the revision request via e-mail.

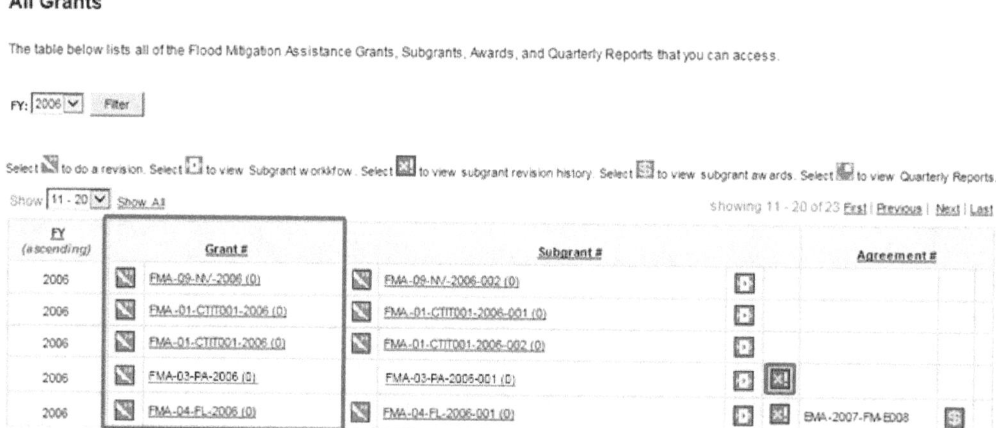

Once a revision is requested, no further processing of the subapplication in the Workflow will be possible until the Applicant resubmits it. When the subapplication is resubmitted, the queue will appear in your Inbox, and then you can check out the subapplication to ensure that your requested revisions were made. Until then, the subapplication will be available only from the All Grants screen. You may select the **Revision History** icon to view the revisions requested.

# Subapplication Revision History

The Subgrant Revision History screen shows a record of Revision Requests for a particular subapplication, as well as any revisions to the application.

The history of a subapplication's revisions can be accessed by either one of the two following methods:

- Selecting the Subgrant # link from the Inbox screen or All Grants screen, and then selecting the Revision History link
- Selecting the Revision History icon associated with the subapplication on the All Grants screen

Alex will demonstrate how to access a subapplication's Revision History by selecting the Revision History icon from the All Grants screen.

Scroll down to see slideshow captions.

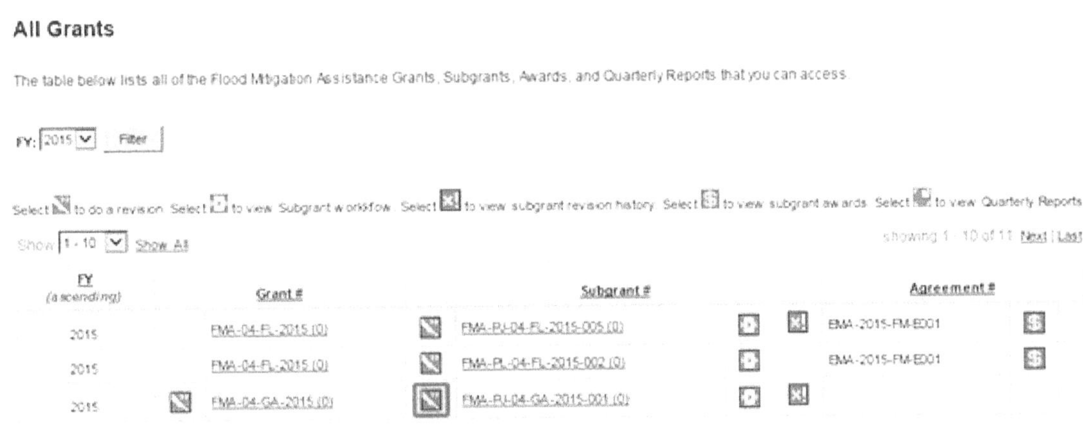


From the All Grants screen, select the **Revision History** icon associated with the subapplication.

**Revision History:**

FMA-PJ-04-GA-2015-001 (0): Property Action (Subgrantee) 5.15

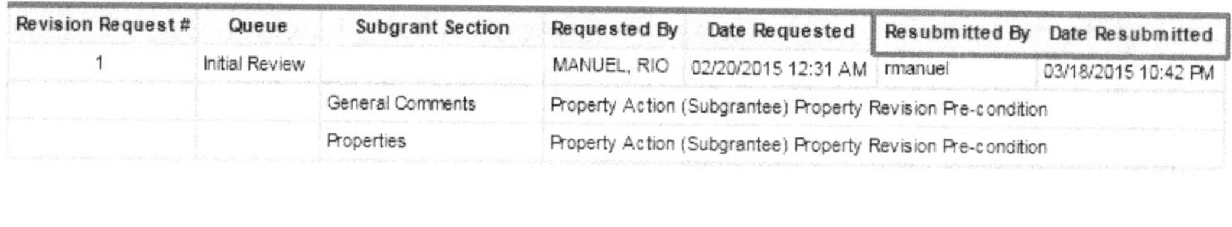

| Revision Request # | Queue | Subgrant # | Requested By | Date Requested | Resubmitted By | Date Resubmitted |
|---|---|---|---|---|---|---|
| 2 | Grant | | RIO, MANUEL | 07/02/2015 06:25 PM | rmanuel | 07/02/2015 07:28 PM |
| | | General Comments | Add Planning Subgrant for V5.15.02 Testing Validation Warning | | | |
| | | Subgrants may be added? | Yes | | | |

| Revision Request # | Queue | Subgrant # | Requested By | Date Requested | Resubmitted By | Date Resubmitted |
|---|---|---|---|---|---|---|
| 1 | Grant | | RIO, MANUEL | 03/18/2015 10:46 PM | rmanuel | 03/18/2015 11:04 PM |
| | | General Comments | Attach Property Action GA as SG | | | |
| | | Subgrants may be added? | Yes | | | |

| Revision Request # | Queue | Subgrant Section | Requested By | Date Requested | Resubmitted By | Date Resubmitted |
|---|---|---|---|---|---|---|
| 1 | Initial Review | | RIO, MANUEL | 02/20/2015 12:31 AM | rmanuel | 03/18/2015 10:42 PM |
| | | General Comments | Property Action (Subgrantee) Property Revision Pre-condition | | | |
| | | Properties | Property Action (Subgrantee) Property Revision Pre-condition | | | |

The Revision History screen displays. Subapplication Revision Requests are displayed below application Revision Requests. The history includes the subapplication number and title, the **Revision Request #**, the **Queue** from which the revision was requested, the subapplication section that required a revision, general and section-specific comments, the requester's name, and the date requested.

| Revision Request # | Queue | Subgrant Section | Requested By | Date Requested | Resubmitted By | Date Resubmitted |
|---|---|---|---|---|---|---|
| 1 | Initial Review | | MANUEL, RIO | 02/20/2015 12:31 AM | rmanuel | 03/18/2015 10:42 PM |
| | | General Comments | Property Action (Subgrantee) Property Revision Pre-condition | | | |
| | | Properties | Property Action (Subgrantee) Property Revision Pre-condition | | | |

Close

If the subapplication has been resubmitted, then the user name of the Applicant who resubmitted it and the **Date Resubmitted** are listed. Select the **Close** button to return to the All Grants screen.

# Out-of-Queue Application Revision Requests

After an application has been processed through the Receipt and Delegate queue, there are no more queues for the application. After the Receipt and Delegate queue, each subapplication moves through each queue of the Pre-Award Eligibility Workflow. So, to request a revision to an application after the Receipt and Delegate queue has been completed, you will have to make an application revision request "out-of-queue." Note that an out-of-queue application revision request does not impact the processing of the application or its associated subapplications in the Pre-Award Eligibility Workflow queues. Alex will show you how to request a revision to an application out-of-queue.

Scroll down to see slideshow captions.

**All Grants**

The table below lists all of the Flood Mitigation Assistance Grants, Subgrants, Awards, and Quarterly Reports that you can access.

FY: 2017 ▾  Filter

Select ▦ to do a revision. Select ▦ to view Subgrant workflow. Select ▦ to view subgrant revision history. Select ▦ to view subgrant awards. Select ▦ to view Quarterly Reports

| FY (ascending) | Grant # | Subgrant # | Agreement # |
|---|---|---|---|
| 2017 | ▦ FMA-04-KY-2017 (0) | ▦ FMA-PJ-04-KY-2017-001 (0) ◫ (Paper Application) | ▦ ▦ |

You can request an out-of-queue revision to an application from the All Grants screen by selecting the **Revision** icon to the left of the application number in the Grant # column.

**Revision Request**

FMA-04-KY-2017 (0)  Columbia DEM Flood Mitigation Assistance Grant

Please enter general comments describing the reason(s) for requesting revision and indicate whether or not Subgrants may be added to this Grant

* General Comments:

> You may attach a Management Costs subapplication to request up to 10% of the total of the Planning and Project subapplications submitted. Note that management costs must be cost-shared.

* Revision Deadline Date: [        ] 🗓

* Subgrants may be added: Select ▾

Fields marked with a red asterisk (*) are required

Just as when submitting a revision request for an application "in queue," (that is, from within the Receipt and Delegate queue), you must provide comments to the Applicant by entering them in the **General Comments** field. For this application, we will enter the comment, "You may attach a Management Costs subapplication to request up to 10% of the total of the planning and project subapplications submitted. Note that management costs must be cost-shared."

**Revision Request**

FMA-04-KY-2017 (0)  Columbia DEM Flood Mitigation Assistance Grant

Please enter general comments describing the reason(s) for requesting revision and indicate whether or not Subgrants may be added to this Grant

* General Comments:

> You may attach a Management Costs subapplication to request up to 10% of the total of the Planning and Project subapplications submitted. Note that management costs must be cost-shared.

* Revision Deadline Date: [11/30/2017] × 🗓

* Subgrants may be added: Select ▾

Fields marked with a red asterisk (*) are required

Then enter a revision deadline date in the **Revision Deadline Date** field. Enter the date of "11/30/2017." Keep in mind that the deadline you set is simply a suggested timeframe and FEMA may choose to accept revisions submitted after the revision deadline date.

## Revision Request

FMA-PJ-03-PA-2003 (0): Pennsylvania FMA Project Application for FY-2003

Please enter general comments, select the Subgrants that need to be revised, and enter comments describing the reason(s) for requesting revision.

* General Comments:

You may attach a Management Costs subapplication to request up to 10% of the total of the planning and project subapplications submitted. Note that management costs must be cost-shared.

* Revision Deadline Date: 11/30/2017

| Select | Subgrant # | Reason(s) for Revision Request |
|--------|-----------|-------------------------------|
| ☐ | FMA-PJ-03-PA-2003-001 (0) | |

Fields marked with a red asterisk (*) are required.

Continue    Cancel

If the Receipt and Delegate queue has not yet been completed, you may check the box in the **Select** column for each subapplication attached to the application that requires revisions. Then, provide the reason for the revision request. After the Receipt and Delegate queue has been completed, individual subapplication revision requests must be made either from a Workflow queue or from the All Grants screen. This revision does not involve a submitted subapplication, therefore, no box is selected.

## Revision Request

FMA-PJ-01-CTIT001-2005 (0): FMA Project Grant Application 02-01-05

Please enter general comments describing the reason(s) for requesting revision and indicate whether or not Subgrants may be added to this Grant.

* General Comments:

You may attach a Management Costs subapplication to request up to 10% of the total of the Planning and Project subapplications submitted. Note that management costs must be cost-shared.

* Revision Deadline Date: 06/00/0000

Select
Yes
No

* Subgrants may be added: Yes

Fields marked with a red asterisk (*) are required.

Continue    Cancel

If the Receipt and Delegate queue has been completed, you will also have the option of allowing the Applicant to attach additional subapplications to his or her application by selecting "Yes" from the **Subgrants May Be Added** drop-down menu. Select the **Continue** button.

## Confirmation

FMA-04-KY-2017 (0): Columbia DEM Flood Mitigation Assistance Grant

Grantee was successfully notified of revision request.

Return to Inbox

You will receive a **Confirmation** screen that the Applicant was notified of the revision request. Select the **Return to Inbox** to continue reviewing subapplications.

# Out-of-Queue Subapplication Revision Requests

In some instances, it may be necessary to request revisions to subapplications when the Revise button is not available from a Workflow queue screen. Such "out-of-queue" subapplication Revision Requests do not impact the processing of the subapplication in the Pre-Award Eligibility Workflow queues.

Alex will demonstrate the process for requesting out-of-queue subapplication revisions.

Scroll down to see slideshow captions.

You can request revision to a subapplication out-of-queue from the All Grants screen by selecting the **Revise** icon to the left of the subapplication number in the Subgrant # column.

### Revision Request

FMA-PJ-04-FL-2016-001 (0): An FMA project

Please enter general comments, select the Subgrant sections that need to be revised and enter comments describing the reason(s) for requesting revision.

* General Comments:

Please revise the Cost Estimate and Cost Share sections.

* Revision Deadline Date:

| Select | Subgrant Section | Reason(s) for Revision Request |
| --- | --- | --- |
|  | Subapplicant |  |
|  | Contact |  |

Just as when making subapplication revision requests from Pre-Award Eligibility Workflow queues, you must provide comments to the Applicant by entering them in the **General Comments** field. For this subapplication, enter the comment, "Please revise the Cost Estimate and Cost Share sections."

**Revision Request**

FMA-PJ-04-FL-2016-001 (0): An FMA project

Please enter general comments, select the Subgrant sections that need to be revised and enter comments describing the reason(s) for requesting revision.

* **General Comments:**

> Please revise the Cost Estimate and Cost Share sections.

* **Revision Deadline Date:** 04/11/2018

Set the **Revision Deadline** date. For this subapplication, enter a revision deadline date of "04/11/2018." Keep in mind that the deadline you set is simply a suggested timeframe and FEMA may choose to accept revisions submitted after the revision deadline date.

| | Section | Reason |
|---|---|---|
| ☐ | Schedule | |
| ☑ | Cost Estimate | Please revise the Cost Estimate to add more details to the elevation project budget. |
| ☑ | Cost Share | Please provide more details about other agency funding type. |
| ☐ | Cost Effectiveness | |
| ☐ | Environmental/Historic Preservation | |
| ☐ | Evaluation | |
| ☐ | Comments and Attachments | |

Fields marked with a red asterisk (*) are required.

Continue    Cancel

Check the box(es) in the **Select** column next to the sections of the subapplication for which you are requesting revision. This enables you to limit access to only those sections of the subapplications for which you are authorizing revisions, and you will only need to review these revised sections as opposed to the entire subapplication. You must enter **Reasons for Revision Request** for each section selected. For this subapplication, we will select the Cost Estimate and Cost Share sections. For the Cost Estimate section, enter, "Please revise the Cost Estimate to add more details to the elevation project budget." For the Cost Share section, enter, "Please provide more details about other agency funding type." Then, select the **Continue** button.

## Confirmation



A **Confirmation** screen will appear displaying a message that the Applicant was notified of the revision request. Select the **Return to Inbox link.**

# Lesson 8 Summary

In this lesson, you learned about:

- Requests for rework
- Requests to revise an application
- Requests to revise a subapplication
- Viewing the application Revision History
- Viewing a subapplication Revision History
- Requesting out-of-queue revisions to applications
- Requesting out-of-queue revisions to subapplications

Some key points from this lesson include:

- From the Pre-Award Review queue, a user may request a rework of a previous queue(s).
- A request to revise an application or subapplication allows changes to be made by the Applicant or Subapplicant.
- From the Pre-Award Eligibility screen, Headquarters PDM Coordinators or Headquarters FMA Coordinators can request that a subapplication be reset.

# Lesson 9 Overview

Once a subapplication has successfully passed through all of the Pre-Award Eligibility Workflow queues, it is eligible to be processed for a subaward.

When you're done with this lesson, you'll be able to identify:

- The components of an award package
- The reasons to amend an award package


# eGrants User Scenario

Listen to Alex
Audio transcript

**Team Leader:** Alex Salazar, Flood Mitigation Assistance (FMA) Program Coordinator

**Your Role:** New FMA Program Analyst

**Office:** FEMA Regional Office

**Challenge:** FMA and Pre-Disaster Mitigation (PDM) subapplications have been selected for award.

**To Date:** You learned about the processes for submitting requests to rework, reset, and revise subapplications.

**The Next Step:** Alex will explain how to create award packages.

Hello. It's Alex here. Once an application or subapplication has completed the Pre-Award Eligibility queues, it next moves to the Award Workflow queues. This queue is where the funding is obligated and the official documentation of the federal award is created. I will show you how to create and amend Award Packages for approved federal awards.

# Creating an Award Package

There are three types of award packages:

- Standard award package: Used to obligate funds to approved subapplications that have not yet been funded
- Additional obligation award package: Used to obligate additional funds to a subaward

- De-obligation award package: Used to return funds from an obligated subaward

| | |
|---|---|
| **Note** | You will need to validate the vendor with the FEMA Finance Center (FFC) before submitting the award package. The FEMA Finance Center will need to know the Recipient's name, its Data Universal Numbering System (DUNS) number, and a previous federal award number that it may have had in the Integrated Financial Management Information System (IFMIS). The FEMA Finance Center will check to see if a current record exists or if a new one must be created. The information can be forwarded to the <u>Records Maintenance mailbox</u> with the Subject: MT eGrants Grantee Validation. The email address is FEMA-Finance-RecordsMaintenance@fema.dhs.gov. |

# Create/Amend Award Package Workflow Queue

The eGrants Internal System allows FEMA to electronically manage the process of creating, reviewing, and amending award packages for applications and subapplications that were approved in the Pre-Award Eligibility Workflow. The Awards Workflow is the process for preparing and reviewing these award packages.

Once subapplications have been approved in the Pre-Award Eligibility Workflow, they can be selected to be included in a federal award. The Awards Workflow begins with the Create/Amend Award Package queue. This queue may entail creating an initial award package for an initial obligation or creating an amendment to an existing award package that may involve an additional obligation, no obligation, or a de-obligation. If an initial award package is created, it is forwarded to the Regional Director Review queue. The Regional Director may disapprove the award package and send it back to the Create/Amend Award Package queue, or he or she may approve the award package, which then submits the obligation to Generic Financial Services (GFS) and the Integrated Financial Management Information System (IFMIS) for obligation approval. If a subaward has a federal share of $1 million or more, the Notification Coordination queue will need to be completed and will take place after the Regional Director Review queue.

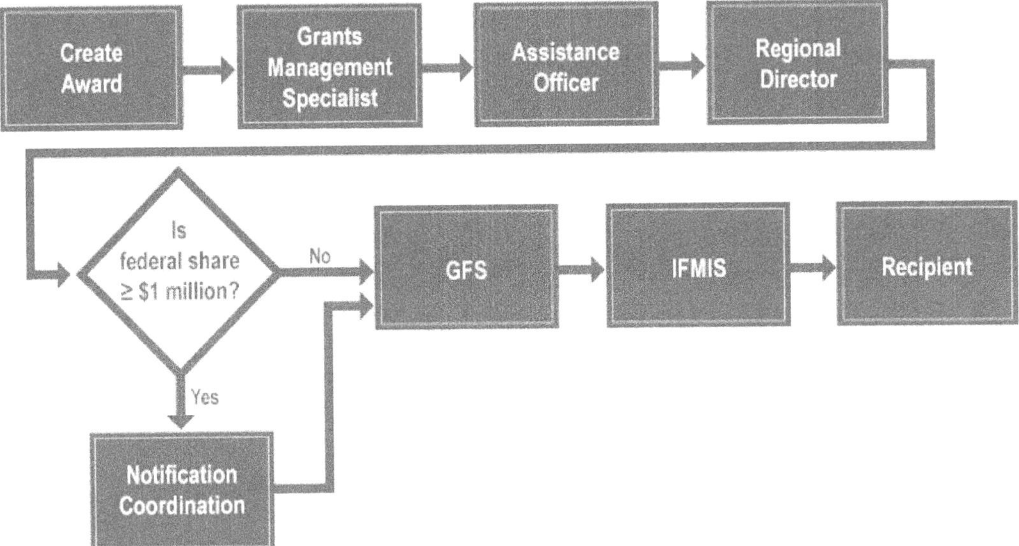


Select this link for the full text of the image.

# Creating a New Award

Assistance Officers and Grants Management Specialists can both create an award package in the Create/Amend Award Package queue, but only Assistance Officers can submit the award package to the Regional Director for review. The Submit button is unavailable to Grants Management Specialists. They must check in the queue so that it can be submitted by an Assistance Officer.

Alex will explain how a Grants Management Specialist creates a new award for a FMA subapplication.

Scroll down to see slideshow captions.

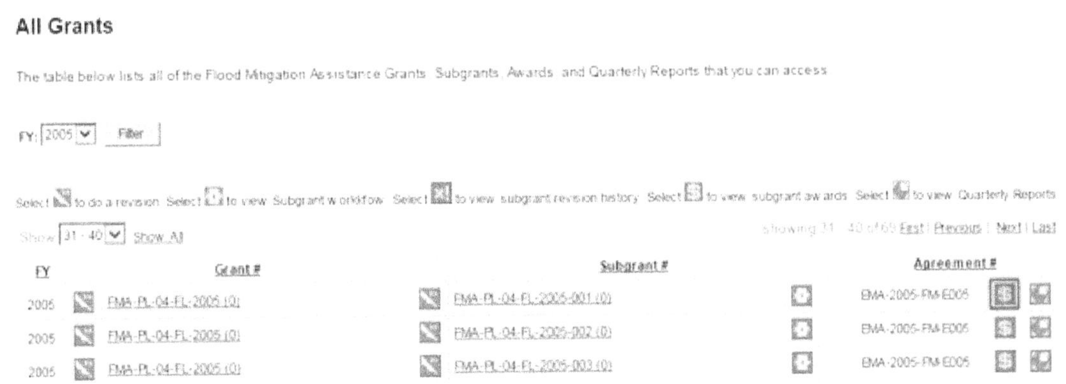

**All Grants**

The table below lists all of the Flood Mitigation Assistance Grants, Subgrants, Awards, and Quarterly Reports that you can access.

FY: 2005   Filter

Select ✎ to do a revision. Select ▣ to view Subgrant workflow. Select ▣ to view subgrant revision history. Select ▣ to view subgrant awards. Select ▣ to view Quarterly Reports.

Show 31 - 40   Show All                                                    showing 31 - 40 of 69  First | Previous | Next | Last

| FY | Grant # | Subgrant # | Agreement # | | |
|---|---|---|---|---|---|
| 2005 | FMA-PL-04-FL-2005 (0) | FMA-PL-04-FL-2005-001 (0) | EMA-2005-FM-E005 | | |
| 2005 | FMA-PL-04-FL-2005 (0) | FMA-PL-04-FL-2005-002 (0) | EMA-2005-FM-E005 | | |
| 2005 | FMA-PL-04-FL-2005 (0) | FMA-PL-04-FL-2005-003 (0) | EMA-2005-FM-E005 | | |

To create an award package, the Grants Management Specialist selects the **Subgrant Award** icon to the right of an eligible subapplication on the All Grants screen.

The Awards screen appears. This screen lists all the award packages that have been created for an application. To create a new award package for an eligible subapplication, the Grants Management Specialist selects the **Create** button.

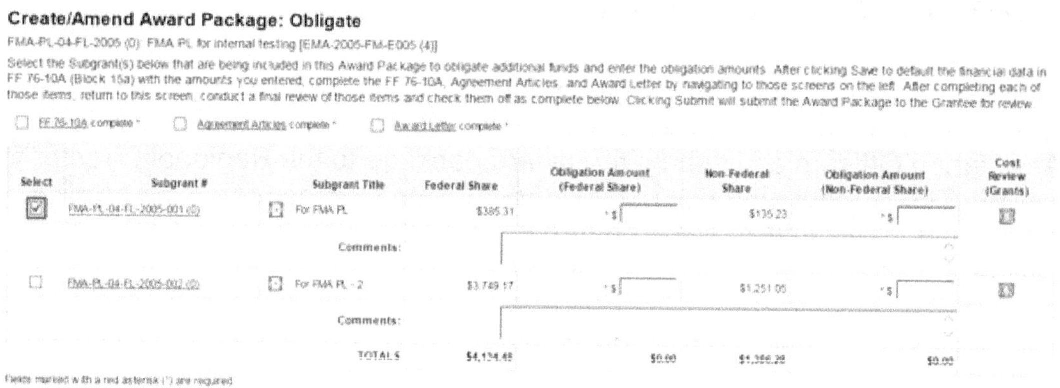

The Create/Amend Award Package: Obligate screen appears. The Grants Management Specialist checks the box in the **Select** column that corresponds with the subapplication which is eligible for an award package. More than one checkbox may be selected to create an award package that includes multiple subapplications.

**Create/Amend Award Package: Obligate**

FMA-PJ-04-FL-2005 (0) FMA PL for internal testing [EMA-2005-FM-E005 (4)]

Select the Subgrant(s) below that are being included in this Award Package to obligate additional funds and enter the obligation amounts. After clicking Save to default the financial data in FF 76-10A (Block 15a) with the amounts you entered, complete the FF 76-10A, Agreement Articles, and Award Letter by navigating to those screens on the left. After completing each of those items, return to this screen, conduct a final review of those items and check them off as complete below. Clicking Submit will submit the Award Package to the Grantee for review.

☐ FF 76-10A complete *    ☐ Agreement Articles complete *    ☐ Award Letter complete *

| Select | Subgrant # | Subgrant Title | Federal Share | Obligation Amount (Federal Share) | Non-Federal Share | Obligation Amount (Non-Federal Share) | Cost Review (Grants) |
|---|---|---|---|---|---|---|---|
| ☑ | FMA-PL-04-FL-2005-001 (0) | For FMA PL | $385.31 | * $ 385.31 | $135.23 | * $ 135.23 | |
| | Comments: | | | | | | |
| ☐ | FMA-PL-04-FL-2005-002 (0) | For FMA PL - 2 | $3,749.17 | * $ | $1,251.05 | * $ | |
| | Comments: | | | | | | |
| | TOTALS | | $4,134.48 | $0.00 | $1,386.28 | $0.00 | |

Fields marked with a red asterisk (*) are required.

Submitted To: FMS        User: RIO, MANUEL        Status: Pending        Date: 07/05/2017 06:05 PM

Attachments    Comments    Save    Submit

The federal share for this subapplication is $385.31. The Grants Management Specialist enters the amount "385.31" in the **Obligation Amount (Federal Share)** text field. The non-federal share for this subapplication is $135.23, so he or she enters "135.23" in the **Obligation Amount (Non-Federal Share)** text field. Then he or she selects the **Save** button.

# Award Package — Part 1

The Grants Management Specialist creates the three documents that constitute the award package. These documents are the:

- FEMA Form (FF) 76-10A
- Agreement Articles
- Award Letter

The links on the Awards screen sidebar menu will open screens that allow him or her to create these documents. The Agreement Articles and Award Letter can also be created outside of eGrants and uploaded to the award package.

Alex will explain how a Grants Management Specialist creates Part 1 of the award package: the FF 76-10A.

Scroll down to see slideshow captions.

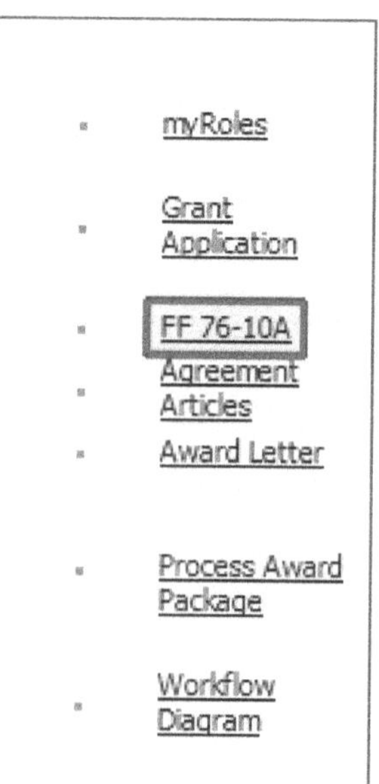


The Grants Management Specialist can access all three parts of the award package by using the links on the Awards screen sidebar menu. To create Part 1 of the awards package, the FEMA Form FF-76-10A form, he or she selects the **FF-76-10A** link.

### Edit Award Package: FF 76-10A

FMA-04-FL-2010 (0): FL FMA 2010 Test 2 [EMA-2010-FM-E001 (2)]

| IFMIS Information | | | | |
| --- | --- | --- | --- | --- |
| Please select the Commitment Number and enter a Vendor ID that will be used to obligate funds in IFMIS for this Grant. | | | | |
| * Commitment #: 819934N   Click here to view Funding Summary for Commitment. | | | * Vendor ID:                    Search | |
| 1. Agreement No. | 2. Amendment No. | 3. Recipient No. | 4. Type of Action * | 5. Control No. |
| EMA-2010-FM-E001 | 2 | 56-7890123 | ☐ Grant  ☐ Award<br>☐ CA  ☐ Amendment | A234567NFM001A |

The Edit Award Package: FF 76-10A screen displays. It is already auto-populated with the Federal and Non-Federal Share information entered earlier. The Grants Management Specialist selects a Commitment number from the **Commitment #** drop-down menu. For this subapplication he or she selects "819934N." Some Commitment numbers may already have vendors linked to them and the number will appear in the **Vendor ID** field. This Commitment number doesn't have a vendor directly linked to it, so the Grants Management Specialist selects the **Search** link in the Vendor ID field.

The Vendor Search screen displays. The Grants Management Specialist can search by **State, Vendor ID, Vendor Name,** or a combination of these categories. The "State" option defaults to the state indicated on the application. The drop-down criteria options for Vendor ID and Vendor name include: Equals, Begins With, and Contains. The Grants Management Specialist has validated the vendor with the FEMA Financial Center, so he or she selects "=" and types the Vendor ID number "SFL153" in the text field. Then, he or she selects the **Search** button.

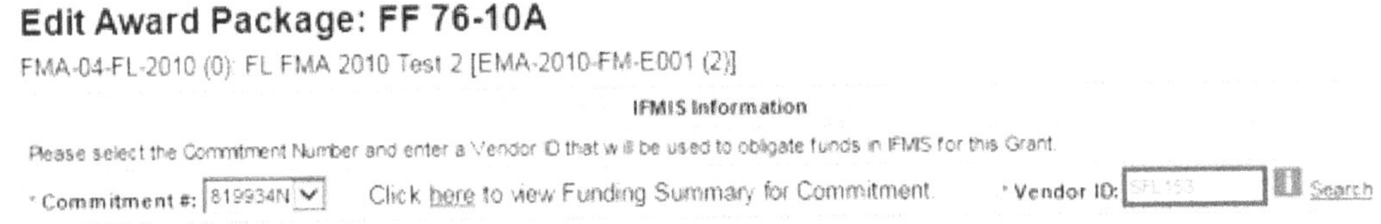


Information on vendors that meet the search criteria are displayed. The Grants Management Specialist selects the radio button to the left of the appropriate **Vendor.** Then, he or she selects the **Return** button to return to the FF 76-10A form.

**Edit Award Package: FF 76-10A**

FMA-04-FL-2010 (0) FL FMA 2010 Test 2 [EMA-2010-FM-E001 (2)]

IFMIS Information

Please select the Commitment Number and enter a Vendor ID that will be used to obligate funds in IFMIS for this Grant.

* Commitment #: 819934N     Click here to view Funding Summary for Commitment.     * Vendor ID: SFL153     Search

The FF 76-10A screen displays. The **Vendor ID** field is updated.

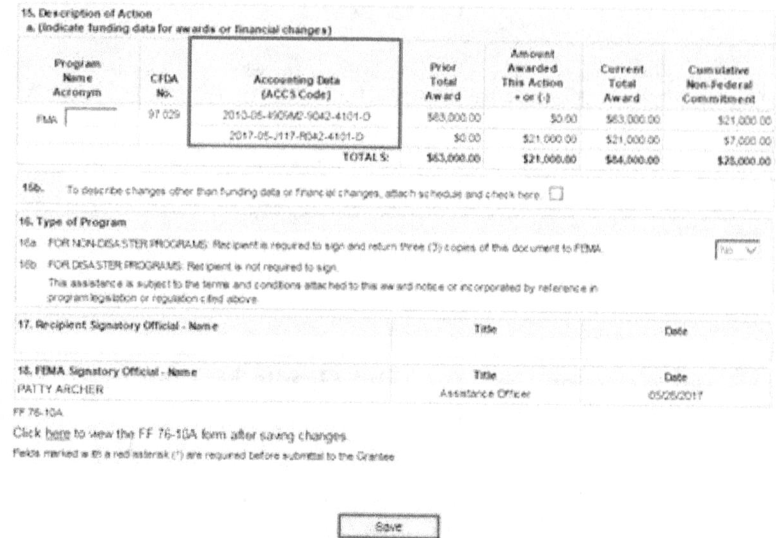

Scrolling down, the **Accounting Classification Code Structure** (ACCS) information displayed in Field 15 is auto-populated by the Commitment ID. The Grants Management Specialist completes all the remaining required fields, then selects the **Save** button.

# Award Package — Part 2 and Part 3

The second part of the award package is the Agreement Articles. This document is the official agreement between FEMA and the Applicant regarding the funding of the federal award and its subawards. It details the laws that govern the agreement, the responsible parties, the funding, period(s) of performance, limitations, reporting procedures, closeout, and other stipulations.

The third part of the award package is the Award Letter. The letter, addressed to the Applicant Point of Contact, officially acknowledges the obligation to fund the federal award, the availability of funds, reporting requirements, and the federal award closeout requirements.

Alex will demonstrate how a Grants Management Specialist attaches the Agreement Articles and the Award Letter to an award package.

Scroll down to view slideshow captions.

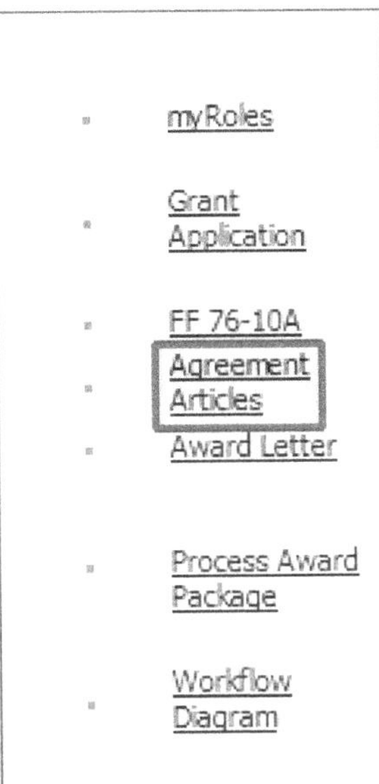



The second component in the award package are the Agreement Articles. To attach a copy of them to the award package, the Grants Management Specialist selects the **Agreement Articles** link from the sidebar menu.

**Edit Award Package: Agreement Articles**

FMA-PL-03-PA-2004 (0)  tin paper fma plan 03.04.05 [EMP-2005-FM-E001 (1)]

Please indicate whether the Agreement Articles will be the standard template or an attachment that you specify. The attachment will be used for the Agreement Articles in the Award Package.

○ Use Standard Template

If necessary, enter additional articles above and beyond the standard Agreement Articles. Additional articles will be appended to the standard Agreement Articles.

Additional Articles:

⦿ Attach Agreement Articles

* File: [                                                    ] [ Browse ]

The field marked with a red asterisk (*) is required before submittal to Grantee if attaching Agreement Articles.

The Edit Award Package: Agreement Articles screen appears. The Grants Management Specialist can choose to use the Standard Template to create the Agreement Articles or attach a file that contains the Agreement Articles from his or her computer. To begin, the Grants Management Specialist selects the **Attach Agreement Articles** radio button. Then, he or she selects the **Browse** button.

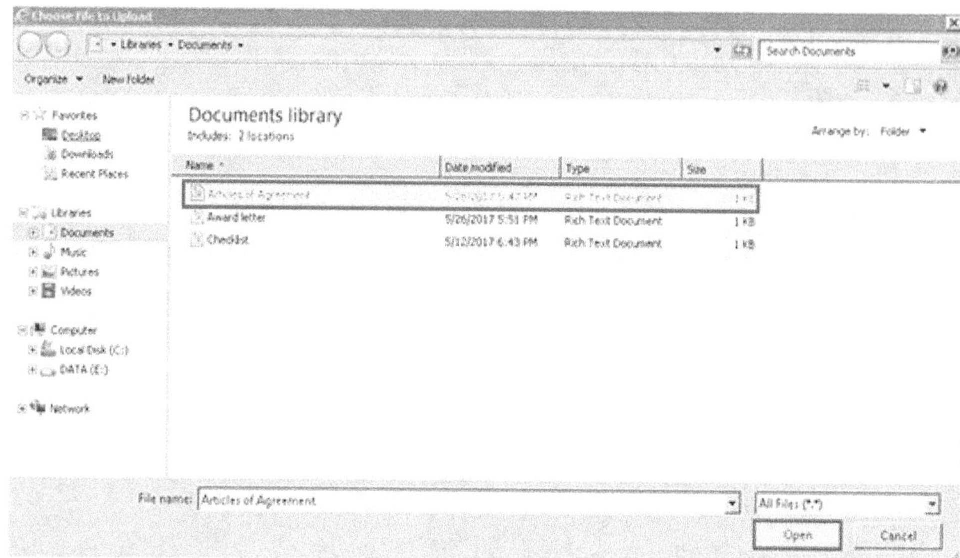

A file explorer window appears. The Grants Management Specialist navigates to find the **Articles of Agreement document** on his or her computer to select it. Then he or she selects the **Open** button to upload it to eGrants.

## Edit Award Package: Agreement Articles

FMA-04-FL-2010 (0): FL FMA 2010 Test 2 [EMA-2010-FM-E001 (2)]

The attachment selected will be used for the Agreement Articles in the Award Package.

| **Attach Agreement Articles** |
| --- |
| * File: `C:\Users\asalazar\Documents\Articles of Agreement.doc`    Browse... |

The field marked with a red asterisk (*) is required before submittal to Grantee if attaching Agreement Articles.

* Assistance Officer: Patty Archer

The field marked with a red asterisk (*) is required before submittal to the Grantee.

Click here to view the entire Agreement Articles after saving changes.

Save

The Agreement Articles **file name** appears on the screen. The Grants Management Specialist now enters the name of the **Assistance Officer,** Patty Archer, then selects **Save.** Now, it's time for the Grants Management Specialist to create the Award Letter.

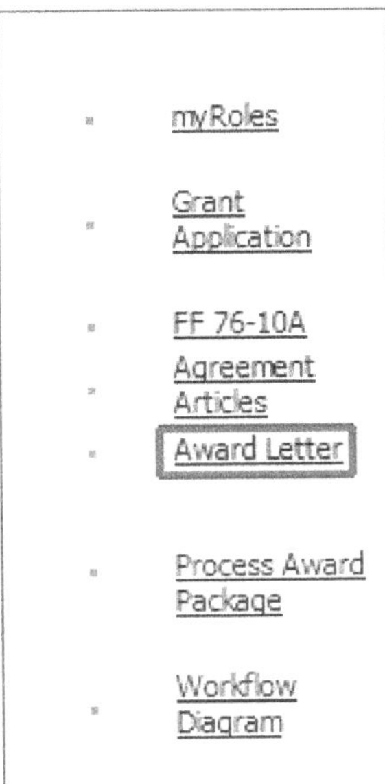


To create the third component in the award package, the Grants Management Specialist selects the **Award Letter** link from the sidebar menu.

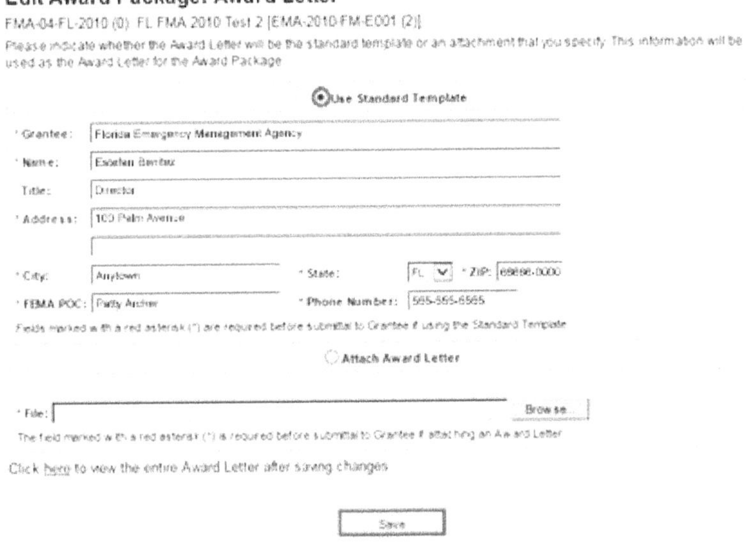


The Edit Award Package: Award Letter page displays. The Grants Management Specialist can select either the Use Standard Template radio button and complete the required fields, or select the Attach Award Letter radio button and attach an Award Letter. For this subapplication, the Grants Management Specialist selects the **Use Standard Template** radio button. The Recipient information is auto-populated from the application. Then, he or she selects the **Save** button. The three parts of the award package are now complete. The Grants Management Specialist now needs to Check In the subapplication so the Assistance Officer can review the award package.

# Grants Office Cost Review

After the award package has been completed, the Assistance Officer must check out the queue in order to review the eligibility of each budget line item in the subapplication and three parts of the award package.
Alex will explain how an Assistance Officer performs the cost review in eGrants.
Scroll down to see slideshow captions.

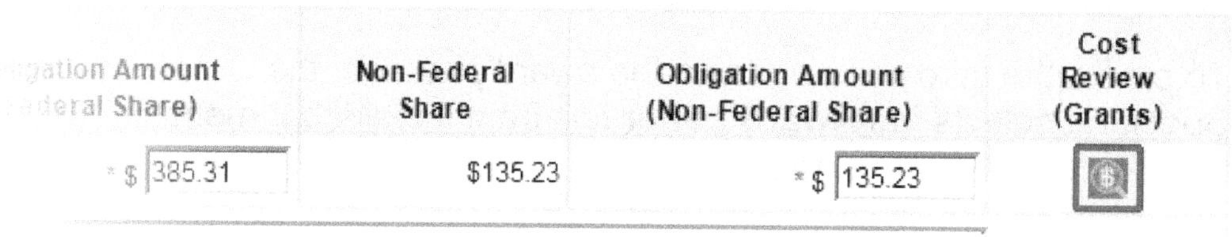


| gation Amount (eral Share) | Non-Federal Share | Obligation Amount (Non-Federal Share) | Cost Review (Grants) |
|---|---|---|---|
| * $ 385.31 | $135.23 | * $ 135.23 | |

To begin the Cost Review process, the Assistance Officer first Checks Out the application and selects the Create/Amend Award link. Then he or she selects the **Cost Review (Grants)** icon for each subapplication included in the award package.

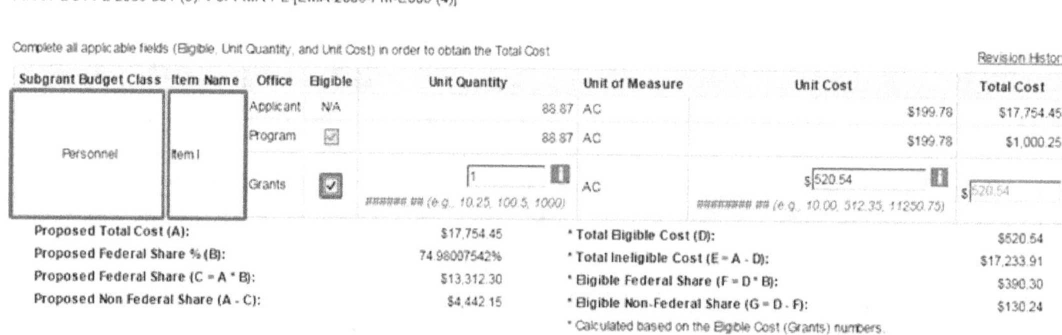


| Subgrant Budget Class | Item Name | Office | Eligible | Unit Quantity | Unit of Measure | Unit Cost | Total Cost |
|---|---|---|---|---|---|---|---|
| | | Applicant | N/A | 88.87 | AC | $199.78 | $17,754.45 |
| Personnel | Item I | Program | ☑ | 88.87 | AC | $199.78 | $1,000.25 |
| | | Grants | ☑ | 1 | AC | $ 520.54 | $ 520.54 |



| | | | |
|---|---|---|---|
| Proposed Total Cost (A): | $17,754.45 | * Total Eligible Cost (D): | $520.54 |
| Proposed Federal Share % (B): | 74.98007542% | * Total Ineligible Cost (E = A - D): | $17,233.91 |
| Proposed Federal Share (C = A * B): | $13,312.30 | * Eligible Federal Share (F = D * B): | $390.30 |
| Proposed Non Federal Share (A - C): | $4,442.15 | * Eligible Non-Federal Share (G = D - F): | $130.24 |

* Calculated based on the Eligible Cost (Grants) numbers.

The Cost Review (Grants) screen displays. The Assistance Officer reviews each **item** in each **Subgrant Budget Class** to determine its eligibility and selects the **checkbox** for each eligible item.

## Cost Review (Grants)

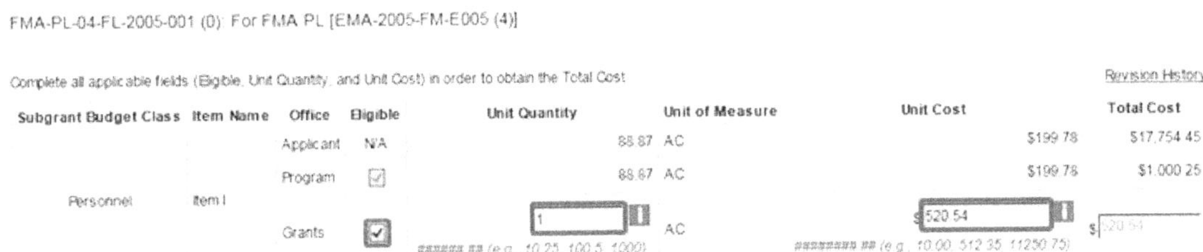

The Assistance Officer then reviews the amounts for individual **unit quantities, units of measure, unit costs,** and the **total cost** for each eligible item.

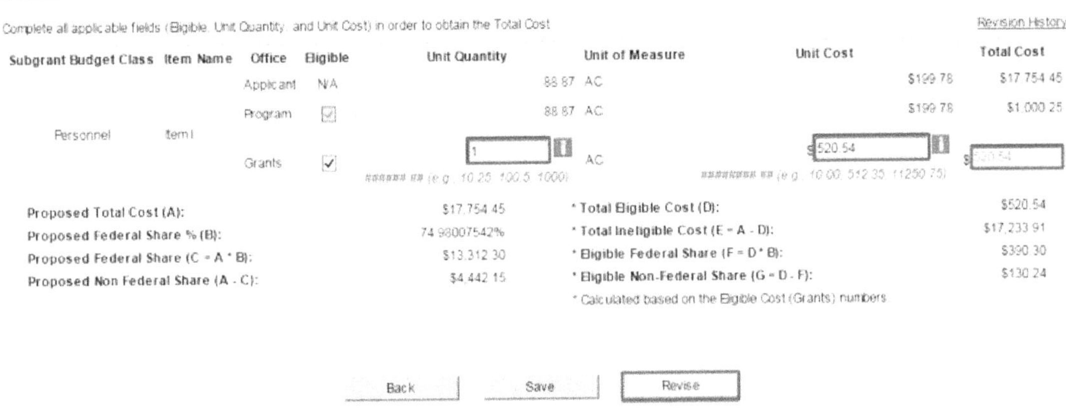

If any corrections or adjustments need to be made, the Assistance Officer can make them in the associated text fields. He or she would then select the **Revise** button, which will bring up the Revision Request screen, to return the subapplication to the Applicant for revisions.

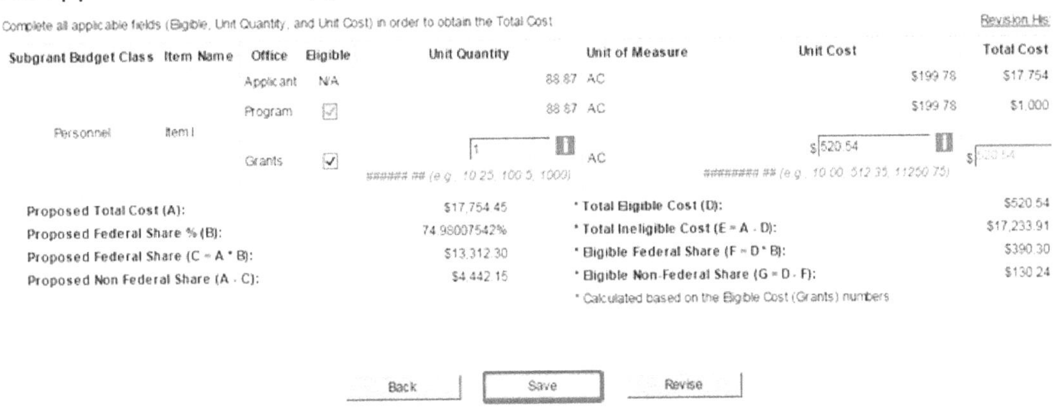

When the review is complete, the Assistance Officer selects the **Save** button.

# Deleting an Award Package

An award package can only be deleted if it has not yet been submitted to the IFMIS.

To delete an award package, a Grants Management Specialist selects the Award icon for a subapplication from either the All Grants or Inbox screens. The Awards screen will display the list of award packages for the subawards within a federal award. He or she selects the Delete icon in the Delete column to remove the award package. The Delete icon will not appear if the award package has already been submitted to IFMIS.

Select this link for the full text of the image.

# Approving an Award Package

The Regional Director reviews the obligated federal share and non-federal share amounts, the FF 76-10A, Agreement Articles, and Award Letter before submitting the obligated federal share amount to GFS and IFMIS for disbursement.

The Regional Director is ready to review and submit the award package for a Flood Mitigation Assistance (FMA) subapplication.

Scroll down to see slideshow captions.

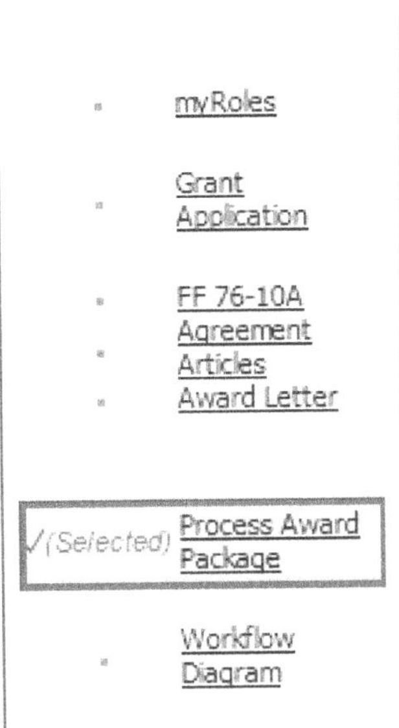


The Regional Director needs to review all three parts of the award package to make sure everything is complete and accurate. He or she selects the **Process Award Package** link on the sidebar menu.

## Process Award Package

FMA-04-FL-2010 (0): FL FMA 2010 Test 2 [EMA-2010-FM-E001 (2)]

| Queue | User | Status | Status Date |
|---|---|---|---|
| Create/Amend Award Package * | REVIEWER, NEW | Pending | 12/23/2013 10:52 PM |
| GFS Obligation | | Not Ready | 12/23/2013 10:52 PM |
| IFMIS Obligation | | Not Ready | 12/23/2013 10:52 PM |

* Completing this step sends an obligation to IFMIS.

The Process Award Package screen appears. The Regional Director selects the **Create/Amend Award Package** link in the Queue column.

**Create/Amend Award Package: Obligate**

FMA-04-FL-2010 (0): FL FMA 2010 Test 2 [EMA-2010-FM-E001 (2)]

Select the Subgrant(s) below that are being included in this Award Package to obligate additional funds and enter the obligation amounts. After clicking Save to default the financial data in FF 76-10A (Block 15a) with the amounts you entered, complete the FF 76-10A, Agreement Articles, and Award Letter by navigating to those screens on the left. After completing each of those items, return to this screen, conduct a final review of those items and check them off as complete below. Clicking Submit will submit the Award Package to the Grantee for review.

☑ FF 76-10A complete *   ☑ Agreement Articles complete *   ☑ Award Letter complete *

| Select | Subgrant # | | Subgrant Title | Federal Share | Obligation Amount (Federal Share) | Non-Federal Share | Obligation Amount (Non-Federal Share) | Cost Review (Grants) |
|---|---|---|---|---|---|---|---|---|
| ☑ | FMA-FL-04-FL-2010-001 (0) | 📄 | test1 PL | $21,000.00 | * $ 21000.00 | $7,000.00 | * $ 7000.00 | 📄 |
| | Comments: | | | | | | | |
| ☐ | FMA-FL-04-FL-2010-005 (0) | 📄 | test3 PL | $21,000.00 | * $ | $7,000.00 | * $ | 📄 |
| | Comments: | | | | | | | |
| ☐ | FMA-FL-04-FL-2010-006 (0) | 📄 | New Test Threville PL 2007 044 | $21,000.00 | * $ | $7,000.00 | * $ | 📄 |
| | Comments: | | | | | | | |
| | | | TOTALS | $63,000.00 | $0.00 | $21,000.00 | $0.00 | |

Fields marked with a red asterisk (*) are required.

| Submitted To: FMS | User: SALAZAR, ALEX | Status: Pending | Date: 12/23/2013 10:52 PM |
|---|---|---|---|

[ Attachments... ]   [ Comments... ]   [ Save ]   [ Submit ]

The Create/Amend Award Package: Obligate screen appears. To review the award package documents for completion and accuracy, the Regional Director selects each link for the **FF 76-10A** form, **Agreement Articles,** and the **Award Letter.** If the review is satisfactory, the Regional Director selects the **Complete** checkbox to the left of each document title. To approve the award package, the Regional Director selects the **Submit** button.

## Confirmation

Award Package FMA-04-FL-2010 (0): FL FMA 2010 Test 2 [EMA-2010-FM-E001 (2)] was successfully sent to IFMIS.

[ Return to Inbox ]

A confirmation screen appears. The obligated federal share amount has now been sent to IFMIS for disbursement. To approve another award package, the Regional Director selects the **Return to Inbox** link.

# Notification Coordination

Issuing a federal award that includes one or more subawards with a federal share of $1 million or greater must be coordinated with the appropriate members of Congress. If the federal share of a subaward is $1 million or greater, the Notification Coordination queue is triggered to document the Large Project Notification (LPN) process and must be completed. Users with the PDM or FMA Coordinator role may complete the Notification Coordination queue.

The Notification Coordination queue is initiated concurrently with the creation of an award package in the eGrants system. The bulk of the LPN process takes place outside of eGrants, with the system used to document the process and dates of completion.

It is best to wait until after the Notification Coordination is completed to document the process in eGrants, since the eGrants Internal System does not allow date(s) later than the current date to be entered. On the Notification Coordination screen, after the notification has been completed, select the "Yes" option from the Notification Coordination Complete drop-down menu. Enter the date of the notification in the Notification Coordination Date field. After the Regional External Affairs Officer has been notified, select the "Yes" option from the Regional External Affairs Officer Notified drop-down menu. After the press release is issued, enter the date that the press release was issued in the Public News Release Date field. After all of the fields have been completed, select the Save button.

## Notification Coordination

FMA-06-LA-2008 (0): GOHSEP FMA FY 2008 [EMT-2011-FM-E002 (0)]

Notification Coordination Complete: Yes    Notification Coordination Date:

Regional External Affairs Officer Notified: Yes    Public News Release Date:

Select this link for the full text of the image.

# Amending Subawards

Sometimes a subaward needs to be amended because its period of performance, scope of work, or costs have changed. In these instances, the Grants Management Specialist would respond to an Applicant's request by releasing section(s) of the subaward for revision. After revision and resubmission, the subapplication would reappear in the grant program Inbox in the appropriate queue for processing.

- If a longer period of performance is required, the Schedule section would be released for revision and resubmission. If the period of performance change has no impact on project or planning costs, the amended award package would not need to be submitted to IFMIS.
- If the scope of work on a project or planning activity has expanded, the Scope of Work section (and Cost Estimate section, if necessary) would be released for revision and resubmission. If the scope of work change has no impact on project or planning costs, the amended award

package would not need to be submitted to IFMIS. However, if monies are no longer required due to a cancelled project or plan, then the de-obligation award package would need to be submitted to IFMIS.
- If additional funds are required to complete a project, the Cost Share and Cost Estimate sections would be released for revision and resubmission. An additional obligation award package would be completed and submitted to IFMIS.

If any corrections or adjustments need to be made, the Assistance Officer can make them in the associated text fields. He or she would then select the **Revise** button, which will bring up the Revision Request screen, to return the subapplication to the Applicant for revisions.

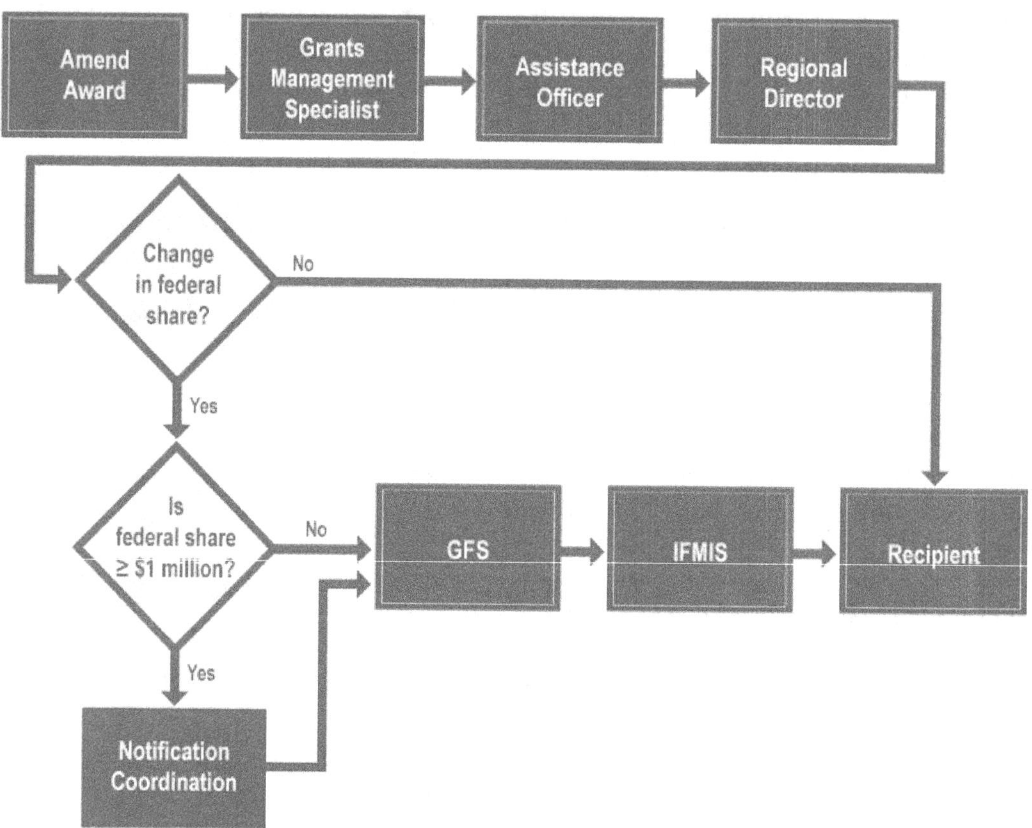


Select this link for the full text of the image.

# Obligate Additional Funds

Once an award package has been processed through IFMIS, it is possible to amend the award to obligate additional funds. This may occur if costs have increased and the originally obligated funds are insufficient to complete the project or plan.

After a subapplication is revised and resubmitted with new federal share and non-federal share amounts, the updated subapplication must complete the Pre-Eligibility Workflow queues before it can be processed for award. (The Pre-Award Eligibility Workflow queues were discussed in Lesson 5.)

Alex will explain how a Grants Management Specialist creates an additional obligation award package for an eligible, revised subapplication.

Scroll down to see slideshow captions.

To begin the process to obligate additional funds, the Grants Management Specialist locates the application, FMA-PL-04-FL-2005, which contains the subaward which requires more funds, on the All Grants screen. Then, he or she selects the **Subgrant Award** icon that corresponds to the subapplication with the "-001" designation.

The Awards screen appears and displays the award packages created for the federal award. To obligate additional funds, the Grants Management Specialist selects the **Obligate** button.

**Create/Amend Award Package: Obligate**

FMA-PL-04-FL-2005 (0) FMA PL for internal testing [EMA-2005-FM-E005 (4)]

Select the Subgrant(s) below that are being included in this Award Package to obligate additional funds and enter the obligation amounts. After clicking Save to default the financial data in FF 76-10A (Block 15a) with the amounts you entered, complete the FF 76-10A, Agreement Articles, and Award Letter by navigating to those screens on the left. After completing each of those items, return to this screen, conduct a final review of those items and check them off as complete below. Clicking Submit will submit the Award Package to the Grantee for review

☐ FF 76-10A complete *    ☐ Agreement Articles complete *    ☐ Award Letter complete *

| Select | Subgrant # | Subgrant Title | Federal Share | Obligation Amount (Federal Share) | Non-Federal Share | Obligation Amount (Non-Federal Share) | Cost Review (Grants) |
|---|---|---|---|---|---|---|---|
| ☑ | FMA-PL-04-FL-2005-001 (0) | For FMA PL | $3,750.00 | * $ | $1,250.00 | * $ | |
| | Comments: | | | | | | |
| ☐ | FMA-PL-04-FL-2005-002 (0) | For FMA PL - 2 | $3,749.17 | * $ | $1,251.05 | * $ | |
| | Comments: | | | | | | |
| | | TOTALS | $7,499.17 | $0.00 | $2,501.05 | $0.00 | |

Fields marked with a red asterisk (*) are required

Submitted To: IFMIS     User: RIO, MANUEL     Status: Pending     Date: 07/05/2017 06:05 PM

[Attachments]   [Comments]   [Save]   [Submit]

The Create/Amend Award Package: Obligate screen appears. The Grants Management Specialist checks the box in the **Select** column for subapplication number FMA-PL-04-FL-2005-001 and enters the new **federal share** and **non-federal share** amounts that have carried over from the revised subapplication. Then, he or she selects the **Save** button. The Assistance Officer will review the revised budget line items. The Grants Management Specialist will complete the three parts of the award package. The Regional Director will review the award package and submit it to IFMIS as before.

**Create/Amend Award Package: Obligate**

FMA-PL-04-FL-2005 (0) FMA PL for internal testing [EMA-2005-FM-E005 (4)]

Select the Subgrant(s) below that are being included in this Award Package to obligate additional funds and enter the obligation amounts. After clicking Save to default the financial data in FF 76-10A (Block 15a) with the amounts you entered, complete the FF 76-10A, Agreement Articles, and Award Letter by navigating to those screens on the left. After completing each of those items, return to this screen, conduct a final review of those items and check them off as complete below. Clicking Submit will submit the Award Package to the Grantee for review

☐ FF 76-10A complete *    ☐ Agreement Articles complete *    ☐ Award Letter complete *

| Select | Subgrant # | Subgrant Title | Federal Share | Obligation Amount (Federal Share) | Non-Federal Share | Obligation Amount (Non-Federal Share) | Cost Review (Grants) |
|---|---|---|---|---|---|---|---|
| ☑ | FMA-PL-04-FL-2005-001 (0) | For FMA PL | $3,750.00 | * $ | $1,250.00 | * $ | |
| | Comments: | | | | | | |
| ☐ | FMA-PL-04-FL-2005-002 (0) | For FMA PL - 2 | $3,749.17 | * $ | $1,251.05 | * $ | |
| | Comments: | | | | | | |
| | | TOTALS | $7,499.17 | $0.00 | $2,501.05 | $0.00 | |

Fields marked with a red asterisk (*) are required

Submitted To: IFMIS     User: RIO, MANUEL     Status: Pending     Date: 07/05/2017 06:05 PM

[Attachments]   [Comments]   [Save]   [Submit]

The Create/Amend Award Package: Obligate screen appears. The Grants Management Specialist checks the box in the **Select** column for subapplication number FMA-PL-04-FL-2005-001 and enters the new **federal share** and **non-federal share** amounts that have carried over from the revised subapplication. Then, he or she selects the **Save** button. The Assistance Officer will review the revised budget line items. The Grants Management Specialist will complete the three parts of the award package. The Regional Director will review the award package and submit it to IFMIS as before.

# Amending to De-Obligate

If it is determined that a mitigation project is cancelled or modified, or other cost reductions are found, the subaward can be amended to de-obligate funds accordingly.

The process to de-obligate funds is the same as for obligating funds, except, select the De-Obligate button on the Awards screen instead of the Obligate button. On the Create/Amend Award Package: De-Obligate screen, select the subapplication number for which funds should be de-obligated. Minus signs will be visible beside the text fields in the De-Obligation Amount columns. Enter the amount to be reduced from the Federal Share and Non-Federal Share in those fields. Then select the Save button to default the financial data from the amounts entered into the FF 76-10A form. The Assistance Officer will review the three parts of the award package before submitting the de-obligation award package to the Regional Director and IFMIS.

### Create/Amend Award Package: De-Obligate

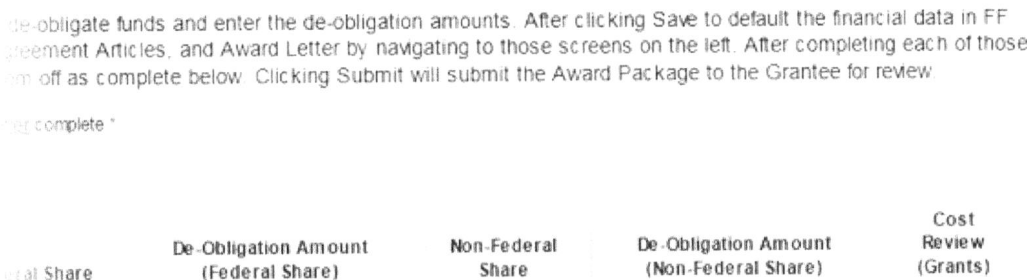

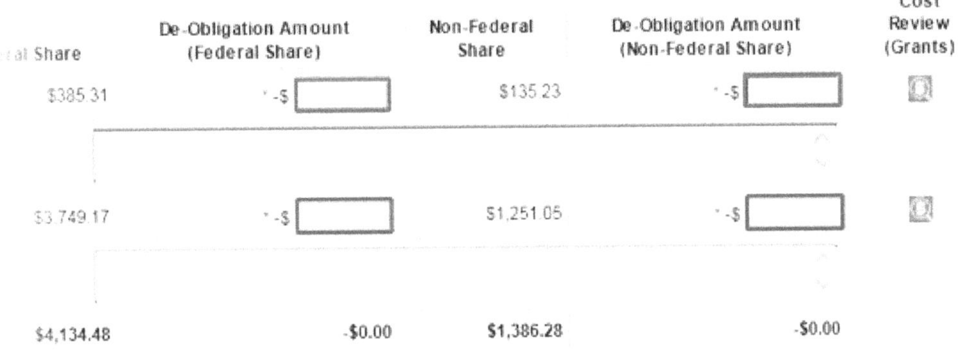

Select this link for the full text of the image.

# Reports

The Reports tab is located at the top of all Workflow queue screens. To run a report for a grant program, users need at least Read Only access. Then, the user will be able to access data only from his or her FEMA Region.

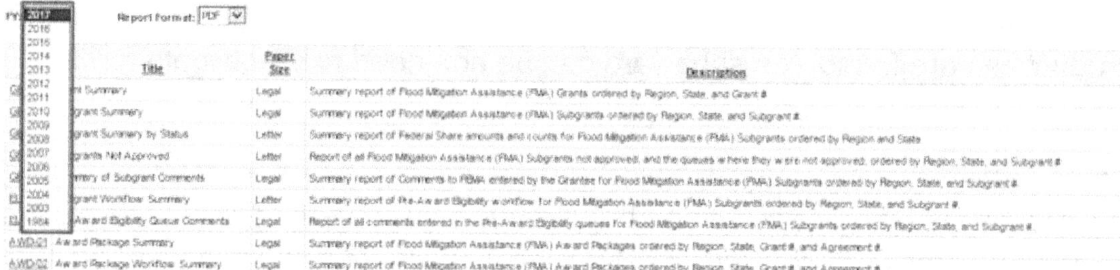

To run a report, first select the fiscal year. For this demonstration, select "2017" from the **FY** drop-down menu.

You can choose to display the report as a PDF or in Microsoft□ Excel format. For this demonstration, select the "PDF" option from the **Report Format** drop-down menu.

Then, select the link for the report in the **ID** column. For this demonstration, select the GEN-02 Subgrant Summary report.

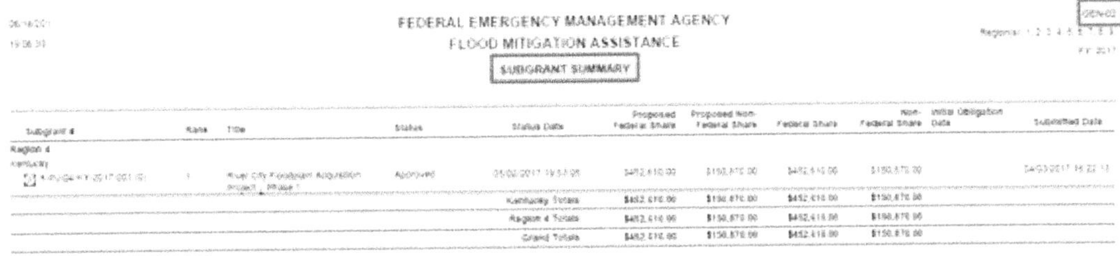

The selected report opens in a new window and can be saved to your computer.

# Searching for Awards

The Search tab allows you to search for federal awards and subawards available to you based on your eGrants roles. You can search within four categories: Grants (federal awards), Subgrants (subawards), Award Packages, and Quarterly Reports by selecting the corresponding link in the sidebar menu. General search criteria include Fiscal Year (FY), Region, and/or State. Additional search criteria are available depending on the search category. Also, for each criterion, you may select "=," "Begins with," "Contains," or "Ends with."

Alex will demonstrate how to perform a search for a project subaward.

Scroll down to see slideshow captions.

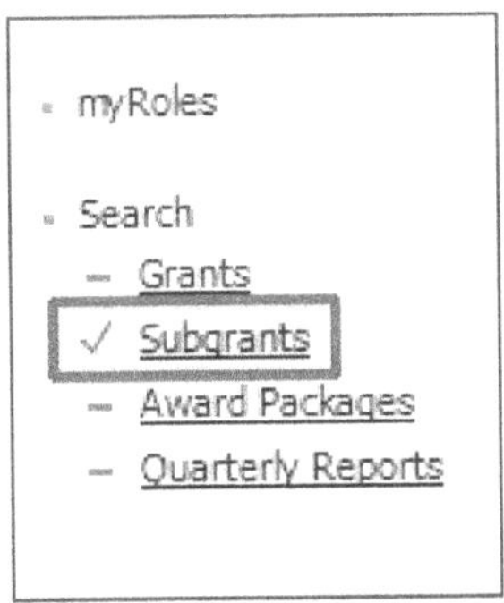


For this demonstration, let's search for a subaward from the State of Connecticut for Fiscal Year 2010. First, select the **Subgrants** link from the sidebar menu to display the search criteria for subawards.

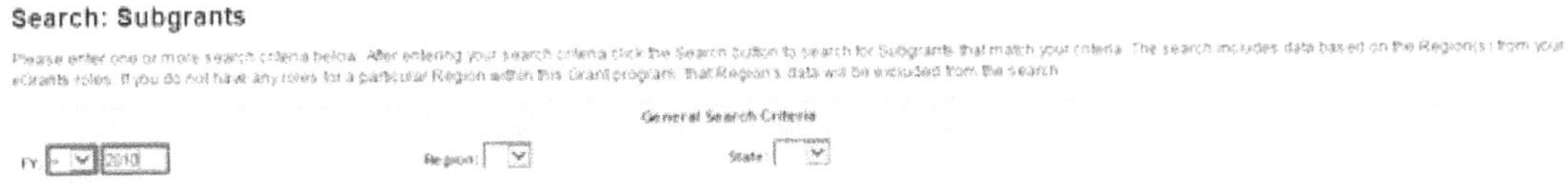

Then, for the search criteria, enter "2010" in the **FY** text field.

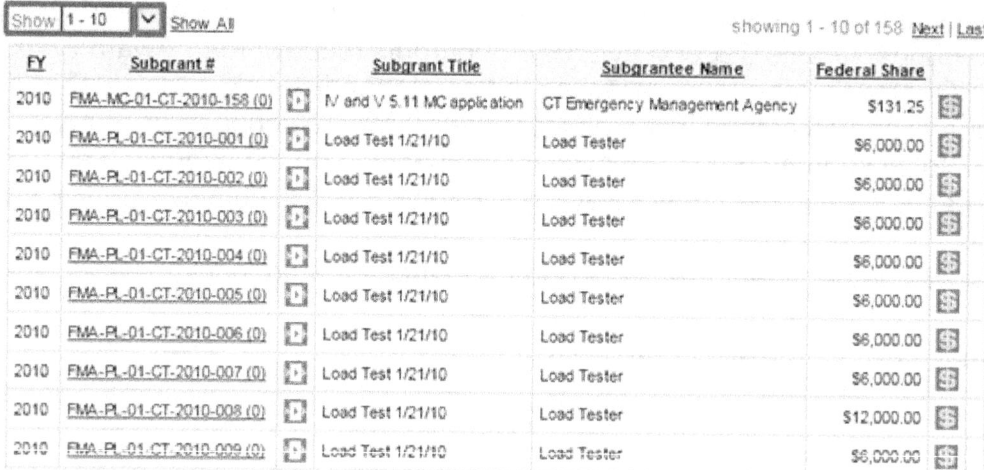

Select "CT" from the **State** drop-down menu. Then, select the **Search** button at the bottom of the screen.

The Search Results: Subgrants screen opens, displaying up to the first 10 results of the search you performed.

You can select the set of 10 results to display from the **Show** drop-down menu or you can choose to display all of the subawards by selecting the **Show All** link. You can also use the **First, Previous, Next,** and **Last** links to navigate through groups of 10 subawards.

# Search Results: Subgrants

158 Subgrant(s) match your search criteria.

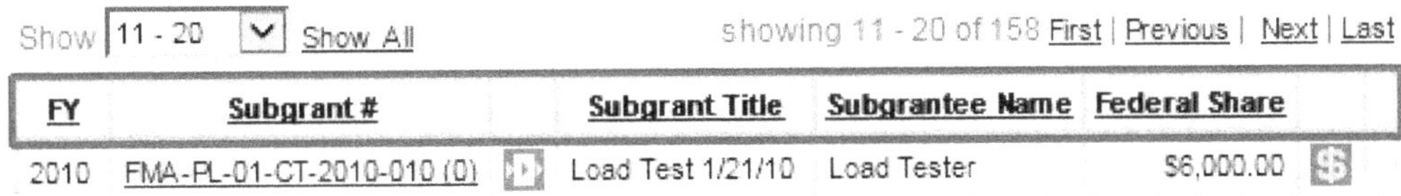

You can sort the results displayed on the screen by clicking a **column title.**

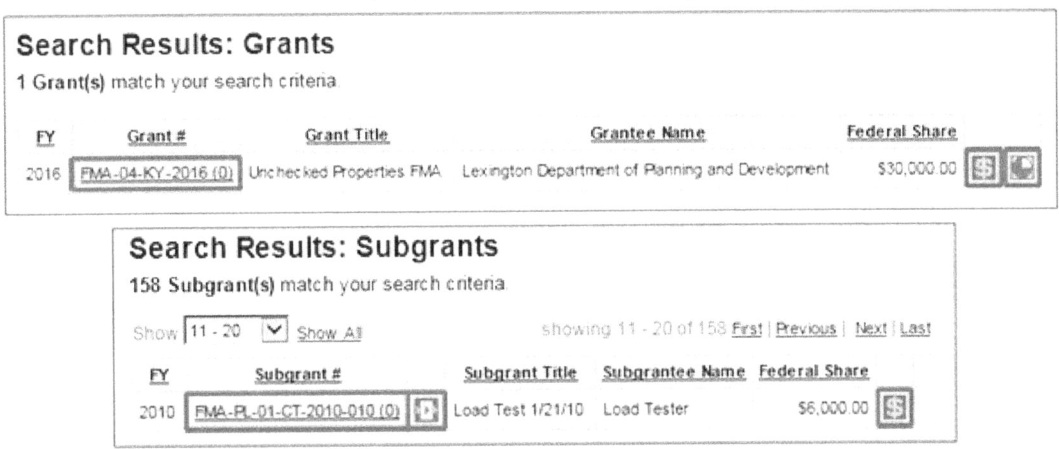

In addition, you can select the links and icons available for any of the specific results: the application number link in the **Grant #** column, the subapplication number link in the **Subgrant #** column, or the **Subgrant (Pre-Award Eligibility) Workflow** icon, **Awards** icon, or **Quarterly Report** icon to navigate to those screens for additional information.

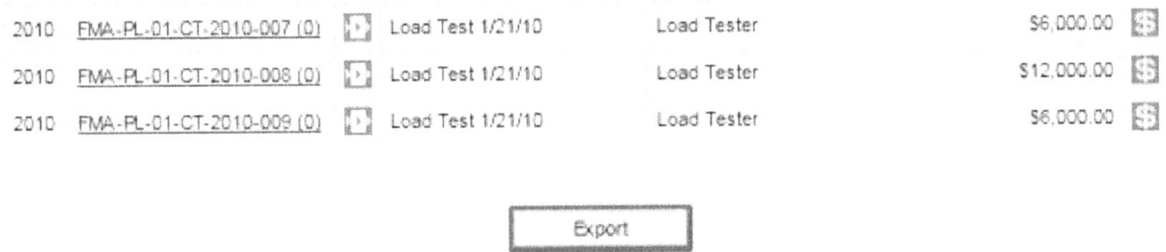

You can also export the search results to a spreadsheet by selecting the **Export** button at the bottom of the screen.

# Lesson 9 Summary

You have now completed Lesson 9: Awards Workflow.

There are several key points to remember when processing a subapplication for a subaward.

- There are three types of award packages:
    - **Standard Award Package:** for previously unfunded, approved subapplications
    - **Additional Obligation Award Package:** for awarding additional funds to a subaward
    - **De-obligation Package:** to return funds from a subaward
- Award packages have three components: the FF-76-10A, Agreement Articles, and Award Letter.
- Award packages can be amended or deleted if they haven't been submitted to the IFMIS for approval.
- Federal share funds can be obligated, increased, or de-obligated.
- The funding of large projects (i.e., individual subapplications of $1 million or more in federal share funds) must be coordinated with members of Congress in an external process that is documented in eGrants.
- You can select the Search tab to find a federal award, subaward, award package, or quarterly report.
- You can select the Reports tab to run a report on the grant programs in the FEMA Region to which you have access.

# Lesson 10 Overview

This lesson describes the Quarterly Reports Workflow of the eGrants Internal System.

At the end of this lesson, you should be able to identify:

- The Quarterly Reports Workflow queues

# eGrants User Scenario

**Team Leader:** Alex Salazar, Flood Mitigation Assistance (FMA) Program Coordinator

**Your Role:** New FMA Program Analyst

**Office:** FEMA Headquarters

**Challenge:** Recipients are required to submit quarterly financial status and performance reports on their federal awards.

**To Date:** You have learned the process for creating and amending an award package.

Listen to Alex
Audio transcript

**The Next Step:** Alex will show you how to view and process Quarterly Performance Reports.

Hi. It's Alex. Each quarter, recipients are required to report on the performance and financial status of projects and plans funded by their federal award. They submit their financial status reports through the Payment and Reporting System. But they submit their performance reports through eGrants. I will show you how to process both the financial status and performance quarterly reports in the Quarterly Reports Workflow queue.

## Quarterly Reports

Unless stated differently in the award documents, Recipients are required to submit quarterly performance and financial reports throughout the period of performance of their federal award. Quarterly Reports are due to FEMA no later than 30 days after the end of each federal fiscal quarter (see due dates below) following the date that the federal award was issued.

Quarterly Performance Reports must be submitted through eGrants. Quarterly Financial Status Reports are created and submitted through the Payment and Reporting System (PARS), which is outside of the eGrants system.

| Period Covered | Report Due Date |
| --- | --- |
| October 1 – December 31 | January 30 |
| January 1 – March 31 | April 30 |
| April 1 – June 30 | July 30 |
| July 1 – September 30 | October 30 |

# Quarterly Reports Workflow Queues

The eGrants Internal System provides FEMA users with the functionality to review the Recipient's quarterly reports.
The FEMA Quarterly Reports Workflow has two queues:

- An Assistance Officer documents the review of both the Quarterly Performance Report and Quarterly Financial Status Report in the Quarterly Report Program Review queue.
- A Grants Management Specialist documents the review of the Quarterly Financial Report in the Quarterly Report Grants Review queue. If the Grants Management Specialist is not satisfied with the outcome of the Quarterly Report Program Review queue, he or she can request that the queue be reworked.

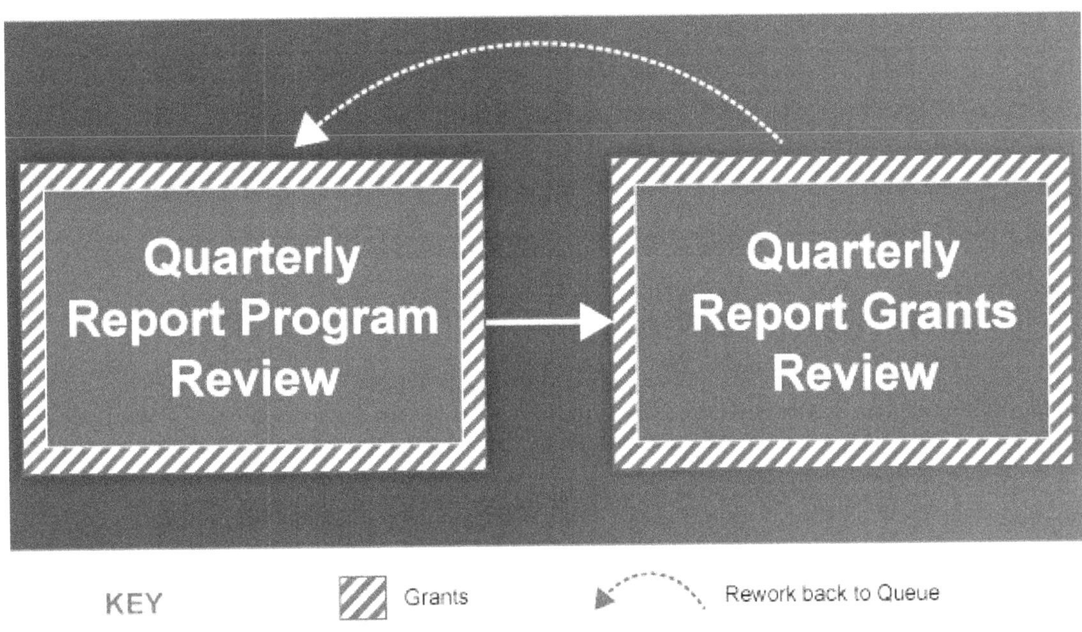


# Quarterly Reports in the Inbox

Quarterly reports received from Recipients are displayed in the Inbox, similar to how applications are displayed. The quarterly report number is displayed in the Subgrant/Quarterly Report # column.

Quarterly report numbers use the following format: *Program Prefix (PDM or FMA) – FEMA Region – State, Territory, or Tribal Code – Fiscal Year – Quarterly Report number.* Performance reports are indicated with a (P) and financial status reports are marked with an (F).

The fiscal quarters are numbered -01 through –xx, with -xx being the last quarter of the period of performance for the federal award, as stated in the FF 76-10A in the award package.

For example, the first Quarterly Performance Report for a FMA federal award for the State of Arkansas in Fiscal Year 2017 would appear as: FMA-10-AR-2017-QR-01 (P).

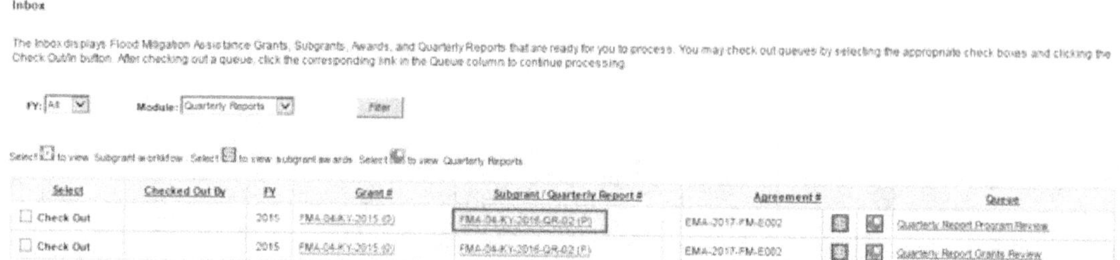

Select this link for the full text of the image.

# View Quarterly Reports

Alex will demonstrate how to view quarterly reports from the Inbox and other screens.
Scroll down to see slideshow captions.

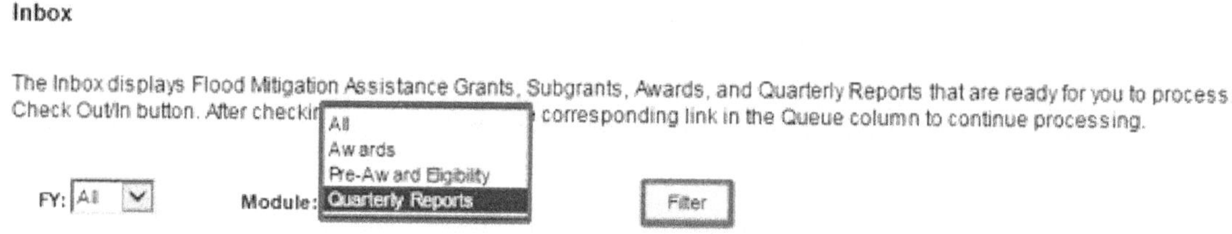

To see the list of Quarterly Reports Workflow queues that are ready for processing in the Inbox, select the **Quarterly Reports** option from the Module drop-down menu. Then, select the **Filter** button.

Just as with applications, you may view and print individual quarterly reports without checking out the Quarterly Review queue by clicking on the **Subgrant/Quarterly Report #** link.

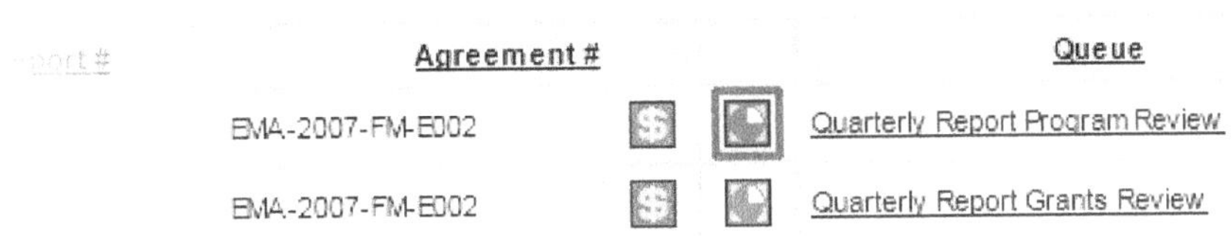


Another way to view and print individual quarterly reports is to select the **Quarterly Reports** icon associated with the report on the Inbox or All Grants screens. The Quarterly Reports icon looks like a pie chart.

The third way you can view and print individual quarterly reports is to select the **Quarterly Reports** tab from the menu at the top of any Pre-Award Eligibility Workflow screen.

# Quarterly Reports Screen

The Quarterly Reports screen allows you to view all of the quarterly reports submitted for a federal award, whether or not they are pending review.

Alex will demonstrate how to view the status of quarterly reports for a federal award.

Scroll down to see slideshow captions.

**Quarterly Reports**

FMA-04-KY-2016 (0) Unchecked Properties FMA

The table below lists all the Quarterly Reports submitted by the Grantee for this Grant. Clicking the View icon will display the Quarterly Report queues. Clicking the form icon will display the Financial Report or the Performance Report. Clicking the Attachments icon will list all of the attachments associated with a report.

Show [11 - 20] Show All                                                                                 showing 11 - 20 of 15  First | Previous | Next | Last

| FY | Quarter | Report # | Report Type | Period Covered | Date Due | Date Submitted | Submittal Status | View | Report |
|---|---|---|---|---|---|---|---|---|---|
| 2017 | 3 | FMA-04-KY-2016-QR-02 (P) | Performance | 03/30/2017 – 06/30/2017 | 07/30/2017 | 04/14/2017 | On time | | |
| 2017 | 3 | FMA-04-KY-2016-QR-02 (F) | Financial | 03/30/2017 – 06/30/2017 | 07/30/2017 | 04/14/2017 | On time | | |

The Quarterly Reports screen displays in order, starting with the most recent, the quarterly reports submitted by the Recipient. Up to the first 10 are displayed and, as in the Inbox and All Grants screens, you can select to view groups of 10 by selecting them in the **Show** drop-down menu, or navigating among them using the **First, Previous, Next,** and **Last** links. Or you can select the **Show All** link to display all of the reports on a single screen.

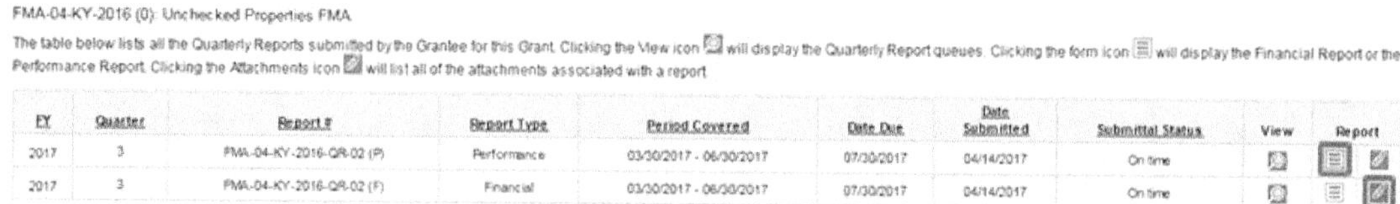

To open a report in a new window, select the **Form** icon, which looks like a piece of lined paper. To view the attachments associated with a report select the **Attachments** icon, which looks like a paper clip.

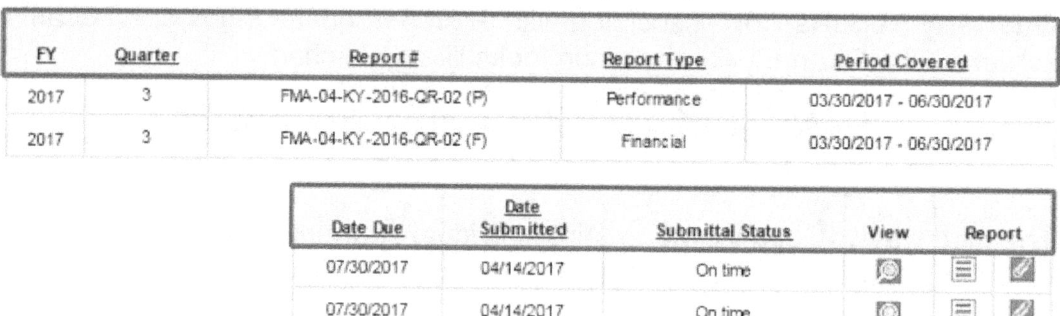

You can see the **FY, Quarter, Report #, Report Type, Period Covered, Date Due, Date Submitted,** and **Submittal Status** displayed for each Quarterly Report received.

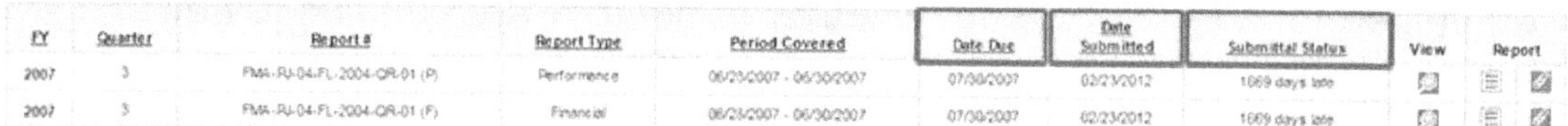

The **Due Date** is the date 30 days past the end date of the quarter period covered. If a report was submitted after the Due Date, the Submittal Status will indicate how may days late it was submitted, and all information on the screen will be in red.

# Process Quarterly Reports Screen

The Process Quarterly Reports screen provides the status of the Quarterly Report Workflow queues.

Alex will demonstrate how to view the status of the Quarterly Report Workflow queues.

Scroll down to see slideshow captions.

... the Quarterly Report queues. Clicking the form icon ☰ will display the Financial Report or the

| Date Due | Date Submitted | Submittal Status | View | Report |
|---|---|---|---|---|
| 07/30/2017 | 04/14/2017 | On time | | |
| 07/30/2017 | 04/14/2017 | On time | | |

From the Quarterly Reports screen, select the icon in the **View** column.

## Process Quarterly Report

FMA-04-KY-2016 (0): Unchecked Properties FMA

Report #:  FMA-04-KY-2016-QR-02    Period Covered:  03/30/2017 - 06/30/2017 (FY 2017/Q3)

| Queue | Approved | User | Status | Status Date |
|---|---|---|---|---|
| Quarterly Report Program Review | Pending | REVIEWER, NEW | Pending | 06/05/2017 12:22 PM |
| Quarterly Report Grants Review | Pending | | Pending | 04/14/2017 06:07 PM |

The Process Quarterly Reports screen displays. This is where we can view the status of the Quarterly Report Workflow queues for the quarterly report.

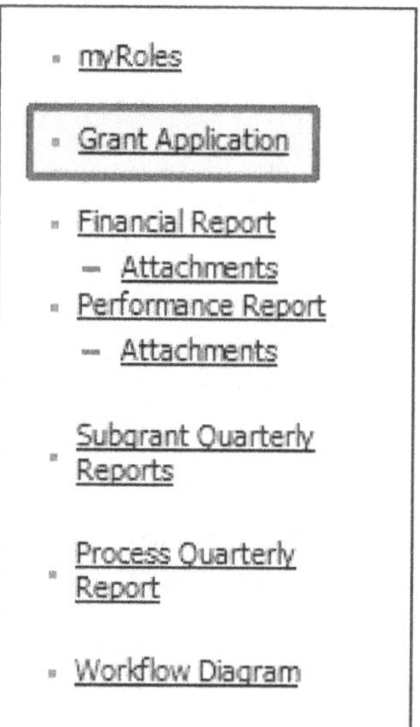


Select the **Grant Application** link in the sidebar menu to view the federal award in a new window for reference.

# Quarterly Report Program Review Queue

The Quarterly Report Program Review queue allows you to document the programmatic review of both the Quarterly Performance Report and Quarterly Financial Report for a federal award.
Users with the PDM Coordinator or FMA Coordinator role can process the Quarterly Report Program Review queue.
Alex will demonstrate how to process the queue.

Scroll down to see slideshow captions.

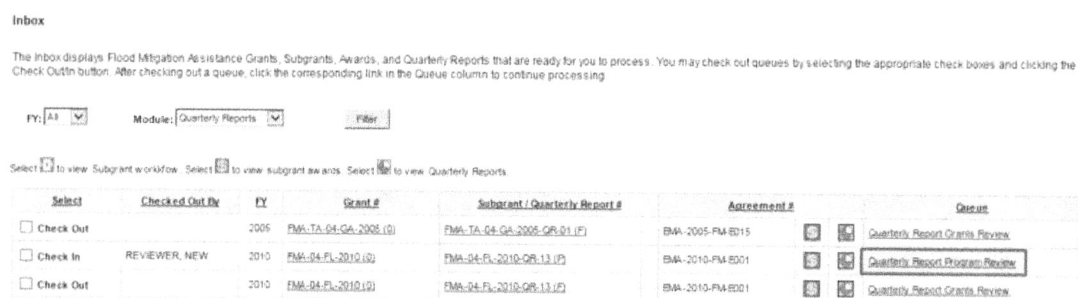

In order to view the Quarterly Report Program Review queue, you should first check it out and then select the **Quarterly Report Program Review** link in the Queue column. In this case, we are going to review the Quarterly Report # FMA-04-FL-2010-QR-13 (P).

**Quarterly Report Program Review**

FMA-04-FL-2010 (0) FL FMA 2010 Test 2

Report #:  FMA-04-FL-2010-QR-13 (P)          Period Covered:          06/07/2010 - 06/30/2013 (FY 2013/Q3)



| Question | Answer |
|---|---|
| Do the accomplishments described in the Performance Report corroborate the outlays in the Financial Report? | Yes |
| Are the program requirements (e.g., environmental/historic conditions, draft plan submittal for review and contracts in place within required timeframes, etc.) being met? | Yes |
| Are the activities identified in the Subgrant Scopes of Work being achieved in the timeframes established in the Work Schedules? | Yes |

The Quarterly Report Program Review screen appears. This screen allows you to document the programmatic review of the quarterly reports.

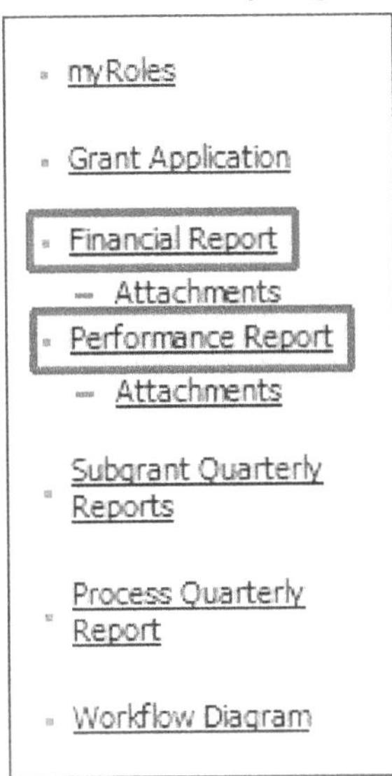


The **sidebar menu** on the left of the Quarterly Report Program Review screen provides links to view the financial and performance reports.

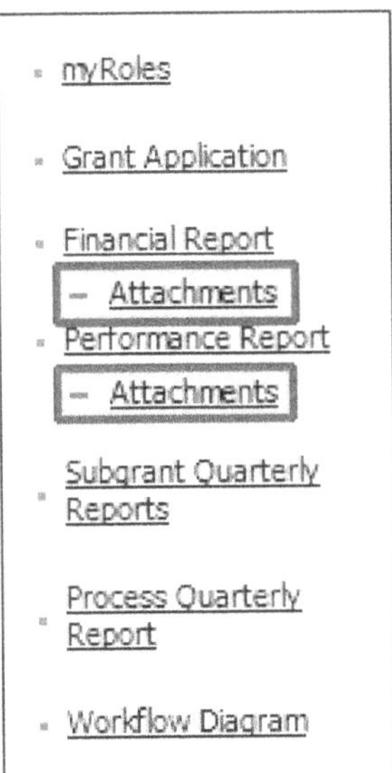

Select the **Attachments** links in the sidebar menu to view any associated attachments that were submitted by the Recipient.

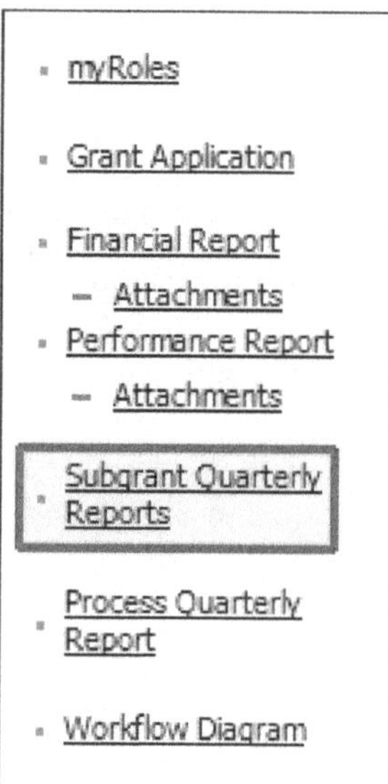


Select the **Subgrant Quarterly Reports** link in the sidebar menu to view any subaward quarterly reports that have been submitted. The documents will open in a new window for reference while you are performing the review.

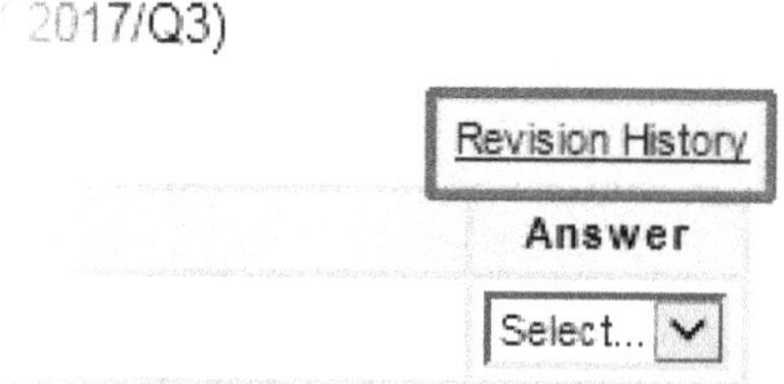


Selecting the **Revision History** link displays any revision requests that were made from this queue.

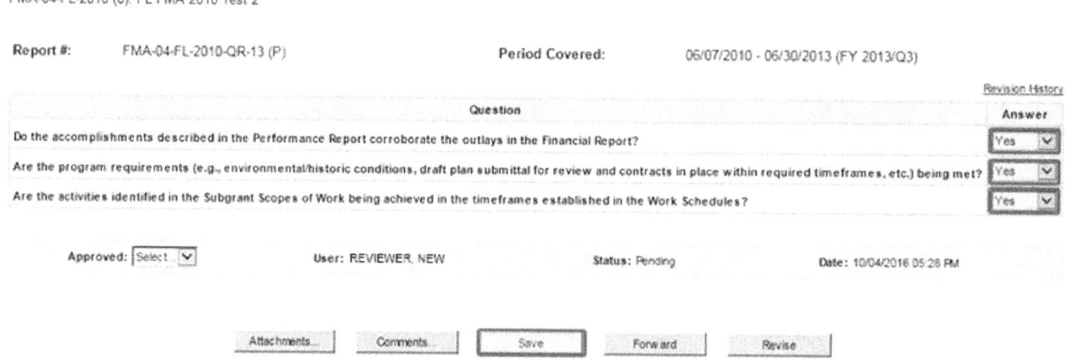

**Quarterly Report Program Review**

FMA-04-FL-2010 (0): FL FMA 2010 Test 2

| Report #: | FMA-04-FL-2010-QR-13 (P) | Period Covered: | 06/07/2010 - 06/30/2013 (FY 2013/Q3) |
|---|---|---|---|

Revision History

| Question | Answer |
|---|---|
| Do the accomplishments described in the Performance Report corroborate the outlays in the Financial Report? | Yes |
| Are the program requirements (e.g., environmental/historic conditions, draft plan submittal for review and contracts in place within required timeframes, etc.) being met? | Yes |
| Are the activities identified in the Subgrant Scopes of Work being achieved in the timeframes established in the Work Schedules? | Yes |

Approved: Select    User: REVIEWER, NEW    Status: Pending    Date: 10/04/2016 05:28 PM

Attachments...    Comments...    Save    Forward    Revise

To respond to each question, select "Yes" or "No" from the **Answer** drop-down menu. For this report, we will select "Yes" for all three questions. When all of the questions have been completed, select the **Save** button.

Approved: Select ⌄     User: REVIEWER, NEW     Status: Pending     Date: 10/04/2016 05:28 PM

Attachments...   Comments...   Save   Forward   Revise

As in the Pre-Eligibility Workflow queues, you can attach relevant documents, add comments, and request a revision from the Recipient by selecting the **Attachments, Comments,** and **Revise** buttons at the bottom of the screen.

**Quarterly Report Program Review**

FMA-04-FL-2010 (0) FL FMA 2010 Test 2

Report #:     FMA-04-FL-2010-QR-13 (P)          Period Covered:     06/07/2010 - 06/30/2013 (FY 2013/Q3)

Revision History

| Question | Answer |
|---|---|
| Do the accomplishments described in the Performance Report corroborate the outlays in the Financial Report? | Yes ⌄ |
| Are the program requirements (e.g., environmental/historic conditions, draft plan submittal for review and contracts in place within required timeframes, etc.) being met? | Yes ⌄ |
| Are the activities identified in the Subgrant Scopes of Work being achieved in the timeframes established in the Work Schedules? | Yes ⌄ |

Approved: [Select / Yes / No]     User: REVIEWER, NEW     Status: Pending     Date: 10/04/2016 05:28 PM

Attachments...   Comments...   Save   Forward   Revise

When the review is complete, select "Yes" or "No" from the **Approved** drop-down menu. For this report, we are going to approve this queue by selecting "Yes." Select the **Forward** button to move the quarterly report to the Quarterly Report Grants Review queue.

**Confirmation**

FMA-04-FL-2010 (0) FL FMA 2010 Test 2

Report #:   FMA-04-FL-2010-QR-13 (P)          Period Covered:     06/07/2010 - 06/30/2013 (FY 2013/Q3)

The Quarterly Report was successfully forwarded from Quarterly Report Program Review. Processing for the Quarterly Report is complete

Return to Inbox

A **Confirmation** message appears. Select the **Return to Inbox** link to process more quarterly reports.

# Quarterly Report Grants Review Queue

The Quarterly Report Grants Review queue allows the Assistance Officer to document the financial review of the quarterly reports for a federal award. If the Assistance Officer concurs with the financial data in the report and concurs with the results of the previous Quarterly Report Program Review Queue, then the Assistance Officer can approve the review and select the Forward button to complete the queue.

If the Assistance Officer disagrees with the results of the previous Quarterly Report Program Review queue, he or she can send the report back to the Program Review queue for rework. In this case, the Assistance Officer would select "No" from the Approved drop-down menu, select the Comments button to add comments, and then select the Save button. If the Assistance Officer detects errors in the financial data in the report, he or she can send a revision request to the Recipient to correct the errors. In this case, the Assistance Officer would select "No" from the Approved drop-down menu, select the Comments button to add comments, and then select the Revise button. The Rework and Revise functionalities were covered in Lesson 8.

## Quarterly Report Grants Review

FMA-04-FL-2010 (0): FL FMA 2010 Test 2

**Report #:**   FMA-04-FL-2010-QR-13 (F)       **Period Covered:**   06/07/2010 - 06/30/2013 (FY 2013/Q3)

Revision History

|  | Award Information on File (in eGrants) | Financial Report (from Applicant) |
|---|---|---|
| Federal Share %/Non-Federal Share % | 75/25 | 0/0 |
| Federal Share | $84,000.00 | $0.00 |
| Non-Federal Share | $28,000.00 | $0.00 |

| Question | Answer |
|---|---|
| Did you review the Financial Report? | Yes |

Approved: Yes [Select... / No]       **User:** REVIEWER, NEW       **Status:** Pending       **Date:** 10/04/2016 05:26 PM

[Attachments...]   [Comments...]   [Save]   [Forward]   [Revise]

Select this link for the full text of the image.

# Lesson 10 Summary

In this lesson, you learned about the:

- Quarterly Reports functionality
- Review queues for quarterly reports

Some key points from this lesson:

- Recipients are required to report their obligations and expenditures on a quarterly basis to FEMA for monitoring.
- Quarterly reports are due on January 30, April 30, July 30, and October 30.
- Recipients attach and submit Quarterly Performance Reports in eGrants. However, Quarterly Financial Status Reports are submitted through the PARS system.
- There are two parts to the Quarterly Report Workflow Queue: The Quarterly Report Program Review for reviewing both the performance and financial reports, and the Quarterly Report Grants Review for reviewing just the financial report.
- If necessary, an Assistance Officer can rework a report back to the Program Review queue, or a revision request can be sent to the Recipient from either the Program Review or Grants Review queues.
- The Quarterly Reports screen displays the submission status of a quarterly report.
- The Process Quarterly Reports screen displays the status of a report in the Quarterly Report Workflow queue.

# Lesson 11 Overview

When we're done with this lesson, you'll be able to identify:

- The Closeout process for subawards and federal awards

# eGrants User Scenario

**Team Leader:** Alex Salazar, Flood Mitigation Assistance (FMA) Program Coordinator

**Your Role:** New FMA Program Analyst

**Office:** FEMA Regional Office

**Challenge:** A federal award needs to be closed after its period of performance has ended.

**To Date:** You have learned how to view and process Quarterly Performance and Financial Status Reports.

Listen to Alex
Audio transcript

**The Next Step:** Alex will explain the Closeout process for federal awards and subawards.

Hi. It's Alex. FEMA is required to document the final financial status of a federal award and its associated subawards at the end of their periods of performance. I will explain the close out process for federal awards and subawards.

# Subaward Closeout

A subaward can be closed out after the final awarded amount has been obligated and its period of performance has ended. Mitigation Specialists are able to close out subawards. To begin the Closeout process, a Subrecipient notifies the Recipient that the subaward is ready to be closed. The Recipient works with the Subrecipient as needed to complete a subaward closeout package. The Recipient submits the closeout package to FEMA when it is complete. The package contains the final quarterly reports, as well as specific documentation depending on the project type and type of subaward. A FEMA Mitigation Specialist reviews the documentation to verify that all the closeout requirements have been met.

Alex will demonstrate how to close out a subaward.

Scroll down to see slideshow captions.

To close out a subaward, select the **Closeout** link on the Inbox screen.

Closeout

Please select one or more Grant Applications or Subgrant Applications to close and enter the Close Date and the Final Federal Share amount.
Provide comments and/or attachments as needed for each Grant or Subgrant by clicking on the corresponding icon.
Selecting a Grant Application or Subgrant Application with a Closed Status will **re-open** it when the Save button is clicked.
When you have completed data entry for all selected Grant and Subgrant Applications, click the Save button.

FY: 2010 ☑  Filter

Fields marked with a red asterisk (*) are required before Saving, if the row is selected.

Enter Dates as MM/DD/YYYY (e.g., 04/15/2015)

Enter Final Fed Share as ########.## (e.g., 15712.35, 121250.75)

Select [icon] to view Subgrant workflow. Select [icon] to view subgrant awards. Select [icon] to view Quarterly Reports.

Select [icon] to access close out attachments. Select [icon] to access close out comments. Select [icon] to access subgrant properties

| Select Grant | Select Subgrant | Grant/Subgrant Application # (Ascending) | Title | Status | Close Date | Final Federal Share | | | | |
|---|---|---|---|---|---|---|---|---|---|---|
| ☐ | | FMA-04-FL-2010 (0) | FL FMA 2010 Test 2 | Obligated | | $84,000.00 | | | | |
| | ☑ | FMA-PL-04-FL-2010-006 (0) | New Test Thrnville FL 2007 046 | Obligated | * | * 21000 | | | | |

The Closeout screen appears. Check the box in the **Select Subgrant** column associated with the subaward number to be closed out.

Select [icon] to access close out attachments. Select [icon] to access close out comments. Select [icon] to access subgrant properties

| Select Grant | Select Subgrant | Grant/Subgrant Application # (Ascending) | Title | Status | Close Date | Final Federal Share | | | | |
|---|---|---|---|---|---|---|---|---|---|---|
| ☐ | | FMA-04-FL-2010 (0) | FL FMA 2010 Test 2 | Obligated | | $84,000.00 | | | | |
| | ☑ | FMA-PL-04-FL-2010-006 (0) | New Test Thrnville FL 2007 046 | Obligated | * 06/19/2017 | * 21000 | | | | |

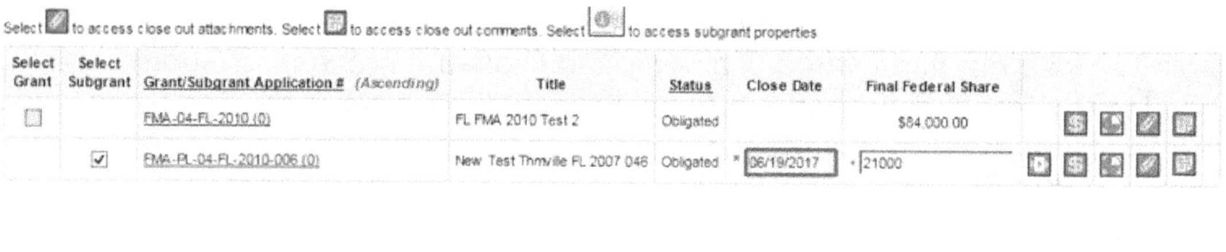


Enter the **Close Date.** For this subaward, enter the date" 06/19/2017."

The **Final Federal Share** text field is already completed with the final obligated amount of $21,000. Select **Save.**

## Closeout Confirmation

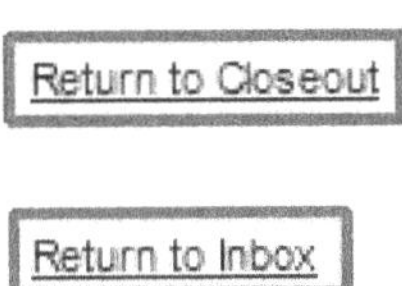

The selected actions were performed for the following grants

FMA-PL-04-FL-2010-006 was successfully closed

Return to Closeout

Return to Inbox

The Closeout Confirmation screen displays. Select the **Return to Closeout** link to continue to close out subawards, or select the **Return to Inbox** link.

**All Grants**

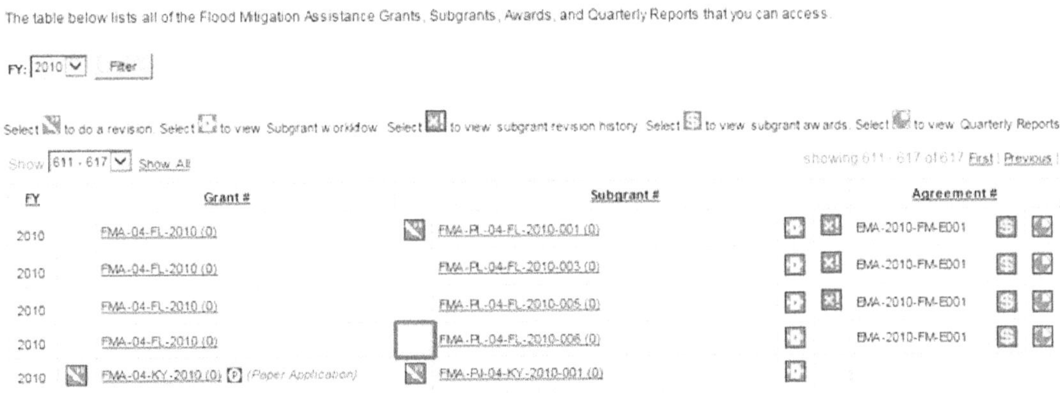



After the subaward is closed, no revisions will be possible, so the **Revision Request** icon will **not** be displayed beside the subaward number on the All Grants screen.

# Federal Award Closeout

The federal award can be closed out after all subawards associated with that federal award have been closed out. FEMA personnel use a checklist to verify that all requirements have been met and to ensure the documentation is complete. The Recipient submits a federal award closeout package, which contains the final quarterly reports and other documentation as evidence of compliance.

The Effective Date is the day when it is recorded in the eGrants system that the federal award is closed. The Effective Date is used as the basis for records retention requirements, per records management regulations.

When a federal award is closed out, all reports that display a Status field will show the federal award as being closed out. Also, after a federal award has been closed out, its associated subawards will not be displayed in the Inbox.

Alex will demonstrate how to close out a federal award.

Scroll down to see slideshow captions.

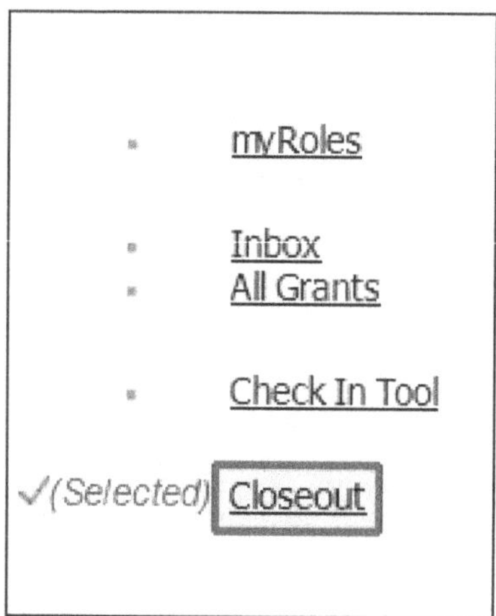



After all subawards associated with a federal award have been closed out, you can close out the federal award. Select the **Closeout** link on the Sidebar menu.

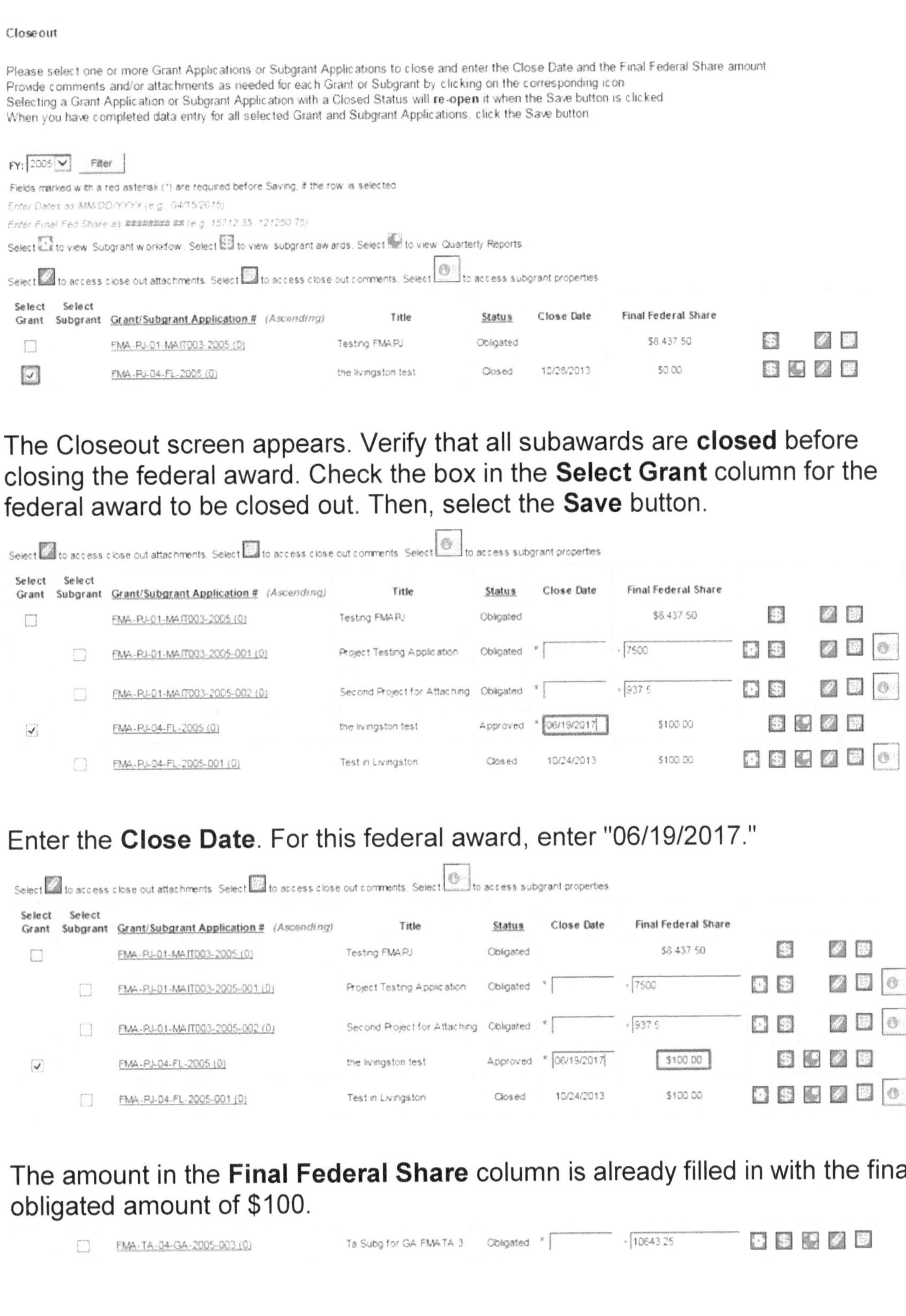

The Closeout screen appears. Verify that all subawards are **closed** before closing the federal award. Check the box in the **Select Grant** column for the federal award to be closed out. Then, select the **Save** button.

Enter the **Close Date**. For this federal award, enter "06/19/2017."

The amount in the **Final Federal Share** column is already filled in with the final obligated amount of $100.

Select the **Save** button.

The **Closeout Confirmation** screen appears. Select the **Return to Closeout** link to continue to close out more subawards, or select the **Return to Inbox** link.

# Reopening Federal Awards

If needed, you can reopen a federal award that has been closed out. As indicated in the directions on the Closeout screen, check the box in the Select Grant column associated with the federal award to be re-opened and then select the Save button. The Closeout confirmation screen will display with a message stating the federal award was successfully re-opened. When a Gen-01 Report is run, the application will display an Approved status.

Closeout

Please select one or more Grant Applications or Subgrant Applications to close and enter the Close Date and the Final Federal Share amount
Provide comments and/or attachments as needed for each Grant or Subgrant by clicking on the corresponding icon
Selecting a Grant Application or Subgrant Application with a Closed Status will **re-open** it when the Save button is clicked.
When you have completed data entry for all selected Grant and Subgrant Applications, click the Save button.

FY: 2005    Filter

Fields marked with a red asterisk (*) are required before Saving, if the row is selected.
Enter Dates as MM/DD/YYYY (e.g. 04/15/2015)
Enter Final Fed Share as ######.## (e.g. 15712.35, 121250.75)
Select ⬚ to view Subgrant workflow. Select ⬚ to view subgrant awards. Select ⬚ to view Quarterly Reports.
Select ⬚ to access close out attachments. Select ⬚ to access close out comments. Select ⬚ to access subgrant properties.

| Select Grant | Select Subgrant | Grant/Subgrant Application #  (Ascending) | Title | Status | Close Date | Final Federal Share | | | | | |
|---|---|---|---|---|---|---|---|---|---|---|---|
| | ☐ | FMA-PJ-01-MAIT003-2005-002 (G) | Second Project for Attaching | Obligated | * | * 937.5 | | | | | |
| ☑ | | FMA-PJ-04-FL-2005 (O) | the livingston test | Closed | 06/19/2017 | $100.00 | | | | | |

Export    Save

**Closeout Confirmation**

The selected actions were performed for the following grants

FMA-PJ-04-FL-2005 was successfully re-opened

Return to Closeout

Return to Inbox

<u>Select this link for the full text of the image.</u>

# Re-opening Subawards

If needed, a subaward can be re-opened after it has been closed out. If the federal award has been closed, it must be re-opened before the subaward can be re-opened.

On the Closeout screen, check the box in the Select Subgrant column for the subaward to be re-opened, then select the Save button. The Closeout confirmation screen will display a message stating that the subaward was successfully re-opened.

Select this link for the full text of the image.

# Lesson 11 Summary

You have completed Lesson 11.

Before you move on to the last lesson in the course, let's review what you learned in this lesson:

- After the final awarded amount has been obligated for a subaward and its period of performance has been completed, it can be closed out in eGrants.
- After all subawards have been closed out, a federal award can be closed out.
- If needed, a federal award that has been closed out can be re-opened.
- Subawards can be re-opened only if the federal award is re-opened first.

# Lesson 12 Overview

This lesson describes the role of Headquarters Flood Mitigation Assistance (FMA) Coordinator or Pre-Disaster Mitigation (PDM) Coordinator in managing the structure for each PDM and FMA federal award cycle in eGrants.

At the end of this lesson, you should be able to identify:

- How eGrants supports hazard mitigation grant program administration

# eGrants User Scenario

**Team Leader:** Alex Salazar, Flood Mitigation Assistance (FMA) Program Coordinator

**Your Role:** New FMA Program Analyst

**Office:** FEMA Regional Office

**Challenge:** The FEMA Headquarters FMA Coordinators and Headquarters PDM Coordinators use eGrants to structure and manage FEMA Hazard Mitigation Assistance (HMA) grant programs.

**To Date:** You have learned how to close out federal awards and subawards.

**The Next Step:** Alex will describe the Program Administration functionalities in eGrants.

Listen to Alex
Audio transcript

Hello. It's Alex again. Each year, Congress appropriates funding for the Mitigation grant programs. Grant program managers, like me, need to set funding limits and enter accounting codes in the eGrants system. I'd like you to understand how a grant program is managed, so I will demonstrate the program administration functions in eGrants.

# Program Administration—ACCS Codes

The Program Administration functionalities allow users with Headquarters PDM Coordinator and FMA Coordinator roles to manage the respective grant programs. One Program Administration function is to enter the Accounting Classification Code Structure (ACCS) codes for grant programs. The ACCS codes are used by the eGrants system to lookup the commitment numbers from FEMA's Generic Financial Interface (GFI) based on the grant program for each award. ACCS codes must be entered before any federal awards can be obligated. The ACCS codes are entered annually and may carry over from the previous fiscal year.

Alex will demonstrate how to enter and edit annual ACCS codes in eGrants.

Scroll down to see slideshow captions.

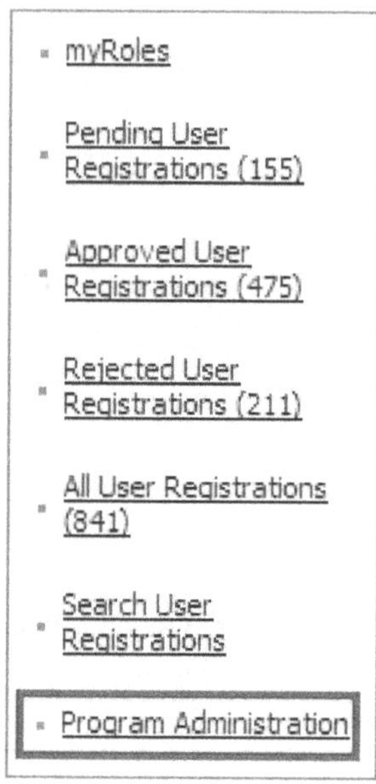

From the eGrants Homepage, select the **Program Administration** link in the sidebar menu. Only Headquarters PDM Coordinators and Headquarters FMA Coordinators can view the Program Administration link.

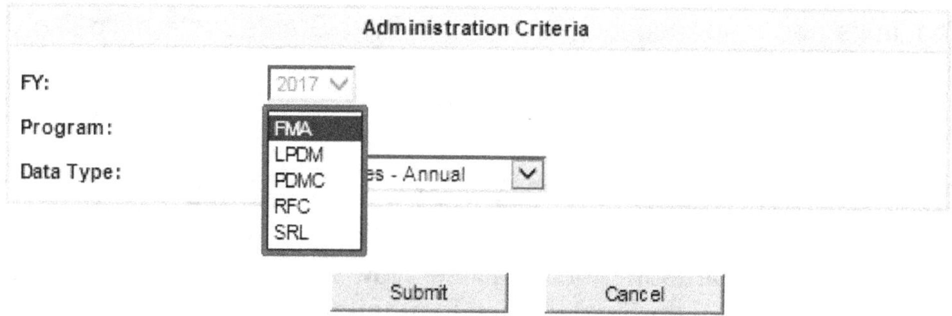

On the Program Administration screen, the current fiscal year (FY) is selected by default in the **FY** drop-down menu, because you can only edit current fiscal year information. Only programs for which you have roles will appear in the **Program** drop-down menu. In this demonstration, five options are available: FMA, LPDM, PDMC, RFC, and SRL. Select the "FMA" option.

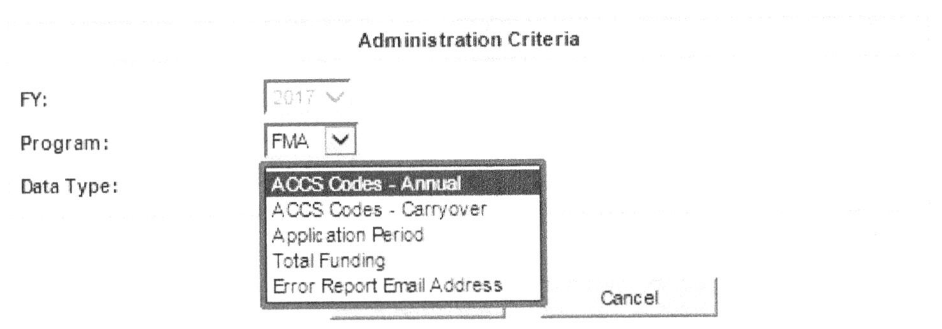



The options that are available in the **Data Type** drop-down menu are determined by the grant program selected. In this demonstration, the task options are: Accounting Classification Code Structure (ACCS) Codes—Annual, ACCS Codes—Carryover, Application Period, Total Funding, or Error Report Email Address. Select the "ACCS Codes—Annual" option.

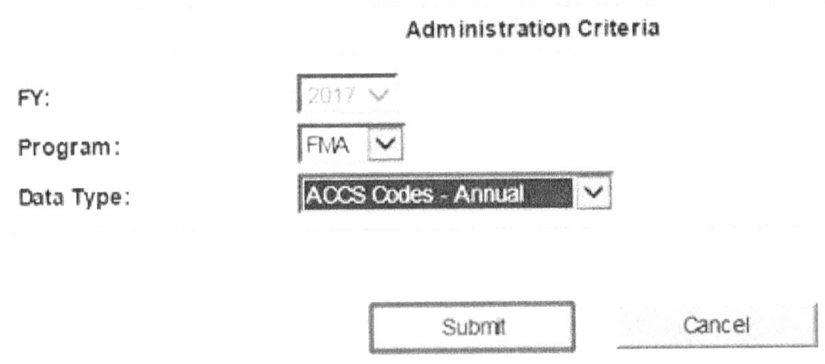



Select the **Submit** button to process the request.

# Program Administration - ACCS Codes - Annual

Please click the Add button to enter the Fund Code and Program Code from the ACCS code for FMA. Only one annual ACCS code may be entered. Click the edit icon to edit the code as necessary.

| ACCS Codes - Annual for FMA | | | | | | |
|---|---|---|---|---|---|---|
| FY | Fund Code | Program Code | Organization Code | Object Class | Fund Type | Edit |
| No Record, Please click the Add button to enter the Fund Code and Program Code. | | | | | | |

Add     Cancel

The Program Administration—ACCS Codes—Annual screen appears. Select the **Add** button to enter the Fund Code and the Program Code.

## Program Administration - Modify ACCS Codes (Annual)

Enter the Fund Code and Program Code from the annual ACCS code and then click the Save button.

| ACCS Codes Input Fields | |
|---|---|
| FY: | 2017 |
| Program: | FMA |
| Fund Code: | 05 |
| Program Code: | 5300M2 |

Save     Cancel

The Program Administration—Modify ACCS Codes (Annual) screen appears. To add the ACCS Code—Annual for FY 2017, enter "05" into the **Fund Code** field and enter "5300M2" into the Program Code field. Select the **Save** button to make the changes.

## Program Administration - ACCS Codes - Annual

Please click the Add button to enter the Fund Code and Program Code from the ACCS code for FMA. Only one annual ACCS code may be entered. Click the edit icon to edit the code as necessary.

| ACCS Codes - Annual for FMA | | | | | | |
|---|---|---|---|---|---|---|
| FY | Fund Code | Program Code | Organization Code | Object Class | Fund Type | Edit |
| 2017 | 5 | 5300M2 | R012-R102 | 4101 | D | |

Cancel

The **Fund Code** and **Program Code** that you entered have been added to the list of annual ACCS codes. The other fields are automatically populated by the eGrants system.

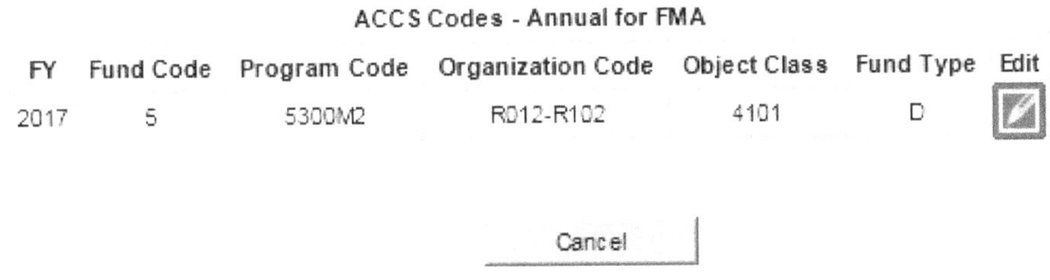

### Program Administration - ACCS Codes - Annual

Please click the Add button to enter the Fund Code and Program Code from the ACCS code for FMA. Only one annual ACCS code may be entered. Click the edit icon to edit the code as necessary.

ACCS Codes - Annual for FMA

| FY | Fund Code | Program Code | Organization Code | Object Class | Fund Type | Edit |
|----|-----------|--------------|-------------------|--------------|-----------|------|
| 2017 | 5 | 5300M2 | R012-R102 | 4101 | D |  |

Cancel

To edit the ACCS Codes-Annual, select the **Edit** icon.

### Program Administration - Modify ACCS Codes (Annual)

Enter the Fund Code and Program Code from the annual ACCS code and then click the Save button.

ACCS Codes Input Fields

| | |
|---|---|
| FY: | 2017 |
| Program: | FMA |
| Fund Code: | 5 |
| Program Code: | 5300M2 |

Save    Cancel

On the Program Administration—Modify ACCS Codes (Annual) screen, you can update the **Fund Code** or the **Program Code,** or both. Select **Save** to make the change(s).

# ACCS Codes—Carryover Functionality

To fund federal awards that have periods of performance that will continue into the next fiscal year, the ACCS fund code and program code they are associated with must "carry over" to the next year. Headquarters FMA Coordinators and Headquarters PDM Coordinators can also enter ACCS—Carryover Codes into eGrants.

Alex will demonstrate how to enter and edit annual ACCS codes in eGrants.

Scroll down to see slideshow captions.

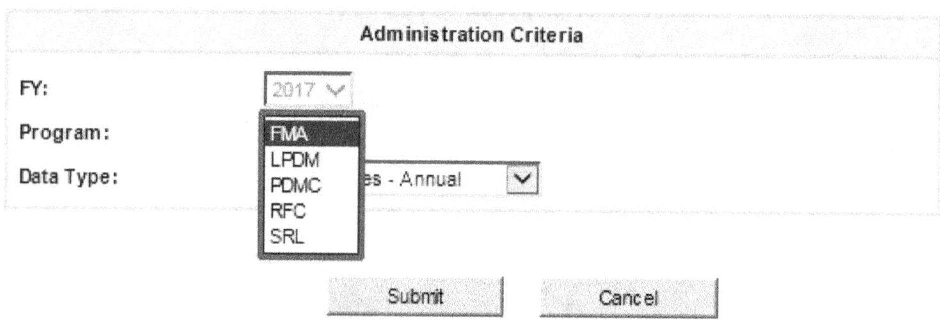

From the Program Administration screen, select the "FMA" option from the **Program** drop-down menu.

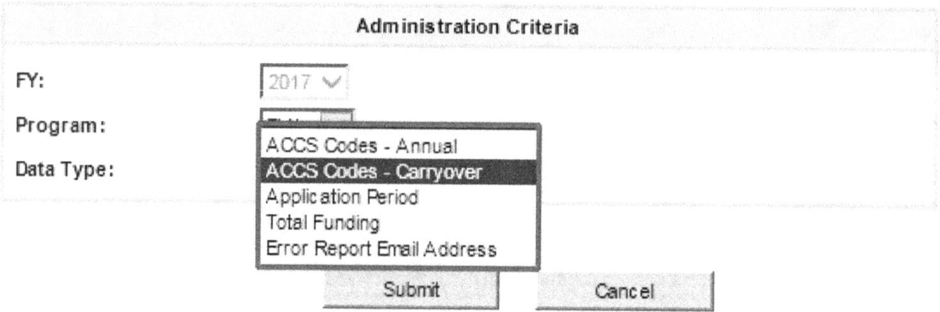

Select **ACCS Codes—Carryover** from the **Data Type** drop-down menu. Remember, the options that are available in the Data Type drop-down menu are determined by what grant program you have selected. Select the **Submit** button to process the request.

## Program Administration - ACCS Codes - Carryover

Please click the Add button to enter the Fund Code and Program Code from the ACCS code for FMA.
More than one carryover ACCS code may be entered. Click the edit icon next to an ACCS code to edit the code as necessary.

ACCS Codes - Carryover for FMA

| FY | Fund Code | Program Code | Organization Code | Object Class | Fund Type | Edit |
|---|---|---|---|---|---|---|
| 2017 | 5 | K117 | R012-R102 | 4101 | D | |
| 2017 | 5 | 3117 | R012-R102 | 4101 | D | |
| 2017 | 5 | J117 | R012-R102 | 4101 | D | |

Add    Cancel

On the Program Administration—ACCS Codes—Carryover screen, select the
**Add** button to enter the Carryover Fund Code and Program Code.

## Program Administration - Modify ACCS Codes (Carryover)

Enter the Fund Code and Program Code from the carryover ACCS code to be added and then click the Save button.

ACCS Codes Input Fields

FY:                          2017
Program:                     FMA
Fund Code:                   5
Program Code:                5302M2

Save    Cancel

The Program Administration—Modify ACCS Codes (Carryover) screen
appears. From here, you can add the carryover ACCS Codes. To carry over
the FY 2017 fund code and program code into FY 2018, enter "05" in the **Fund
Code** text field and "5302M2" in the **Program Code** text field. Then, select the
**Save** button.

# Program Administration - ACCS Codes - Carryover

Please click the Add button to enter the Fund Code and Program Code from the ACCS code for FMA.
More than one carryover ACCS code may be entered. Click the edit icon next to an ACCS code to edit the code as necessary.

| FY | Fund Code | Program Code | Organization Code | Object Class | Fund Type | Edit |
|---|---|---|---|---|---|---|
| 2017 | 5 | K117 | R012-R102 | 4101 | D | |
| 2017 | 5 | 3117 | R012-R102 | 4101 | D | |
| 2017 | 5 | 5302M2 | R012-R102 | 4101 | D | |
| 2017 | 5 | J117 | R012-R102 | 4101 | D | |

ACCS Codes - Carryover for FMA

Add     Cancel

The **Carryover Fund Code** and **Program Code** that you entered have been added to the list of Carryover ACCS codes. The other fields are automatically populated by the eGrants system

## Program Administration - ACCS Codes - Carryover

Please click the Add button to enter the Fund Code and Program Code from the ACCS code for FMA.
More than one carryover ACCS code may be entered. Click the edit icon next to an ACCS code to edit the code as necessary.

| FY | Fund Code | Program Code | Organization Code | Object Class | Fund Type | Edit |
|---|---|---|---|---|---|---|
| 2017 | 5 | K117 | R012-R102 | 4101 | D | |
| 2017 | 5 | 3117 | R012-R102 | 4101 | D | |
| 2017 | 5 | 5302M2 | R012-R102 | 4101 | D | |
| 2017 | 5 | J117 | R012-R102 | 4101 | D | |

ACCS Codes - Carryover for FMA

To edit the Carryover ACCS Codes, select the **Edit** icon.

## Program Administration - Modify ACCS Codes (Carryover)

Enter the Fund Code and Program Code from the carryover ACCS code to be added and then click the Save button.

ACCS Codes Input Fields

| | |
|---|---|
| **FY:** | 2017 |
| **Program:** | FMA |
| **Fund Code:** | 5 |
| **Program Code:** | 5302M2 |

Save     Cancel

Input the updated **Fund Code** or **Program Code**. Then, select **Save** to make the change.

# Application Period Functionality

The Application Period controls how long an application for a grant program is available to Applicants in the eGrants External System.

Hope Samuels, a Headquarters PDM Coordinator, will demonstrate how to enter the start and end dates for the PDM Application Period in eGrants.

Scroll down to see slideshow captions.

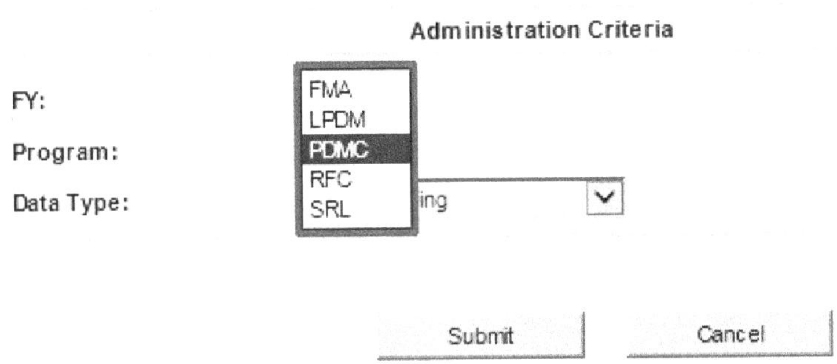


On the Program Administration screen, the current fiscal year is selected by default in the **FY** drop-down menu. The **Program** drop-down menu has five options. I select the "PDMC" option.

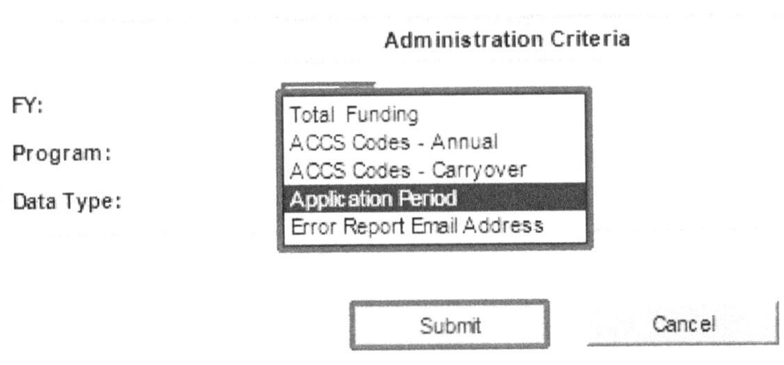


To enter, view, or update the PDM application period, I select the "Application Period" option from the **Data Type** drop-down menu. Then, I select the **Submit** button.

# Program Administration - Application Period

Please click the Update button to enter the Application Period Dates and Times for Grant Program PDMC and FY 2016.

| | | Application Period | |
|---|---|---|---|
| FY | Program | Start Date | End Date |
| 2016 | PDMC | 03/01/2017 02:00 PM | 03/30/2017 05:00 PM |

Update          Cancel

Any application period that has previously been set will appear on the Program Administration—Application Period screen. I select the **Update** button to enter or modify the **Start Date** and **End Date**. I can enter the dates and times based on Eastern Standard Time (EST) and the eGrants Internal System will automatically convert the date and time to the time zone at each user's location.

## Program Administration - Modify (Application Period )

Enter the Application Period Start and End Dates and Times and then click the Save button to save the information.

| | Application Period Input Fields |
|---|---|
| FY: | 2016 |
| Program: | PDMC |
| Start Date: | 03/01/2017  02:00  PM |
| End Date: | 04/30/2017 ×  05:00  PM |

Note: Application Period Start Time and End Time will be entered using Eastern Standard Time (EST).

Save          Cancel

For this demonstration, I will edit the End Date. I select the **End Date** text field, and change the month from "03" to "04". I select the **Save** button to save the change.

## Program Administration - Application Period

Please click the Update button to enter the Application Period Dates and Times for Grant Program PDMC and FY 2016.

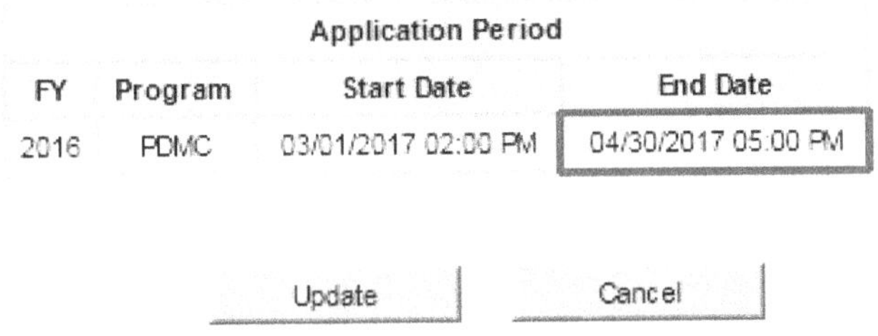

The change appears on the Application Period screen.

# PDM Total Funding Functionality

For the PDM grant program, the funding amount available for selected subapplications must be entered each fiscal year.

Hope Samuels, a Headquarters PDM Coordinator, will demonstrate how to record the annual total funding amount available for PDM federal awards.

Scroll down to see slideshow captions.

## Program Administration

Please select the Fiscal Year (FY), Program, and Data Type in order to administer the program's FY requirements. Please note that only the current FY ACCS Codes may be modified.

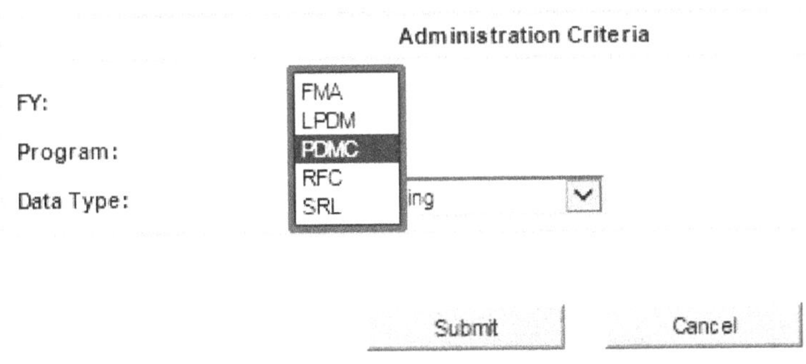

To set the total funding limit for the Pre-Disaster Mitigation grant program, select the **Program** drop-down menu. Select the "PDMC" option.

# Program Administration

Please select the Fiscal Year (FY), Program, and Data Type in order to administer the program's FY requirements.Please note that only the current FY ACCS Codes may be modified.

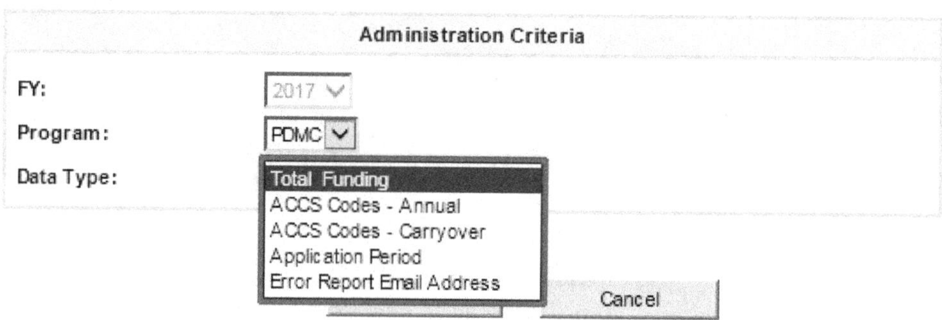

For this demonstration, the **Data Type** drop-down menu now has five options: Total Funding, ACCS Codes – Annual, ACCS Codes – Carryover, Application Period, and Error Report Email Address. Select the "Total Funding" item.

# Program Administration

Please select the Fiscal Year (FY), Program, and Data Type in order to administer the program's FY requirements.Please note that only the current FY ACCS Codes may be modified.

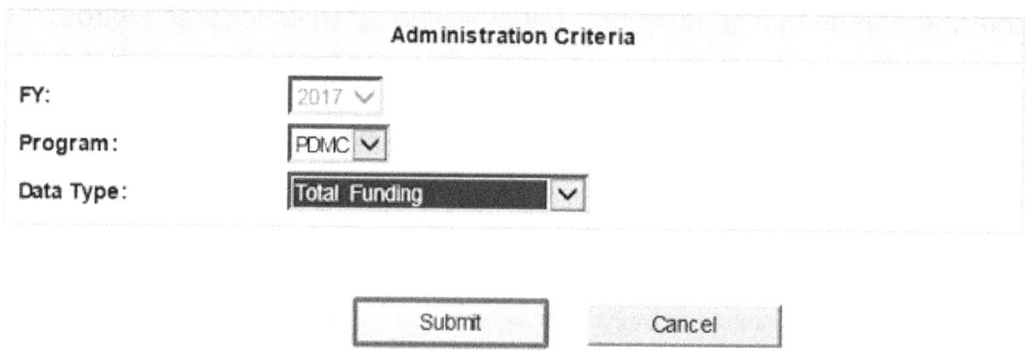

Select the **Submit** button to process your request.

# Program Administration - PDMC Total Funding

Please click the Add or Edit button to enter the available amount for PDMC for the FY 2017. The Selection for Award queue will not function without this data.

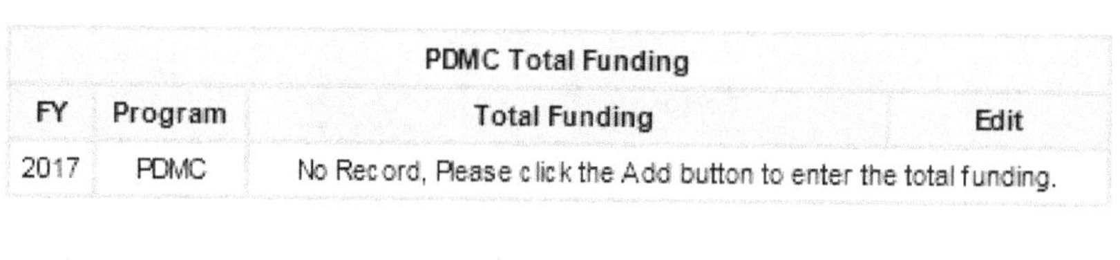

| PDMC Total Funding | | | |
|---|---|---|---|
| FY | Program | Total Funding | Edit |
| 2017 | PDMC | No Record, Please click the Add button to enter the total funding. | |

On the Program Administration – PDMC Total Funding screen, select the **Add** button to add the Total Funding amount.

## Program Administration - Modify PDMC Total Funding

Please enter the total funding available for PDMC for the FY 2017. The Selection for Award queue will not function without this data.

PDMC Total Funding

FY:                2017

Program:           PDMC

Total Funding:     $ 3000000    ×

Save            Cancel

Enter the appropriate amount in the **Total Funding** field. In this example, we will enter "3,000,000" into the Total Funding field. Select the **Save** button to save the change you made.

## Program Administration - PDMC Total Funding

Please click the Add or Edit button to enter the available amount for PDMC for the FY 2017. The Selection for Award queue will not function without this data.

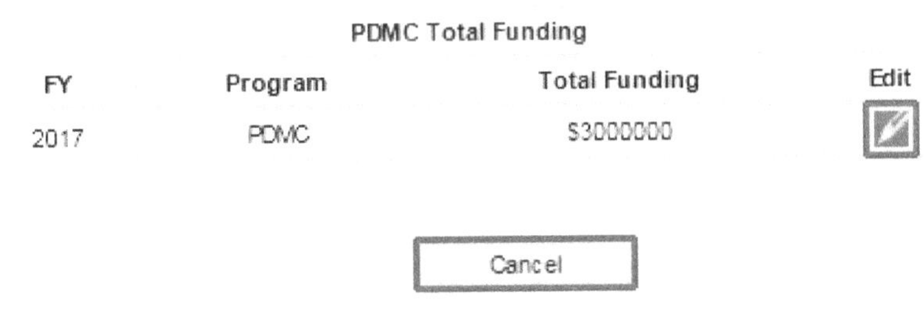

| FY | Program | Total Funding | Edit |
|----|---------|---------------|------|
| 2017 | PDMC | $3000000 | |

Cancel

You can also edit the Total Funding amount by selecting the **Edit** icon on the Program Administration – PDMC Total Funding screen. Select the **Cancel** button to return to the Program Administration screen.

# Lesson 12 Summary

In this lesson, you learned about the:

- Reports functionality
- Program Administration functionalities including setting:
  - Accounting Classification Code Structure (ACCS) codes
  - Application periods

- o   Total Funding limits

Some key points from this lesson are:

- Only users with the Headquarters PDM Coordinator or the Headquarters FMA Coordinator role will have access to the Program Administration functionality to enter or edit the ACCS codes, application period, and PDM Total Funding.
- The start and end dates of the application period for each grant program control the availability of applications to Applicants in the eGrants External System.
- Each fiscal year, federal awards cannot be made until an ACCS code is entered for the grant program.